101 Great, Ready-to-Use Book Lists for Teens

101 Great, Ready-to-Use Book Lists for Teens

Nancy J. Keane

LIBRARIES UNLIMITED

AN IMPRINT OF ABC-CLIO, LLC
Santa Barbara, California • Denver, Colorado • Oxford, England

Library of Congress Cataloging-in-Publication Data

Keane, Nancy J.
  101 great, ready-to-use book lists for teens / Nancy J. Keane.
    pages cm
  Includes bibliographical references and index.
    ISBN 978–1–61069–134–5 (pbk.) — ISBN 978–1–61069–135–2 (ebook) 1. Teenagers—Books and reading—United States. 2. Young adults' libraries—Book lists. 3. High school libraries—Book lists. 4. Young adult literature—Bibliography. I. Keane, Nancy J. Big book of teen reading lists. II. Title. III. Title: One hundred one great, ready-to-use book lists for teens. IV. Title: One hundred and one great, ready-to-use book lists for teens.
  Z1037.K287   2012
  028.5′5—dc23   2011051428

ISBN: 978–1–61069–134–5
EISBN: 978–1–61069–135–2

16 15 14 13 12   1 2 3 4 5

This book is also available on the World Wide Web as an eBook.
Visit www.abc-clio.com for details.

Libraries Unlimited
An Imprint of ABC-CLIO, LLC

ABC-CLIO, LLC
130 Cremona Drive, P.O. Box 1911
Santa Barbara, California 93116-1911

This book is printed on acid-free paper ∞

Manufactured in the United States of America

*Dedicated to my children, Aureta and Alex,
and my grandchildren, Aiden and Jordan.*

Contents

Acknowledgments

I wish to thank the people who have helped with this endeavor. First, I would like to thank all the authors who have given us these marvelous stories to enjoy. With so many children's books in print, it is always difficult to limit the entries. Without these extraordinary people, this would have been a thankless task. As it was, I have spent numerous entertaining hours wrapped up in the books.

I would also like to thank the many librarians and teachers whom I have the pleasure to contact each day. They have introduced me to books I may have missed. The many wonderful, dedicated teachers I have had the privilege of knowing also influenced this work tremendously. I have been fortunate to work with a talented group of educators.

I would also like to thank my marvelous editor, Barbara Ittner. She has worked with me from the beginning of this manuscript, offering both advice and support. She is truly amazing!

Most importantly, I would like to thank my family. My children, Aureta and Alex, and my grandchildren, Aiden and Jordan, are always there to share a story or two.

Introduction

Whether teachers use basal readers, leveled reading, or a literature-based program, there is a need to extend the reading materials for children beyond the current materials. But how do you find those supplemental materials easily? This book represents an attempt to create valuable reading lists to support the extended reading demands.

Everyday librarians and teachers plan activities for children that involve using literature. Before starting this task, they may have some books in mind—but perhaps not. It is time consuming to search for books that support the theme of a lesson. Studies have shown that the average librarian has a working repertoire of twenty to thirty titles to recommend at any one time.[1] This book represents an attempt to create valuable reading lists to support adults in their work with teens and young adults.

An unlimited number of reading lists could be developed to assist professionals in their work. The lists in this book have been chosen in consultation with teachers and public librarians, and through discussions on professional e-mail lists. The book is meant to serve as an extension to the previous work, *The Big Book of Teen Reading Lists* (2006). As such, it is divided into **Readalikes-**related lists, **Genre-**related lists, **Characters-**related lists, **Books about Self**–related lists, **Setting**–related lists, **Subjects-**related lists, **Teaching Literary Elements**–related lists, and **Professional Resources**–related lists. In addition to my own lists, Donna Zecha has contributed lists to this work as well.

The books suggested were all in print as of August 2011. Although the emphasis is on books published within the last ten years, older titles are included if they are still in print and represent a valuable addition to the list. Information included for each title includes the author, title, publisher, date of publication, and number of pages. The Lexile level of the book is supplied when available. A short annotation, taken from the Library of Congress cataloging database, is provided as well. The interest level of the book is indicated by IL and a grade level. For example, IL K–3 indicates that the main audience for the book is kindergarten through third grade, although these books may also be valuable for older readers. IL 3–6 books are appropriate for grades three through six; IL 5–8 books are meant for grades five through eight; IL YA indicates that the book is geared toward young adults; IL AD indicates adult-level material, typically consisting of teacher-level material to use with students or adult books that are appropriate for students. Non-fiction books are designated by the notation "(Non-fiction)." Because twelve to eighteen years of age is a large span in terms of maturity, it is strongly suggested that teachers and librarians review materials recommended for older students before using them with younger children. It is important to look beyond recommended interest level when suggesting books to students.

We hope that teachers and librarians will find this resource valuable for suggesting reading materials to teens and young adults. The lists provided in this book can be used in a variety of ways. For example, they can be photocopied and handed out to students as suggested reading. They can be enlarged and posted in the library, put on the library website or published in the library's newsletter; or used to create book displays. Add your school or library logo, or even some copyright free clip art to personalize the list. Have fun. Be creative. Be resourceful.

However you use the lists, it is hoped that you will find them to be valuable resources and aids for suggesting reading materials.

Note

1. Eaton, G. (2002, October 28). How to do a book talk. University of Rhode Island. Retrieved from http://www.uri.edu/artsci/lsc/Faculty/geaton/MSLMAtalk/

Part 1

Genres

Biography in Picture Book Format

Barton, Chris. *The Day-Glo Brothers: The True Story of Bob and Joe Switzer's Bright Ideas and Brand-New Colors.* Charlesbridge, c2009. 42p. IL 3–6, Lexile: 990 (Non-fiction)

   Illustrations and easy-to-follow text describe how brothers Bob and Joe Switzer invented fluorescent paint and colors; explains how fluorescence works.

Bryant, Jennifer. *A River of Words: The Story of William Carlos Williams.* Eerdmans Books for Young Readers, 2008. 34p. IL 3–6, Lexile: 820

   An illustrated biography of American poet William Carlos Williams, who studied to become a doctor, yet still found time to write poetry.

Corey, Shana. *Mermaid Queen: The Spectacular True Story of Annette Kellerman, Who Swam Her Way to Fame, Fortune, & Swimsuit History!* Scholastic Press, 2009. 42p. IL K–3, Lexile: 650 (Non-fiction)

   An illustrated biography of Annette Kellerman, an early feminist who overcame a childhood illness to become internationally recognized for her swimming, invention of water ballet, and introduction of the modern swimsuit for women.

Gerstein, Mordicai. *The Man Who Walked between the Towers.* Roaring Brook Press, c2003. 40p. IL K–3, Lexile: 480 (Non-fiction)

   A lyrical evocation of Philippe Petit's 1974 tightrope walk between the World Trade Center towers.

Grimes, Nikki. *Talkin' About Bessie: The Story of Aviator Elizabeth Coleman.* Orchard Books, 2002. 48p. IL 3–6, Lexile: 970 (Non-fiction)

   A biography of the woman who became the first licensed African American pilot.

Halfmann, Janet. *Seven Miles to Freedom: The Robert Smalls Story.* Lee & Low Books, c2008. 40p. IL 3–6, Lexile: 870 (Non-fiction)

   A biography of Robert Smalls, who, during the Civil War, commandeered the Confederate ship *Planter* to carry his family and twelve other slaves to freedom; Smalls went on to become a member of the U.S. Congress and worked toward African American advancement.

Jackson Issa, Kai. *Howard Thurman's Great Hope.* Lee & Low Books, c2008. 32p. IL 3–6, Lexile: 840 (Non-fiction)

   A biography of Howard Thurman, which describes how he obtained a scholarship to attend an out-of-town high school, went on to graduate college, and became a civil rights leader for the African American community.

Johnson, Jen Cullerton. *Seeds of Change: Planting a Path to Peace.* Lee & Low Books, c2010. 40p. IL 3–6, Lexile: 820 (Non-fiction)

   Examines the life of Nobel Peace Prize winner and environmentalist Wangari Maathai, who took a stand in favor of women's rights in her native Kenya and started an effort to restore Kenya's ecosystem.

Kerley, Barbara. *Walt Whitman: Words for America.* Scholastic Press, 2004. 42p. IL 3–6, Lexile: 970 (Non-fiction)

   A biography of the American poet, whose compassion led him to nurse soldiers during the Civil War, to give voice to the nation's grief at President Abraham Lincoln's assassination, and to capture the true American spirit in verse.

Biography in Picture Book Format

Kerley, Barbara. *What to Do About Alice?: How Alice Roosevelt Broke the Rules, Charmed the World, and Drove Her Father Teddy Crazy!* Scholastic Press, 2008. 44p. IL K–3, Lexile: 800 (Non-fiction)
> An illustrated biography of Alice Roosevelt Longworth, focusing on her experiences while her father was president of the United States.

Krull, Kathleen. *Harvesting Hope: The Story of Cesar Chavez.* Harcourt, c2003. 48p. IL K–3, Lexile: 800 (Non-fiction)
> A biography of Cesar Chavez, from age ten, when he and his family lived happily on their Arizona ranch, to age thirty-eight, when he led a peaceful protest against California migrant workers' miserable working conditions.

Krull, Kathleen. *Wilma Unlimited: How Wilma Rudolph Became the World's Fastest Woman.* Harcourt Brace, c1996. 44p. IL 3–6, Lexile: 730 (Non-fiction)
> A biography of the African American woman who overcame crippling polio as a child to become the first woman to win three gold medals in track in a single Olympic Games.

Lasky, Kathryn. *One Beetle Too Many: The Extraordinary Adventures of Charles Darwin.* Candlewick Press, 2009. 40p. IL 3–6, Lexile: 1050 (Non-fiction)
> Describes the life and work of the renowned nineteenth-century biologist, who transformed conventional Western thought with his theory of natural evolution.

Levine, Ellen. *Henry's Freedom Box.* Scholastic Press, 2007. 40p. IL K–3, Lexile: 380
> A fictionalized account of how in 1849 a Virginia slave, Henry "Box" Brown, escaped to freedom by shipping himself in a wooden crate from Richmond to Philadelphia.

Matthews, Elizabeth. *Different like Coco.* Candlewick Press, 2007. 36p. IL K–3, Lexile: 990 (Non-fiction)
> An illustrated look at the life of fashion designer Coco Chanel, discussing her youth in France and the development of her own unique style, which caught on around the world.

Medina, Tony. *Love to Langston.* Lee & Low Books, c2002. 34p. IL K–3. Lexile: NP (Non-fiction)
> A series of poems written from the point of view of the poet Langston Hughes, offering an overview of key events and themes in his life.

Moss, Marissa. *Mighty Jackie: The Strike-Out Queen.* Simon & Schuster Books for Young Readers, c2004. 32p. IL K–3, Lexile: 770 (Non-fiction)
> An account of Jackie Mitchell, a seventeen-year-old girl who pitched against Babe Ruth and Lou Gehrig in an exhibition game in 1931, becoming the first professional female pitcher in baseball history.

Novesky, Amy. *Me, Frida.* Abrams Books for Young Readers, 2010. 32p. IL 3–6
> A fictionalized account of how artist Frida Kahlo found her own voice and style when her famous husband, Diego Rivera, was commissioned to paint a mural in San Francisco, California, in the 1930s and she found herself exploring the city on her own.

Biography in Picture Book Format

Pena, Matt de la. *A Nation's Hope: The Story of Boxing Legend Joe Louis.* Dial Books for Young Readers, c2011. 40p. IL K–3 (Non-fiction)
An illustrated introduction to the life and accomplishments of professional boxer Joe Louis.

Rabin, Staton. *Mr. Lincoln's Boys: Being the Mostly True Adventures of Abraham Lincoln's Trouble-Making Sons, Tad and Willie.* Viking, 2008. 36p. IL K–3, Lexile: 710 (Non-fiction)
An illustrated story recounting the adventures of Abraham Lincoln and his two sons, focusing on the years when Lincoln was U.S. president.

Rappaport, Doreen. *Martin's Big Words: The Life of Dr. Martin Luther King, Jr.* Jump at the Sun/ Hyperion Books for Children, c2001. 34p. IL 3–6, Lexile: 410 (Non-fiction)
A look at the life of Dr. Martin Luther King, Jr., explaining his work to bring about a peaceful end to segregation.

Rockwell, Anne F. *Only Passing Through: The Story of Sojourner Truth.* Dell Dragonfly Books, 2002, c2000. 38p. IL 3–6, Lexile: 790 (Non-fiction)
An illustrated biography of nineteenth-century abolitionist Sojourner Truth, who was born into slavery and fought for the rights of African Americans and women.

Stone, Tanya Lee. *Elizabeth Leads the Way: Elizabeth Cady Stanton and the Right to Vote.* Henry Holt, 2008. 32p. IL K–3, Lexile: 700 (Non-fiction)
A brief biography of the life and achievements of Elizabeth Cady Stanton, the nineteenth-century women's rights activist who fought for a woman's right to vote.

Weatherford, Carole Boston. *Jesse Owens: Fastest Man Alive.* Walker, Distributed to the trade by Holtzbrinck, 2007. 32p. IL 3–6, Lexile: 880 (Non-fiction)
A biography of Jesse Owens, the African American track and field athlete who won four gold medals at the 1936 Berlin Olympic Games.

Weatherford, Carole Boston. *Moses: When Harriet Tubman Led Her People to Freedom.* Jump at the Sun/Hyperion Books for Children, c2006. 41p. IL K–3, Lexile: 660
A fictionalized account of Harriet Tubman's escape from slavery for freedom in Philadelphia, where she turned her talents to leading others along the Underground Railroad.

White, Linda Arms. *I Could Do That!: Esther Morris Gets Women the Vote.* Farrar, Straus, Giroux, 2005. 38p. IL K–3, Lexile: 780 (Non-fiction)
An account of Esther Morris, a woman whose "can-do" attitude shaped her life, helping her become instrumental in making Wyoming the first state to allow women to vote in 1869, and who then became the first woman to hold public office in the United States.

Winter, Jonah. *Roberto Clemente: Pride of the Pittsburgh Pirates.* Atheneum Books for Young Readers, c2005. 36p. IL K–3, Lexile: 800 (Non-fiction)
Presents a children's illustrated biography of baseball great Roberto Clemente, who played for the Pittsburgh Pirates from 1955 until his untimely death in an airplane crash in 1972.

Biography in Picture Book Format

Yaccarino, Dan. *The Fantastic Undersea Life of Jacques Cousteau.* Knopf, 2009. 33p. IL K–3, Lexile: 840 (Non-fiction)
> A pictorial biography of Jacques Cousteau, covering his adventures aboard the ship *Calypso* with his team of scientists, diving equipment, and waterproof cameras, and his work to protect the oceans from pollution.

Yolen, Jane. *All Star!: Honus Wagner and the Most Famous Baseball Card Ever.* Philomel Books, c2010. 34p. IL K–3, Lexile: 880 (Non-fiction)
> A biography of the personal and professional life of American Major League Baseball shortstop Honus Wagner, who played mostly for the Pittsburgh Pirates from 1897 to 1917.

Yolen, Jane. *Lost Boy: The Story of the Man Who Created Peter Pan.* Dutton Children's Books, c2010. 40p. IL K–3, Lexile: 970 (Non-fiction)
> An illustrated exploration of the childhood and adult life of J. M. Barrie, the author of *Peter Pan.*

Yoo, Paula. *Sixteen Years in Sixteen Seconds: The Sammy Lee Story.* Lee & Low Books, c2005. 32p. IL 3–6, Lexile: 880 (Non-fiction)
> Presents the true story of Dr. Sammy Lee and his desire to become an Olympic diver in an age when racism and prejudice ruled in America, and describes how he honored his father's wishes to become a doctor as well.

Alternating Narration

Younger Teens

Avi. *Never Mind!: A Twin Novel.* HarperTrophy, 2005, c2004. 200p. IL 5–8, Lexile: 620
Twelve-year-old New York City twins Meg and Edward have nothing in common, so they are just as shocked as everyone else when Meg's hopes for popularity and Edward's mischievous schemes coincidentally collide in a hilarious showdown.

Creech, Sharon. *The Wanderer.* HarperCollins Publishers, c2000. 305p. IL 3–6, Lexile: 830
Thirteen-year-old Sophie and her cousin Cody record their transatlantic crossing aboard the *Wanderer,* a forty-five-foot sailboat, on which, along with their uncles and another cousin, the children are en route to visit their grandfather in England.

Fleischman, Paul. *Whirligig.* Square Fish, 2010, c1998. 133p. IL YA, Lexile: 760
While traveling to each corner of the country to build a whirligig in memory of the girl whose death he caused, sixteen-year-old Brian finds forgiveness and atonement.

Frost, Helen. *The Braid.* Farrar, Straus and Giroux, 2006. 95p. IL YA, Lexile: 730
Two Scottish sisters, living on the western island of Barra in the 1850s, relate, in alternate voices and linked narrative poems, their experiences after their family is forcibly evicted and separated, with one sister accompanying their parents and younger siblings to Cape Breton, Canada, and the other staying behind with other family on the small island of Mingulay.

Grimes, Nikki. *Bronx Masquerade.* Dial Books, c2002. 167p. IL YA, Lexile: 670
While studying the Harlem Renaissance, students at a Bronx high school read aloud poems they have written, revealing their innermost thoughts and fears to their formerly clueless classmates.

Hearn, Julie. *The Minister's Daughter.* Simon Pulse, c2005. 263p. IL YA, Lexile: 860
In 1645 in England, the daughters of the town minister successfully accuse a local healer and her granddaughter of witchcraft to conceal an out-of-wedlock pregnancy; years later, during the 1692 Salem witch trials; their lie has unexpected repercussions.

Hesse, Karen. *Witness.* Scholastic Press, 2001. 161p. IL 5–8, Lexile: NP
A series of poems express the views of various people in a small Vermont town, including a young black girl and a young Jewish girl, during the early 1920s when the Ku Klux Klan is trying to infiltrate the town.

Konigsburg, E. L. *The View from Saturday.* Atheneum Books for Young Readers, c1996. 163p. IL 3–6, Lexile: 870
Four students, with their own individual stories, develop a special bond and attract the attention of their teacher, a paraplegic, who chooses them to represent their sixth-grade class in the Academic Bowl competition.

Myracle, Lauren. *TTYL.* Amulet Books, 2004. 209p. IL YA, Lexile: NP
Chronicles, in "instant message" format, the day-to-day experiences, feelings, and plans of three friends—Zoe, Maddie, and Angela—as they begin tenth grade.

Alternating Narration

Oates, Joyce Carol. *Big Mouth & Ugly Girl.* HarperTempest, c2002. 266p. IL YA, Lexile: 720
When sixteen-year-old Matt is falsely accused of threatening to blow up his high school and his friends turn against him, an unlikely classmate comes to his aid.

Park, Linda Sue. *When My Name Was Keoko.* Clarion Books, c2002. 199p. IL 5–8, Lexile: 610
With national pride and occasional fear, a brother and sister face the increasingly oppressive occupation of Korea by Japan during World War II, which threatens to suppress Korean culture entirely.

Pearsall, Shelley. *All of the Above: A Novel.* Little, Brown, c2006. 234p. IL 3–6 Lexile: 1000
Five urban middle school students, their teacher, and other community members relate how a school project to build the world's largest tetrahedron affects the lives of everyone involved.

Strasser, Todd. *Give a Boy a Gun.* Simon Pulse, c2000. 208p. IL YA, Lexile: 760
Events leading up to a night of terror at a high school dance are told from the point of view of various people involved.

Stroud, Jonathan. *The Amulet of Samarkand.* Miramax Books/Hyperion Books for Children, c2003. 462p. IL 5–8, Lexile: 800
Nathaniel, a young magician's apprentice, becomes caught in a web of magical espionage, murder, and rebellion, after he summons the djinni Bartimaeus and instructs him to steal the Amulet of Samarkand from the powerful magician Simon Loveland.

Van Draanen, Wendelin. *Flipped.* A. A. Knopf, c2001. 212p. IL 5–8, Lexile: 720
In alternating chapters, two teenagers describe how their feelings about themselves, each other, and their families have changed over the years.

Westerfeld, Scott. *The Last Days: A Novel.* Razorbill, c2006. 286p. IL YA, Lexile: 820
Five New York teenagers try to concentrate on their new band while the city suffers from a mysterious epidemic that is turning people into cannibals.

Yolen, Jane. *Armageddon Summer.* Harcourt, 1999, c1998. 266p. IL YA, Lexile: 820
Fourteen-year-old Marina and sixteen-year-old Jed accompany their parents' religious cult, the Believers, to await the end of the world atop a remote mountain, where they try to decide what they themselves believe.

Older Teens

Barkley, Brad. *Scrambled Eggs at Midnight.* Speak, 2006. 262p. IL YA, Lexile: 970
Calliope and Eliot, two fifteen-year-olds in Asheville, North Carolina, begin to acknowledge some unpleasant truths about their parents and form their own ideas about love.

Cohn, Rachel. *Nick & Norah's Infinite Playlist.* Knopf, c2006. 183p. IL YA, Lexile: 1020
High school student Nick O'Leary, a member of a rock band, meets college-bound Norah Silverberg and asks her to be his girlfriend for five minutes to avoid his ex-sweetheart.

Alternating Narration

De Lint, Charles. *The Blue Girl.* Firebird, c2004. 368p. IL YA, Lexile: 800
Seventeen-year-old Imogene decides to reinvent herself after moving to a new town with her family, hoping to leave behind her tough, rebellious nature, befriending the high school outcast, and trying her best to avoid trouble. When she gets on the wrong side of a gang of malicious fairies, Imogene finds herself in more trouble than ever before.

Flinn, Alex. *Fade to Black.* HarperTempest, c2005. 184p. IL YA, Lexile: 590
An HIV-positive high school student who has been hospitalized after being attacked, the bigot accused of the crime, and the only witness, a classmate with Down syndrome, reveal how the assault has changed their lives as they tell of its aftermath.

Giles, Gail. *What Happened to Cass McBride?: A Novel.* Little, Brown, 2006. 211p. IL YA, Lexile: 520
After his younger brother commits suicide, Kyle Kirby decides to exact revenge on the person he holds responsible.

Jenkins, A. M. *Beating Heart: A Ghost Story.* HarperCollins, c2006. 244p. IL YA, Lexile: 730
Following his parents' divorce, seventeen-year-old Evan moves with his mother and sister into an old house, where the spirit of a teenager who died there awakens and mistakes him for her long-departed lover.

Johnson, Angela. *The First Part Last.* Simon & Schuster Books for Young Readers, c2003. 131p. IL YA, Lexile: 790
Bobby's carefree teenage life changes forever when he becomes a father and must care for his adored baby daughter.

Moriarty, Jaclyn. *The Year of Secret Assignments.* Arthur A. Levine Books, 2004. 340p. IL YA, Lexile: 890
Three female students from Ashbury High write to three male students from rival Brookfield High as part of a pen pal program, leading to romance, humiliation, revenge plots, and war between the schools.

Myracle, Lauren. *TTYL.* Amulet Books, 2004. 209p. IL YA, Lexile: NP
Chronicles, in "instant message" format, the day-to-day experiences, feelings, and plans of three friends—Zoe, Maddie, and Angela—as they begin tenth grade.

Pearsall, Shelley. *All of the Above: A Novel.* Little, Brown, c2006. 234p. IL 3–6 Lexile: 1000
Five urban middle school students, their teacher, and other community members relate how a school project to build the world's largest tetrahedron affects the lives of everyone involved.

Rapp, Adam. *33 Snowfish.* Candlewick Press, c2003. 179p. IL YA, Lexile: 1050
A homeless boy, running from the police with a fifteen-year-old, drug-addicted prostitute, her boyfriend who just killed his own parents, and a baby, gets the chance to make a better life for himself.

Stone, Tanya Lee. *A Bad Boy Can Be Good for a Girl.* Wendy Lamb Books, c2006. 228p. IL YA, Lexile: 780
Josie, Nicolette, and Aviva all fall for the same sexy high school senior; while each makes different choices, they are all changed by their experiences of love and sex.

Alternating Narration

Strasser, Todd. *Give a Boy a Gun.* Simon Pulse, c2000. 208p. IL YA, Lexile: 760
Events leading up to a night of terror at a high school dance are told from the point of view of various people involved.

Volponi, Paul. *Black and White.* Viking, 2005. 185p. IL YA, Lexile: 710
Two star high school basketball players, one black and one white, experience the justice system differently after committing a crime together and getting caught.

Westerfeld, Scott. *The Last Days: A Novel.* Razorbill, c2006. 286p. IL YA, Lexile: 820
Five New York teenagers try to concentrate on their new band while the city suffers from a mysterious epidemic that is turning people into cannibals.

Scary Books for Middle School Students

Series

Bellairs, John. *The Curse of the Blue Figurine.* Puffin Books, 2004, c1983. 200p. IL 5–8
Johnny Dixon is plunged into a terrifying mystery-adventure when he removes a blue figurine called an ushabti from church.

Bellairs, John. *The House with a Clock in Its Walls.* Puffin Books, 2004. 179p. IL 5–8
A boy goes to live with his magician uncle in a mansion that has a clock hidden in the walls; the clock is ticking off the minutes until doomsday.

Bellairs, John. *The Mummy, the Will, and the Crypt.* Puffin Books, 2004, c1983. 168p. IL 5–8
Twelve-year-old Johnny Dixon and his friend Professor Childermass look for the hidden will left by an eccentric cereal tycoon, who wished to make life difficult for his heirs after his own death by suicide.

Bruchac, Joseph. *Skeleton Man.* HarperTrophy, 2003, c2001. 114p. IL 5–8, Lexile: 730
After her parents disappear and she is turned over to the care of a strange "great-uncle," Molly must rely on her dreams about an old Mohawk story for her safety—and maybe even for her life.

Gaiman, Neil. *Coraline.* HarperCollins, c2002. 162p. IL 5–8, Lexile: 740
Looking for excitement, Coraline ventures through a mysterious door into a world that is similar, yet disturbingly different from her own, where she must challenge a gruesome entity to save herself, her parents, and the souls of three others.

Hahn, Mary Downing. *The Dead Man in Indian Creek.* Sandpiper, c1990. 130p. IL 5–8, Lexile: 820
When Matt and Parker find a dead man at the edge of Indian Creek and learn the body they found may be a drug-related death, they fear Parker's mother, Pam, and her new boyfriend, Evans, may be involved.

Naylor, Phyllis Reynolds. *Jade Green: A Ghost Story.* Atheneum, c1999. 168p. IL 5–8, Lexile: 1040
While living with her uncle in a house haunted by the ghost of a young woman, recently orphaned Judith Sparrow wonders if her one small transgression is the cause of mysterious happenings.

Nixon, Joan Lowery. *The House on Hackman's Hill.* Scholastic, 1990, c1985. 126p. IL 3–6, Lexile: 780
Jeff and Debbie make their way through the snow to the old Hackman mansion to look for a stolen Egyptian mummy. Soon they are trapped in the house by the snow.

Steampunk

Aiken, Joan. *The Wolves of Willoughby Chase.* Dell Yearling, 2001, c1962. 181p. IL 5–8, Lexile: 1020
Surrounded by villains of the first order, brave Bonnie and gentle cousin Sylvia conquer all obstacles in this Victorian melodrama.

Beddor, Frank. *The Looking Glass Wars.* Speak, c2006. 358p. IL YA, Lexile: 1010
When she is cast out of Wonderland by her evil aunt Redd, young Alyss Heart finds herself living in Victorian Oxford as Alice Liddell; she struggles to keep memories of her kingdom intact until she can return and claim her rightful throne.

Bray, Libba. *A Great and Terrible Beauty.* Delacorte Press, c2003. 403p. IL YA, Lexile: 760
After the suspicious death of her mother in 1895, sixteen-year-old Gemma returns to England, after many years in India, to attend a finishing school where she becomes aware of her magical powers and ability to see into the spirit world.

Conaway, Judith. *20,000 Leagues under the Sea.* Random House, 1994, c1983. 95p. IL 3–6
An adaptation of the nineteenth-century science fiction tale of an electric submarine, its eccentric captain, and the undersea world, which anticipated many of the scientific achievements of the twentieth century.

Dolamore, Jaclyn. *Magic under Glass.* Bloomsbury, 2010. 225p. IL YA, Lexile: 680
A wealthy sorcerer's invitation to sing with his automaton leads seventeen-year-old Nimira, whose family's disgrace brought her from a palace to poverty, into political intrigue, enchantments, and a friendship with a fairy prince who needs her help.

DuPrau, Jeanne. *The City of Ember.* Random House, c2003. 270p. IL 5–8, Lexile: 680
In the city of Ember, twelve-year-old Lina trades jobs on Assignment Day to be a Messenger—a role that allows her to run to new places in her decaying but beloved city, perhaps even to glimpse Unknown Regions.

Foglio, Kaja. *Girl Genius. 1: Agatha Heterodyne & the Beetleburg Clank.* Airship Entertainment, c2010. 86p. IL YA
Agatha Clay, a student at Transylvania Polygnostic University, has trouble concentrating and rotten luck. She seems doomed for a career as a minor lab assistant, but when the university is overtaken and a strange clank stalks the streets, it seems she may have a spark of Mad Science in her after all.

Harland, Richard. *Worldshaker.* Simon & Schuster Books for Young Readers, 2010, c2009. 388p. IL YA, Lexile: 640
Sixteen-year-old Col Porpentine is being groomed as the next Commander of Worldshaker, a juggernaut where elite families live on the upper decks while the Filthies toil below. When Col meets Riff, a Filthy girl on the run, he discovers how ignorant he is of his home and its residents.

Knox, Elizabeth. *Dreamhunter.* Farrar, Straus and Giroux, 2006. 365p. IL YA Lexile: 880
In a world where select people can enter "The Place" and find dreams of every kind to share with others for a fee, a fifteen-year-old girl trains to be a dreamhunter. When her father disappears, she is left to carry on his mysterious mission.

Steampunk

Knox, Elizabeth. *Dreamquake*. Farrar, Straus and Giroux, 2007. 449p. IL YA, Lexile: 850
While investigating the government's involvement in the disappearance of her father, Tziga Hame, and the decline of the art of projecting dreams, dreamhunter Laura learns more about "The Place."

Mieville, China. *Perdido Street Station*. Ballantine Publishing Group, 2001, c2000. 710p. IL AD
New Crobuzon is a squalid city where humans, Re-mades, and arcane races live in perpetual fear—but when an evil monster is let loose, the city's residents must band together to find a way to kill it before they are all destroyed.

Mieville, China. *Un Lun Dun*. Del Rey/Ballantine Books, 2008, c2007. 474p. IL YA, Lexile: 630
Twelve-year-old Zanna and her friend Deeba discover an entrance to a strange world where they encounter killer giraffes, animated umbrellas, ghost children, and flying double-decker buses.

Milford, Kate. *The Boneshaker*. Clarion Books, 2010. 372p. IL 5–8, Lexile: 900
When Jake Limberleg brings his traveling medicine show to a small Missouri town in 1913, thirteen-year-old Natalie senses that something is wrong and, after investigating, learns that her love of automata and other machines make her the only one who can set things right.

Moore, Alan. *The League of Extraordinary Gentlemen*. America's Best Comics, c2000. IL AD
The adventures of the League of Extraordinary Gentlemen, a group composed of characters taken from late-nineteenth-century literature, as they defend Britain against various villains. Includes the text story "Allan and the Sundered Veil" by Alan Moore and illustrated by Kevin O'Neill.

Novik, Naomi. *His Majesty's Dragon*. Del Rey/Ballantine Books, c2006. 356p. IL AD, Lexile: 1030
After capturing a French frigate and seizing its precious cargo, Captain Will Laurence of the HMS *Reliant* befriends the dragon Temeraire and uses his new friend to help defend his country from other airborne dragon forces.

Oppel, Kenneth. *Airborn*. Eos, c2004. 355p. IL YA, Lexile: 760
Matt, a young cabin boy aboard an airship, and Kate, a wealthy young girl traveling with her chaperone, team up to search for the existence of mysterious winged creatures reportedly living hundreds of feet above the Earth's surface.

Reeve, Philip. *Larklight, or, The Revenge of the White Spiders!, Or, To Saturn's Rings and Back!: A Rousing Tale of Dauntless Pluck in the Farthest Reaches of Space*. Bloomsbury Children's Books, 2006. 399p. IL 5–8, Lexile: 1170
In an alternate Victorian England, young Arthur and his sister Myrtle—residents of Larklight, a floating house in one of Her Majesty's outer space territories—uncover a spidery plot to destroy the solar system.

Reeve, Philip. *Starcross, or, The Coming of the Moobs, Or, Our Adventures in the Fourth Dimension!: A Stirring Adventure of Spies, Time Travel and Curious Hats*. Bloomsbury Children's Books, 2007. 368p. IL 5–8, Lexile: 1150
Young Arthur Mumby, his sister Myrtle, and their mother accept an invitation to take a holiday at an up-and-coming resort in the asteroid belt, where they become involved in a dastardly plot involving spies, time travel, and mind-altering clothing.

Steampunk

Richards, Justin. *The Death Collector.* Bloomsbury, 2007, c2006. 320p. IL YA, Lexile: 800
Three teens and a curator of unclassified artifacts at the British Museum match wits with a madman determined to use unorthodox methods to reanimate the dead—both humans and dinosaurs.

Selznick, Brian. *The Invention of Hugo Cabret: A Novel in Words and Pictures.* Scholastic Press, 2007. 533p. IL 3–6, Lexile: 820
When twelve-year-old Hugo, an orphan living and repairing clocks within the walls of a Paris train station in 1931, meets a mysterious toyseller and his goddaughter, his undercover life and his biggest secret are jeopardized.

Sfar, Joann. *The Professor's Daughter.* First Second, 2007. 64p. IL AD
The daughter of a renowned archeologist and the well-preserved Imhotep IV, who has just woken up after a 3,000-year sleep, fall in love, but many things stand in their way, not the least of which is her father, who plans to put Imhotep on permanent display at the British museum.

Stephenson, Neal. *The Diamond Age.* Bantam Books, 2003, c1995. 499p. IL AD
Nell, a street urchin in a neo-Victorian future, is given the power to decode and reprogram the course of humanity when her brother mugs engineer John Percival Hackworth and brings home an illegal interactive device designed to teach girls to think for themselves.

Stevermer, Caroline. *A College of Magics.* Starscape, 2005, c1994. 468p. IL 5–8
Faris Nallaneen, the teenage heir to the small northern dukedom of Galazo, who is still too young to claim her title, is banished by her despotic uncle to the College of Greenlaw; it turns out to be a school for magic, which leads to Faris's involvement in a variety of intrigues.

Stevermer, Caroline. *A Scholar of Magics.* Starscape, 2006, c2004. 426p. IL AD
Wyoming sharpshooter Samuel Lambert comes to England's Glasscastle University to assist with a top-secret project, unaware of the dangerous magic within the castle walls, and finds himself enchanted by the provost's sister.

Ward, James M. *Midshipwizard Halcyon Blithe.* Tor, 2006, c2005. 288p. IL YA
Halcyon Blithe dreams of finding his fortune among those who sail the dragonships, and becomes a midshipwizard on a dragonship, hoping to make a name for himself and achieve immortality.

Webb, Catherine. *The Extraordinary and Unusual Adventures of Horatio Lyle.* Atom, 2007, c2006. 311p. IL YA
Horatio Lyle, a former Special Constable, brings his passion for science and invention into play when he teams up with a reformed pickpocket and a rebellious young gentleman to investigate a conspiracy involving a missing Chinese artifact.

Wooding, Chris. *The Haunting of Alaizabel Cray.* Orchard Books, 2004, c2001. 292p. IL YA, Lexile: 970
As Thaniel, a wych-hunter, and Cathaline, his friend and mentor, try to destroy the terrible creatures that infest the alleys of London's Old Quarter, their lives become entwined with that of Alaizabel Cray, a woman who may be either mad or possessed.

Steampunk

Series

Mowll, Joshua. *Guild of Specialists.* Candlewick Press, 2008– . IL 5–8
The posthumous papers of Rebecca MacKenzie document her adventures, along with those of her brother Doug, in 1920s China as the teenaged siblings are sent to live aboard their uncle's ship; there they become involved in the dangerous activities of a mysterious secret society called the Honourable Guild of Specialists.

Nix, Garth. *The Abhorsen Trilogy.* Eos, 1996–2004. IL YA
A fantasy trilogy following the magical adventures of Sabriel, her father Abhorsen, a powerful necromancer, and their ancestors and descendants in the magical Old Kingdom.

Nix, Garth. *Keys to the Kingdom.* Scholastic Press, 2005. 389p. IL 3–6
One mysterious house is the doorway to a very mysterious world—where one boy is about to venture and unlock a number of fantastical secrets.

Novik, Naomi. *Temeraire.* Del Rey/Ballantine Books, c2006. 365p. IL AD
Captain Will Laurence of HMS *Reliant* befriends the dragon Temeraire and uses his new friend to help defend his country from other air-borne dragon forces.

Reeve, Philip. *Mortal Engines Quartet.* Scholastic Press, c2010. IL YA
Tom, a third-class apprentice in a distant future in which technology has been lost and tiered cities move about the Earth on caterpillar tracks, often absorbing smaller locales, has many dangerous adventures after being pushed off London by Thaddeus Valentine, a historian who is trying to resurrect an ancient atomic weapon.

Slade, Arthur. *Hunchback Assignments.* Wendy Lamb Books, c2009– . IL YA
In Victorian London, fourteen-year-old Modo, a shape-changing hunchback, becomes a secret agent for the Permanent Association, which strives to protect the world from the evil machinations of the Clockwork Guild.

Springer, Nancy. *Enola Holmes Mystery.* Philomel Books, c2006– . IL 5–8
Enola Holmes, the much younger sister of famed detective Sherlock Holmes, must travel to London in disguise to unravel the disappearance of her missing mother.

Updale, Eleanor. *Montmorency.* Orchard Books, 2006. 404p. IL 5–8
Gripping tales of adventure set in Victorian London. Montmorency is a thief leading a double life—as a distinguished gentleman and his degenerate servant.

Whitehouse, Howard. *Mad Misadventures of Emmaline and Rubberbones.* Kids Can Press, c2007. 272p. IL 3–6
Fourteen-year-old tomboy Emmaline Cayley is sent away to St. Grimelda's School for Young Ladies in hopes of ridding her of her unladylike ways.

Vampires for Boys

Enthoven, Sam. *The Black Tattoo.* Razorbill, c2006. 503p. IL YA, Lexile: 800

When his best friend Charlie is possessed by an ancient demon, fourteen-year-old Jack, accompanied by Esme, a girl with superhuman powers, battles foes all over London and into Hell to save him.

Jinks, Catherine. *The Reformed Vampire Support Group.* Harcourt, 2009. 362p. IL YA, Lexile: 750

Fifteen-year-old vampire Nina has been stuck for fifty-one years in a boring support group for vampires, and nothing exciting has ever happened to them—until one of them is murdered and the other group members must try to solve the crime.

Johnson, Pete. *The Vampire Blog.* Yearling, c2011.IL 3–6

On the night of his thirteenth birthday, Matt's parents tell him that he is actually half-vampire and is about to go through his vampire changeover period. Matt has to come to grips with things like fangs, musty breath, and being awake all night, as well as dealing with the everyday life of a thirteen-year-old boy.

Rice, Anne. *Interview with the Vampire.* Knopf, 1976. 371p. IL AD, Lexile: 970

Contains the confessions of a vampire, which are hypnotic, shocking, and erotic.

Sedgwick, Marcus. *My Swordhand Is Singing.* Laurel-Leaf Books, 2007. 205p. IL YA, Lexile: 770

In the dangerous dark of winter in an Eastern European village during the early seventeenth century, Peter learns from a gypsy girl that the Shadow Queen is behind a recent series of murders and reanimations, and his father's secret past may hold the key to stopping her.

Waters, Dan. *Generation Dead.* Hyperion, c2008. 392p. IL YA, Lexile: 820

When dead teenagers who have come back to life start showing up at her high school, Phoebe, a Goth girl, becomes interested in the phenomenon; when she starts dating a "living impaired" boy, they encounter prejudice, fear, and hatred.

Wells, Dan. *I Am Not a Serial Killer.* Tom Doherty Associates, 2010. 271p. IL AD

Fifteen-year-old sociopath John Wayne Cleaver, having set rigid rules by which he must live to prevent himself from becoming a murderer, is intrigued by a body found behind a local laundromat and conducts his own investigation into what he believes are the actions of a serial killer.

Wells, Dan. *Mr. Monster.* Tor, 2010. 287p. IL AD

Young John Wayne Cleaver, who associates his killer instincts with the persona he refers to as "Mr. Monster," has another monster to kill when his disposal of a demon draws another demon to Clayton County and its victims begin to arrive at the mortuary; John must vanquish the new demon and his own Mr. Monster to save Clayton.

Vampires for Boys

Series

Clare, Cassandra. *The Mortal Instruments*. Margaret K. McElderry Books, c2007–c2009. IL YA
Collects the first three novels in Cassandra Clare's *Mortal Instrument* series, in which teenager
Clary Fray, who has the ability to see demons, is almost killed by a monster, becomes involved with
the Shadowhunters, learns terrifying truths about her family, and tries to find a cure for her mother's
enchantment.

Warm and Fuzzy Books for Middle School Students

Birney, Betty. *The Seven Wonders of Sassafras Springs*. Atheneum Books for Young Readers, c2005. 210p. IL 3–6, Lexile: 790
> Eben McAllister searches his small town to see if he can find anything comparable to the real Seven Wonders of the World.

Grisham, John. *Skipping Christmas*. Doubleday, c2001. 177p. IL AD
> Luther and Nora Krank decide to opt out of Christmas, choosing instead to set sail on a Caribbean cruise on December 25, but they learn there are consequences to pay for trying to ignore the holiday frenzy.

Hiaasen, Carl. *Hoot*. Alfred A. Knopf, Distributed by Random House, c2002. 292p. IL 5–8, Lexile: 760
> Roy, who is new to his small Florida community, becomes involved in another boy's attempt to save a colony of burrowing owls from a proposed construction site.

Korman, Gordon. *Schooled*. Hyperion Paperbacks for Children, 2008, c2007. 208p. IL 5–8, Lexile: 740
> Cap lives in isolation with his grandmother, a former hippie; when she falls from a tree and breaks her hip, Cap is sent to a foster home, where he has his first experience in a public school.

Law, Ingrid. *Savvy*. Dial Books for Young Readers, Walton Media, c2008. 342p. IL 5–8, Lexile: 1070
> Recounts the adventures of Mibs Beaumont, whose thirteenth birthday has revealed her "savvy"— a magical power unique to each member of her family—just as her father is injured in a terrible accident.

Osa, Nancy. *Cuba 15: A Novel*. Delacorte Press, 2005, c2003. 277p. IL YA, Lexile: 750
> Violet Paz, a Chicago high school student, reluctantly prepares for her upcoming "quince," a Spanish nickname for the celebration of a Hispanic girl's fifteenth birthday.

Peck, Richard. *A Long Way from Chicago: A Novel in Stories*. Dial Books for Young Readers, c1998. 148p. IL 5–8, Lexile: 750
> A boy recounts his annual summer trips to rural Illinois with his sister during the Great Depression to visit their larger-than-life grandmother.

Rinaldi, Ann. *Wolf by the Ears*. Scholastic, c1991. 252p. IL YA, Lexile: 580
> Harriet Hemings, rumored to be the daughter of Thomas Jefferson and Sally Hemings, one of his black slaves, struggles with the problems facing her—to escape from the velvet cage that is Monticello, or to stay and remain a slave.

Van Draanen, Wendelin. *Flipped*. A. A. Knopf, c2001. 212p. IL 5–8, Lexile: 720
> In alternating chapters, two teenagers describe how their feelings about themselves, each other, and their families have changed over the years.

Warm and Fuzzy Books for Middle School Students

Weeks, Sarah. *So B. It: A Novel.* Laura Geringer Books, c2004. 245p. IL 5–8, Lexile: 860
   After spending her life with her mentally disabled mother and agoraphobic neighbor, twelve-year-old Heidi sets out from Reno, Nevada, to New York to find out who she is.

Zimmer, Tracie Vaughn. *Reaching for Sun.* Bloomsbury Children's Books, 2007. 181p. IL 3–6, Lexile: NP
   Josie, who lives with her mother and grandmother and has cerebral palsy, befriends a boy who moves into one of the rich houses behind her old farmhouse.

Historical Fiction for Middle School Boys

Avi. *Don't You Know There's a War on?* HarperTrophy, 2003, c2001. 200p. IL 3–6, Lexile: 500
In wartime Brooklyn in 1943, eleven-year-old Howie Crispers mounts a campaign to save his favorite teacher from being fired.

Avi. *The Fighting Ground.* Lippincott, c1984. 157p. IL 5–8, Lexile: 580
Thirteen-year-old Jonathan goes off to fight in the Revolutionary War and discovers the real war is being fought within himself.

Bartoletti, Susan Campbell. *The Boy Who Dared.* Scholastic Press, 2008. 202p. IL 5–8, Lexile: 760
In October 1942, seventeen-year-old Helmuth Hubener, imprisoned for distributing anti-Nazi leaflets, recalls his past life and how he came to dedicate himself to bring the truth about Hitler and the war to the German people.

Bruchac, Joseph. *Code Talker: A Novel about the Navajo Marines of World War Two.* Dial Books, c2005. 231p. IL 5–8, Lexile: 910
After being taught in a boarding school run by whites that Navajo is a useless language, Ned Begay and other Navajo men are recruited by the Marines to become Code Talkers, sending messages during World War II in their native tongue.

Buckley-Archer, Linda. *Gideon the Cutpurse: Being the First Part of the Gideon Trilogy.* Simon & Schuster Books for Young Readers, 2006. 404p. IL 5–8, Lexile: 960
Ignored by his father and sent to Derbyshire for the weekend, twelve-year-old Peter and his new friend Kate are accidentally transported back in time to 1763 England, where they are befriended by a reformed cutpurse.

Cadnum, Michael. *The Book of the Lion.* Speak, 2003, c2000. 204p. IL YA, Lexile: 980
In twelfth-century England, after his master, a maker of coins for the king, is brutally punished for alleged cheating, seventeen-year-old Edmund finds himself traveling to the Holy Land as squire to a knight crusader on his way to join the forces of Richard the Lionheart.

Carbone, Elisa Lynn. *Storm Warriors.* Dell Yearling, 2002, c2001. 168p. IL 5–8, Lexile: 890
In 1895, after his mother's death, twelve-year-old Nathan moves with his father and grandfather to Pea Island off the coast of North Carolina, where he hopes to join the all-black crew at the nearby lifesaving station, despite his father's objections.

Choldenko, Gennifer. *Al Capone Does My Shirts.* Putnam's, c2004. 228p. IL 5–8, Lexile: 600
A twelve-year-old boy named Moose moves to Alcatraz Island in 1935 when guards' families were housed there, and has to contend with his extraordinary new environment in addition to life with his autistic sister.

Collier, James Lincoln. *Jump Ship to Freedom.* Bantam Doubleday Dell Books for Young Readers, 1987, c1981. 198p. IL 5–8, Lexile: 850
In 1787, a fourteen-year-old slave, anxious to buy freedom for himself and his mother, escapes from his dishonest master and tries to find help in cashing the soldier's notes received by his father for fighting in the Revolution.

Historical Fiction for Middle School Boys

Collier, James Lincoln. *My Brother Sam Is Dead.* Simon & Schuster Books for Young Readers, 1985, c1974. 216p. IL 5–8, Lexile: 770
> Recounts the tragedy that strikes the Meeker family during the American Revolution, when one son joins the rebel forces while the rest of the family tries to stay neutral in a Tory town.

Conly, Jane Leslie. *Murder Afloat.* Disney/Hyperion Books, c2010. 164p. IL 5–8
> Benjamin Franklin Orville's life is torn asunder when a simple trip to the market goes awry and Benjy is taken by captors with a group of German immigrants to work with the poorly kept crew of the *Ella Dawn,* a North Atlantic oystering vessel.

Crane, Stephen. *The Red Badge of Courage.* Bantam Books, 1983. 138p. IL YA, Lexile: 900
> During his service in the Civil War, a young Union soldier matures to manhood and finds peace of mind as he comes to grips with his conflicting emotions about war.

Curtis, Christopher Paul. *Elijah of Buxton.* Scholastic, 2007. 341p. IL 3–6, Lexile: 1070
> Eleven-year-old Elijah Freeman, the first free-born child in Buxton, Canada, which is a haven for slaves fleeing the American South in 1859, uses his wits and skills to try to bring to justice the lying preacher who has stolen money that was to be used to buy a family's freedom.

Curtis, Christopher Paul. *The Watsons Go to Birmingham—1963: A Novel.* Delacorte Press, c1995. 210p. IL 5–8, Lexile: 1000
> The ordinary interactions and everyday routines of the Watsons, an African American family living in Flint, Michigan, change drastically after they go to visit Grandma in Alabama in the summer of 1963.

DeFelice, Cynthia C. *Weasel.* Avon Books, 1991, c1990. 119p. IL 5–8, Lexile: 870
> Alone in the frontier wilderness in the winter of 1839 while his father is recovering from an injury, eleven-year-old Nathan runs afoul of the renegade killer known as Weasel and makes a surprising discovery about the concept of revenge.

Fleischman, Paul. *Bull Run.* Laura Geringer Book/HarperTrophy, 1995, c1993. 104p. IL 5–8, Lexile: 810
> Northerners, Southerners, generals, couriers, dreaming boys, and worried sisters describe the glory, the horror, the thrill, and the disillusionment of the first battle of the Civil War.

Flood, Bo. *Warriors in the Crossfire.* Front Street, c2010. 142p. IL 5–8, Lexile: 560
> Joseph, living on the island of Saipan during World War II, learns what it means to be a warrior as he and his family struggle to survive in the face of impending invasion.

Hobbs, Will. *Far North.* Morrow Junior Books, c1996. 226p. IL 5–8, Lexile: 820
> After the destruction of their float plane, sixteen-year-old Gabe and his Dene friend, Raymond, struggle to survive a winter in the wilderness of the Northwest Territories of Canada.

Hobbs, Will. *Jason's Gold.* Morrow Junior Books, c1999. 221p. IL 5–8, Lexile: 860
> Fifteen-year-old Jason embarks on a 10,000-mile journey in 1897 in hopes of striking it rich after hearing the news that gold has been discovered in Canada's Yukon Territory.

Historical Fiction for Middle School Boys

Klages, Ellen. *The Green Glass Sea.* Viking, 2006. 321p. IL 5–8, Lexile: 790
While her father works on the Manhattan Project, eleven-year-old gadget lover and outcast Dewey Kerrigan lives in Los Alamos Camp, and becomes friends with Suze, another young girl who is shunned by her peers.

Lisle, Janet Taylor. *The Art of Keeping Cool.* Aladdin Paperbacks, c2000. 250p. IL 5–8, Lexile: 730
In 1942, Robert and his cousin Elliot uncover long-hidden family secrets while staying in their grandparents' Rhode Island town, where they also become involved with a German artist who is suspected of being a spy.

Lytle, Robert A. *A Pitch in Time.* EDCO, c2002. 316p. IL 5–8
A young boy tumbles from his bike and wakes up to find he has traveled back in time to the spring of 1864, where the turbulent times come in conflict with everything he has ever known.

Mazer, Harry. *A Boy at War: A Novel of Pearl Harbor.* Simon & Schuster Books for Young Readers, 2002, c2001. 104p. IL 3–6
While fishing with his friends off Honolulu on December 7, 1941, teenaged Adam is caught in the midst of the Japanese attack. During the chaos of the subsequent days, he tries to find his father, a naval officer who was serving on the U.S.S. *Arizona* when the bombs fell.

Napoli, Donna Jo. *Stones in Water.* Puffin, 1999, c1997. 209p. IL 5–8, Lexile: 630
After being taken by German soldiers from a local movie theater along with other Italian boys, including his Jewish friend, Roberto is forced to work in Germany; he escapes into the Ukrainian winter, before desperately trying to make his way back home to Venice.

Paulsen, Gary. *The Legend of Bass Reeves: Being the True Account of the Most Valiant Marshal in the West.* Wendy Lamb Books, c2006. 137p. IL 5–8, Lexile: 950
The story of Bass Reeves, who was born a slave and later became one of the most respected federal marshals in Oklahoma and Texas.

Paulsen, Gary. *Soldier's Heart: Being the Story of the Enlistment and Due Service of the Boy Charley Goddard in the First Minnesota Volunteers: A Novel of the Civil War.* Delacorte Press, c1998. 106p. IL YA, Lexile: 1000
Eager to enlist, fifteen-year-old Charley has a change of heart after experiencing both the physical horrors and mental anguish of Civil War combat.

Paulsen, Gary. *Woods Runner.* Wendy Lamb Books, c2010. 164p. IL 5–8, Lexile: 870
From his 1776 Pennsylvania homestead, thirteen-year-old Samuel, who is a highly skilled woods-man, sets out toward New York City to rescue his parents from the band of British soldiers and Native Americans who kidnapped them after slaughtering most of their community. Includes historical notes.

Philbrick, W. R. *The Mostly True Adventures of Homer P. Figg.* Blue Sky Press, c2009. 224p. IL 3–6, Lexile: 950
Homer P. Figg escapes from his wretched foster home in Pine Swamp, Maine, and sets out to find his beloved older brother, Harold, who has been illegally sold into the Union Army.

Historical Fiction for Middle School Boys

Preus, Margi. *Heart of a Samurai: Based on the True Story of Nakahama Manjiro.* Amulet Books, 2010. 301p. IL YA, Lexile: 760

In 1841, after being rescued by an American whaler after a terrible shipwreck leaves him and his four companions castaways on a remote island, fourteen-year-old Manjiro, who dreams of becoming a samurai, learns new laws and customs as he becomes the first Japanese person to set foot in the United States.

Scaletta, Kurtis. *Mamba Point.* Knopf, c2010. 271p. IL 5–8

After moving with his family to Liberia, twelve-year-old Linus discovers that he has a mystical connection with the black mamba, one of the deadliest snakes in Africa, which he is told will give him some of the snake's characteristics.

Schmidt, Gary D. *The Wednesday Wars.* Clarion Books, c2007. 264p. IL 5–8, Lexile: 990

During the 1967 school year, on Wednesday afternoons when all his classmates go to either Catechism or Hebrew school, seventh-grader Holling Hoodhood stays in Mrs. Baker's classroom, where they read the plays of William Shakespeare and Holling learns valuable lessons about the world he lives in.

Smith, Roland. *Elephant Run.* Hyperion Books for Children, c2007. 318p. IL 5–8, Lexile: 750

Nick's father and others are taken prisoner when his plantation in Burma is invaded by the Japanese in 1941; Nick and his friend Mya risk their lives to free the captives from the POW camp.

Wilson, John. *Four Steps to Death.* KCP Fiction, c2005. 207p. IL YA

The fates of three young men come together during the Battle of Stalingrad in Russia during World War II.

Humor for Middle School Boys

Adams, Douglas. *The Hitchhiker's Guide to the Galaxy.* Harmony Books, c1979. 215p. IL YA
Seconds before Earth is destroyed to make room for a galactic freeway, a young man is rescued by an alien friend, who whisks him away on a space-traveling adventure.

Angleberger, Tom. *The Strange Case of Origami Yoda.* Amulet Books, 2010. 141p. IL 3–6, Lexile: 760
Sixth-grader Tommy and his friends describe their interactions with a paper finger puppet of Yoda, worn by their weird classmate Dwight, as they try to figure out whether the puppet can really predict the future. The book includes instructions for making an origami Yoda.

Berk, Josh. *The Dark Days of Hamburger Halpin.* Knopf, c2010. 250p. IL YA, Lexile: 820
When Will Halpin transfers from his all-deaf school into a mainstream Pennsylvania high school, he faces discrimination and bullying, but still manages to solve a mystery surrounding the death of a popular football player in his class.

Calame, Don. *Swim the Fly.* Candlewick Press, 2009. 345p. IL YA, Lexile: 620
Swim team members and best friends Matt, Sean, and Coop set themselves the summertime goal of seeing a live girl naked. While the chances of that happening seem very dim, Matt's personal goal to swim the one-hundred-yard butterfly to impress the new girl on the team appears even less likely to be realized.

Crawford, Brent. *Carter Finally Gets It.* Disney Hyperion Books, c2009. 300p. IL YA, Lexile: 760
Awkward freshman Will Carter endures many painful moments during his first year of high school before realizing that nothing good comes easily, focus is everything, and the payoff is usually incredible.

Crawford, Brent. *Carter's Big Break: A Novel.* Hyperion, c2010. 231p. IL YA, Lexile: 940
Fourteen-year-old Will Carter's summer gets off to a bad start when his girlfriend leaves him, but then he is cast opposite a major star, Hilary Idaho, in a small movie being filmed in his town—and things start looking up.

Gill, David Macinnis. *Black Hole Sun.* Greenwillow Books, c2010. 340p. IL YA, Lexile: 610
Sixteen-year-old Durango and his crew of mercenaries are hired by the settlers of a mining community on Mars to protect their most valuable resource from a feral band of marauders.

Going, Kelly. *Fat Kid Rules the World.* G. P. Putnam's Sons, c2003. 187p. IL YA, Lexile: 700
Seventeen-year-old Troy—depressed, suicidal, and weighing nearly three hundred pounds—gets a new perspective on life when Curt, a semi-homeless teen who is a genius on guitar, asks Troy to be the drummer in a rock band.

Jinks, Catherine. *Evil Genius.* Harcourt, 2007, c2005. 486p. IL YA, Lexile: 720
Child prodigy Cadel Piggot, an antisocial computer hacker, discovers his true identity when he enrolls as a first-year student at an advanced crime academy.

Korman, Gordon. *Born to Rock.* Hyperion Paperbacks, 2008, c2006. 261p. IL YA, Lexile: 780
High school senior Leo Caraway, a conservative Republican, learns that his biological father is a punk rock legend.

Humor for Middle School Boys

Korman, Gordon. *Son of the Mob.* Hyperion Paperbacks, 2004, c2002. 262p. IL YA, Lexile: 690
Seventeen-year-old Vince's life is constantly complicated by the fact that he is the son of a powerful Mafia boss, a relationship that threatens to destroy his romance with the daughter of an FBI agent.

Lieb, Josh. *I Am a Genius of Unspeakable Evil and I Want to Be Your Class President.* Razorbill, c2009. 302p. IL YA, Lexile: 780
Twelve-year-old evil genius, Oliver, uses his great brain to become the third richest person in the world. He then finds that overthrowing foreign dictators is easier than getting the kids in his middle school to vote him class president.

Lubar, David. *Dunk.* Graphia, c2002. 260p. IL YA, Lexile: 520
Chad, hoping to work out his frustrations and his anger by taking a summer job as a dunk tank Bozo on the boardwalk at the New Jersey shore, comes to a better understanding of himself and the uses of humor as he undergoes training in the fine art of insults.

Lubar, David. *Sleeping Freshmen Never Lie.* Dutton, c2005. 279p. IL YA, Lexile: 560
While navigating his first year of high school and awaiting the birth of his new baby brother, Scott loses old friends and gains some unlikely new ones as he hones his skills as a writer.

Paulsen, Gary. *How Angel Peterson Got His Name: And Other Outrageous Tales about Extreme Sports.* Dell Yearling, 2004, c2003. 111p. IL 5–8, Lexile: 1180
Author Gary Paulsen relates tales from his youth in a small town in northwestern Minnesota in the late 1940s and early 1950s, such as skiing behind a souped-up car and imitating daredevil Evel Knievel.

Pearce, Jonathan. *A Little Honesty: Aches and Joys of an American Prince.* BalonaBooks, c2005. 226p. IL YA
Sixteen-year-old Zachary Taylor, stuck in summer school, escapes his boredom, as well as the very real problems in his life, by losing himself in daydreams.

Sonnenblick, Jordan. *Notes from the Midnight Driver.* Scholastic Press, 2006. 265p. IL YA, Lexile: 930
After being assigned to perform community service at a nursing home, sixteen-year-old Alex befriends a cantankerous old man who has some lessons to impart about jazz guitar playing, love, and forgiveness.

Van de Ruit, John. *Spud.* Razorbill, c2007. 317p. IL YA
In 1990, thirteen-year-old John "Spud" Milton, a prepubescent choirboy, keeps a diary of his first year at an elite, boys-only boarding school in South Africa, as he deals with bizarre housemates, wild crushes, embarrassingly dysfunctional parents, and much more.

Wizner, Jake. *Spanking Shakespeare.* Random House, c2007. 287p. IL YA, Lexile: 850
Shakespeare Shapiro has always hated his name, which has been a source of teasing all the way through school. He may get his revenge through his memoirs—a school project that has chronicled every detail of his life.

Genres

Humor for Middle School Boys

Series

Kinney, Jeff. *Diary of a Wimpy Kid Series.* Amulet Books, 2008– . IL 5–8
Greg Heffley recounts his day-to-day adventures.

Humor for Young Adults

Abdel-Fattah, Randa. *Does My Head Look Big in This?* Orchard Books, 2007, c2005. 360p. IL YA, Lexile: 850
> Year Eleven at an exclusive prep school in the suburbs of Melbourne, Australia, would be tough enough, but it is further complicated for Amal when she decides to wear the hijab, the Muslim head scarf, full time as a badge of her faith—without losing her identity or her sense of style.

Alexie, Sherman. *The Absolutely True Diary of a Part-time Indian.* Little, Brown, 2009, c2007. 230p. IL YA, Lexile: 600
> Budding cartoonist Junior leaves his troubled school on the Spokane Indian Reservation to attend an all-white farm-town school, where the only other Native American is the school mascot. Includes a foreword by Marcus Zusak, color illustrations, and interviews with author Sherman Alexie and illustrator Ellen Forney.

Brashares, Ann. *The Sisterhood of the Traveling Pants.* Delacorte, c2001. 294p. IL YA, Lexile: 600
> Carmen decides to discard an old pair of jeans, but Tibby, Lena, and Bridget think they are great and decide that whoever the pants fit best will get them. When the jeans fit everyone perfectly, a sisterhood and a memorable summer begin.

Bray, Libba. *Going Bovine.* Delacorte Press, c2009. 480p. IL YA, Lexile: 680
> Cameron Smith, a disaffected sixteen-year-old diagnosed with mad cow disease, sets off on a road trip with a death-obsessed, video-gaming dwarf he meets in the hospital in an attempt to find a cure.

Bruel, Nick. *Bad Kitty.* Roaring Brook Press, 2007. 40p. IL K–3, Lexile: 280
> When a kitten discovers there is no cat food in the house, she decides to become very, very bad.

Cabot, Meg. *All-American Girl.* HarperTeen, 2008, c2002. 398p. IL YA, Lexile: 880
> Sophomore Samantha Madison stops a presidential assassination attempt, is appointed teen ambassador to the United Nations, and catches the eye of the very cute First Son.

Calame, Don. *Swim the Fly.* Candlewick Press, 2009. 345p. IL YA, Lexile: 620
> Swim team members and best friends Matt, Sean, and Coop set themselves the summertime goal of seeing a live girl naked. While the chances of that happening seem very dim, Matt's personal goal to swim the one-hundred-yard butterfly to impress the new girl on the team appears even less likely to be realized.

Crawford, Brent. *Carter Finally Gets It.* Disney Hyperion Books, c2009. 300p. IL YA, Lexile: 760
> Awkward freshman Will Carter endures many painful moments during his first year of high school before realizing that nothing good comes easily, focus is everything, and the payoff is usually incredible.

Gaiman, Neil. *The Graveyard Book.* HarperCollins, c2008. 312p. IL 5–8, Lexile: 820
> The orphan Bod (short for "Nobody") is taken in by the inhabitants of a graveyard as a child of eighteen months and raised lovingly and carefully to the age of eighteen years by the community of ghosts and otherworldly creatures.

Humor for Young Adults

Goldschmidt, Judy. *The Secret Blog of Raisin Rodriguez: A Novel.* Razorbill, c2005. 202p. IL 5–8, Lexile: 670

In a weblog she sends to her best friends back in Berkeley, seventh grader Raisin Rodriguez chronicles her successes—and her even more frequent humiliating failures—as she attempts to make friends at her new Philadelphia school.

Hughes, Mark Peter. *Lemonade Mouth.* Delacorte Press, c2007. 338p. IL YA, Lexile: 800

A diverse group of high school students thrown together in detention form a band to play at a school talent show and end up competing with a wildly popular local rock band.

Jenkins, A. M. *Repossessed.* HarperTeen, c2007. 218p. IL YA, Lexile: 700

A fallen angel, tired of being unappreciated while doing his pointless, demeaning job, leaves Hell, enters the body of a seventeen-year-old boy, and tries to experience the full range of human feelings before being caught and punished. Meanwhile, the boy's family and friends puzzle over his changed behavior.

Jinks, Catherine. *The Reformed Vampire Support Group.* Harcourt, 2009. 362p. IL YA, Lexile: 750

Fifteen-year-old vampire Nina has been stuck for fifty-one years in a boring support group for vampires, and nothing exciting has ever happened to them—until one of them is murdered and the other group members must try to solve the crime.

Klass, David. *Stuck on Earth.* Farrar, Straus, Giroux, 2010. 227p. IL 5–8

On a secret mission to evaluate whether the human race should be annihilated, a space alien inhabits the body of a bullied 14-year-old boy.

Kluger, Steve. *My Most Excellent Year: A Novel of Love, Mary Poppins, & Fenway Park.* Dial Books, c2008. 403p. IL YA, Lexile: 1030

Three teenagers in Boston narrate their experiences of a year of new friendships, first loves, and coming into their own.

Korman, Gordon. *Son of the Mob.* Hyperion Paperbacks, 2004, c2002. 262p. IL YA, Lexile: 690

Seventeen-year-old Vince's life is constantly complicated by the fact that he is the son of a powerful Mafia boss, a relationship that threatens to destroy his romance with the daughter of an FBI agent.

LaRochelle, David. *Absolutely, Positively Not.* Arthur A. Levine Books, 2005. 219p. IL YA, Lexile: 730

Chronicles a teenage boy's humorous attempts to fit in at his Minnesota high school by becoming a macho, girl-loving, *Playboy*-pinup–displaying heterosexual.

Limb, Sue. *Girl, 15, Charming but Insane.* Delacorte Press, 2005, c2004. 214p. IL 5–8, Lexile: 740

Fifteen-year-old Jess, living with her mum, separated from her father in Cornwall, and with a best friend who seems to do everything perfectly, finds her own assets through humor.

Humor for Young Adults

Mackler, Carolyn. *The Earth, My Butt, and Other Big Round Things.* Candlewick Press, 2003. 246p. IL YA, Lexile: 790

> Feeling like she does not fit in with the other members of her family, who are all thin, brilliant, and good-looking, fifteen-year-old Virginia tries to deal with her self-image, her first physical relationship, and her disillusionment with some of the people closest to her.

Martinez, A. Lee. *Gil's All Fright Diner.* Tor, c2005. 268p. IL AD

> Earl and Duke stop in at a roadside diner in Rockwood County, and Loretta, the cafe's owner, asks them to help solve the zombie problem that is troubling the local town.

Medina, Nico. *Fat Hoochie Prom Queen.* Simon Pulse, 2008. 290p. IL YA

> Margarita Diaz's feud with Bridget Benson reaches its boiling point as both girls run for prom queen. As their campaigns turn dirty, the girls learn some surprising truths about each other and themselves.

Meehl, Brian. *Suck It Up.* Delacorte Press, c2008. 323p. IL YA, Lexile: 740

> After graduating from the International Vampire League, a scrawny, teenaged vampire named Morning is given the chance to fulfill his childhood dream of becoming a superhero when he embarks on a League mission to become the first vampire to reveal his identity to humans and to demonstrate how peacefully evolved, blood-substitute–drinking vampires can use their powers to help humanity.

Perkins, Lynne Rae. *As Easy as Falling off the Face of the Earth.* Greenwillow Books, c2010. 352p. IL YA, Lexile: 730

> A teenaged boy encounters one comedic calamity after another when his train strands him in the middle of nowhere, and everything comes down to luck.

Powell, Randy. *Three Clams and an Oyster.* Farrar Straus Giroux, 2006, c2002. 216p. IL YA, Lexile: 630

> During their humorous search to find a fourth player for their flag football team, three high school juniors are forced to examine their long friendship, their individual flaws, and their inability to try new experiences.

Quick, Matthew. *Sorta like a Rock Star: A Novel.* Little, Brown, 2010. 355p. IL YA, Lexile: 1030

> Amber Appleton, living in a school bus with her mother, refuses to give in to despair and continues visiting the elderly at a nursing home, teaching English to Korean women, and caring for a Vietnam veteran and his dog. A fatal tragedy, however, may prove to be one burden too many for the seventeen-year-old girl.

Shusterman, Neal. *Bruiser.* HarperTeen, c2010. 328p. IL YA, Lexile: 820

> Inexplicable events start to occur when sixteen-year-old twins Tennyson and Bronte befriend a troubled and misunderstood outcast, aptly nicknamed Bruiser, and his little brother, Cody.

Sonnenblick, Jordan. *Notes from the Midnight Driver.* Scholastic Press, 2006. 265p. IL YA, Lexile: 930

> After being assigned to perform community service at a nursing home, sixteen-year-old Alex befriends a cantankerous old man who has some lessons to impart about jazz guitar playing, love, and forgiveness.

Humor for Young Adults

Supplee, Suzanne. *Artichoke's Heart.* Dutton Books, c2008. 276p. IL YA, Lexile: 780

When she is almost sixteen years old, Rosemary decides she is sick of being overweight, being mocked at school and at Heavenly Hair (her mother's beauty salon), and feeling out of control. As she slowly loses weight, she realizes that she is able to cope with her mother's cancer, has a boyfriend for the first time, and discovers that other people's lives are not as perfect as they seem from the outside.

Van Draanen, Wendelin. *Flipped.* A. A. Knopf, Distributed by Random House, c2001. 212p. IL 5–8, Lexile: 720

In alternating chapters, two teenagers describe how their feelings about themselves, each other, and their families have changed over the years.

Winerip, Michael. *Adam Canfield of the Slash.* Candlewick Press, 2005. 326p. IL 3–6, Lexile: 830

While serving as co-editors of their school newspaper, middle schoolers Adam and Jennifer uncover fraud and corruption in their school and in the city's government.

Zusak, Markus. *I Am the Messenger.* Knopf, Distributed by Random House, 2006. 357p. IL YA, Lexile: 640

After capturing a bank robber, nineteen-year-old cab driver Ed Kennedy begins receiving mysterious messages that direct him to addresses where people need help, which helps him start to get over his lifelong feeling of worthlessness.

Humorous Historical Fiction for Middle School Students

Curtis, Christopher Paul. *Bud, Not Buddy.* Delacorte Press, c1999. 245p. IL 5–8, Lexile: 950
Ten-year-old Bud, a motherless boy living in Flint, Michigan, during the Great Depression, escapes a bad foster home and sets out in search of the man he believes to be his father—the renowned bandleader, H. E. Calloway of Grand Rapids.

Curtis, Christopher Paul. *The Watsons Go to Birmingham—1963: A Novel.* Delacorte Press, c1995. 210p. IL 5–8, Lexile: 1000
The ordinary interactions and everyday routines of the Watsons, an African American family living in Flint, Michigan, change drastically after they go to visit Grandma in Alabama in the summer of 1963.

Fleischman, Sid. *Bandit's Moon.* Greenwillow Books, 2008, c1998. 184p. IL 3–6, Lexile: 690
Twelve-year-old Annyrose, left behind when her brother joins the Gold Rush, escapes the unscrupulous woman with whom she is staying and sets out on a grand adventure with the notorious bandit Joaquin Murieta and his band of outlaws.

Jinks, Catherine. *Pagan's Crusade.* Candlewick Press, 2003, c1992. 246p. IL YA, Lexile: 560
In twelfth-century Jerusalem, orphaned sixteen-year-old Pagan is assigned to work for Lord Roland, a Templar knight, as Saladin's armies close in on the Holy City.

Karr, Kathleen. *The Great Turkey Walk.* Farrar, Straus and Giroux, 2000, 1998. 199p. IL 5–8, Lexile: 700
In 1860, fifteen-year-old third-grader Simon Green attempts to herd one thousand turkeys from Missouri to Denver, Colorado, in hopes of selling them at a profit.

Peck, Richard. *A Long Way from Chicago: A Novel in Stories.* Dial Books for Young Readers, c1998. 148p. IL 5–8, Lexile: 750
A boy recounts his annual summer trips to rural Illinois with his sister during the Great Depression to visit their larger-than-life grandmother.

Peck, Richard. *A Season of Gifts.* Dial Books for Young Readers, c2009. 164p. IL 5–8, Lexile: 690
Relates the surprising gifts bestowed on twelve-year-old Bob Barnhart and his family, who have recently moved to a small Illinois town in 1958, by their larger-than-life neighbor, Mrs. Dowdel.

Peck, Richard. *A Year Down Yonder.* Dial Books for Young Readers, c2000. 130p. IL 5–8, Lexile: 610
During the recession of 1937, fifteen-year-old Mary Alice is sent to live with her feisty, larger-than-life grandmother in rural Illinois and comes to a better understanding of this fearsome woman.

Philbrick, W. R. *The Mostly True Adventures of Homer P. Figg.* Blue Sky Press, c2009. 224p. IL 3–6, Lexile: 950
Homer P. Figg escapes from his wretched foster home in Pine Swamp, Maine, and sets out to find his beloved older brother, Harold, who has been illegally sold into the Union Army.

Humorous Historical Fiction for Middle School Students

Schlitz, Laura Amy. *Good Masters! Sweet Ladies!: Voices from a Medieval Village*. Candlewick Press, 2007. 85p. IL 3–6, Lexile: NP

> A collection of short one-person plays featuring characters, between ten and fifteen years old, who live in or near a thirteenth-century English manor.

Schmidt, Gary D. *The Wednesday Wars*. Clarion Books, c2007. 264p. IL 5–8, Lexile: 990

> During the 1967 school year, on Wednesday afternoons when all his classmates go to either Catechism or Hebrew school, seventh-grader Holling Hoodhood stays in Mrs. Baker's classroom, where they read the plays of William Shakespeare and Holling learns valuable lessons about the world he lives in.

Teague, Mark. *The Doom Machine: A Novel*. Blue Sky Press, c2009. 376p. IL 5–8, Lexile: 610

> When a spaceship lands in the small town of Vern Hollow in 1956, juvenile delinquent Jack Creedle and prim, studious Isadora Shumway form an unexpected alliance as they try to keep a group of extraterrestrials from stealing eccentric Uncle Bud's space travel machine.

Part 2

Characters

Drinking and Driving

Bunting, Eve. *A Sudden Silence*. Harcourt, 2007, c1988. 135p. IL YA
Jesse Harmon searches for the hit-and-run driver who killed his brother Bry.

Deuker, Carl. *Heart of a Champion: A Novel*. Little, Brown, 2007, c1993. 192p. IL YA
Seth faces a strain on his friendship with Jimmy, who is both a baseball champion and something of an irresponsible fool, when Jimmy is kicked off the team.

Draper, Sharon M. *Tears of a Tiger*. Atheneum, 1994. 162p. IL YA, Lexile: 700
The death of high school basketball star Rob Washington in an automobile accident affects the lives of his close friend Andy, who was driving the car, and many others in the school.

Elkeles, Simone. *Leaving Paradise*. Flux, c2007. 303p. IL YA, Lexile: 680
In the year following a fateful night, Caleb Becker spends his time in juvenile detention, while Maggie Armstrong spends hers in hospitals and physical therapy. When the two come face-to-face once more, they must do their best to mend the past and heal their emotional wounds.

Fleischman, Paul. *Whirligig*. Square Fish, 2010, c1998. 133p. IL YA, Lexile: 760
While traveling to each corner of the country to build a whirligig in memory of the girl whose death he caused, sixteen-year-old Brian finds forgiveness and atonement.

Frank, E. R. *Wrecked*. Simon Pulse, 2007, c2005. 247p. IL YA, Lexile: 680
After a car accident seriously injures her best friend and kills her brother's girlfriend, sixteen-year-old Anna tries to cope with her guilt and grief, while learning some truths about her family and herself.

Green, John. *Looking for Alaska: A Novel*. Dutton, c2005. 221p. IL YA, Lexile: 930
For sixteen-year-old Miles, his first year at Culver Creek Preparatory School in Alabama includes good friends and great pranks, but is defined by his search for answers about life and death after a fatal car crash.

Johnson, Peter. *What Happened*. Front Street, c2007. 133p. IL YA
A sixteen-year-old boy tries to come to grips after he and his brother go for a joyride that ends in a hit-and-run incident.

Kropp, Paul. *Playing Chicken: A Novel*. H.I.P. Books, c2003. 88p. IL YA
Josh, surprised to be invited to a party with a gang of kids involved with alcohol, drugs, and wild behavior, makes the rash decision to attend, and soon finds events spiraling out of control.

Rogers, David. *The Late Great Me: A Full Length Play*. Dramatic Publishing Company, c1977. 127p. IL YA
This play based on Sandra Scoppettone's *The Late Great Me* tells the story of Geri, a sixteen-year-old who gains new confidence with a little help from alcohol, but soon realizes she is no longer in control of herself.

Drinking and Driving

Sonnenblick, Jordan. *Notes from the Midnight Driver.* Scholastic Press, 2006. 265p. IL YA, Lexile: 930

After being assigned to perform community service at a nursing home, sixteen-year-old Alex befriends a cantankerous old man who has some lessons to impart about jazz guitar playing, love, and forgiveness.

Voigt, Cynthia. *Izzy, Willy-Nilly.* Simon Pulse, 2005, c1986. 327p. IL 5–8, Lexile: 790

A car accident causes fifteen-year-old Izzy to lose one leg and face the need to start building a new life as an amputee.

Epic Quest

Alexander, Lloyd. *The Iron Ring.* LRS, 2003, c1997. 373p. IL 5–8
Driven by his sense of dharma, or honor, young King Tamar sets off on a perilous journey, with a significance greater than he can imagine. During his sojourn, he meets talking animals, villainous and noble kings, demons, and the love of his life.

Flinn, Alex. *Beastly.* HarperTeen, c2007. 304p. IL YA, Lexile: 580
In this modern retelling of "Beauty and the Beast" from the point of view of the Beast, a vain Manhattan private school student is turned into a monster and must find true love before he can return to his human form.

Kostick, Conor. *Edda.* Viking, 2011. 440p. IL YA
In the virtual world of Edda, ruler Scanthax decides he wants to invade another virtual world, embroiling the universes of Edda, Saga, and Epic in war, with only three teenagers to try to restore peace.

Kostick, Conor. *Epic.* Viking, 2007, c2004. 364p. IL YA, Lexile: 880
On New Earth, a world based on a video role-playing game, fourteen-year-old Erik persuades his friends to aid him in some unusual gambits both to save Erik's father from exile and to safeguard the futures of all of their families.

Kostick, Conor. *Saga.* Viking, 2008. 367p. IL YA, Lexile: 780
On Saga, a world based on a video role-playing game, fifteen-year-old Ghost lives to break rules. When the Dark Queen who controls Saga plots to enslave its people and those of New Earth, Ghost and her airboarding friends, along with Erik and his friends from Epic, try to stop her.

Michaelis, Antonia. *Dragons of Darkness.* Amulet Books, c2010. 548p. IL YA, Lexile: 800
Two boys from very different backgrounds are thrown together by magic, mayhem, and a common foe as they battle deadly dragons in the wilderness of Nepal.

Nicholson, William. *Seeker.* Harcourt, 2006. 413p. IL YA, Lexile: 750
Having been rejected by the Nomana—the revered warrior-monk order they long to join—sixteen-year-olds Seeker and Morning Star, along with a curious pirate named Wildman, attempt to prove that they are worthy of joining the community.

Paolini, Christopher. *Eragon.* Alfred A. Knopf, c2003. 509p. IL YA, Lexile: 710
In Aagaesia, a fifteen-year-old boy of unknown lineage called Eragon finds a mysterious stone that weaves his life into an intricate tapestry of destiny, magic, and power, peopled with dragons, elves, and monsters.

Yancey, Richard. *The Extraordinary Adventures of Alfred Kropp.* Bloomsbury Publishing, 2005. 339p. IL YA, Lexile: 810
Through a series of dangerous and violent misadventures, teenage loser Alfred Kropp rescues King Arthur's legendary sword Excalibur from the forces of evil.

Epic Quest

Series

Barron, T. A. *Great Tree of Avalon.* Philomel Books, c2004– . IL 5–8.
This trilogy combines gripping adventure, vivid imagery, and profound ideas about humanity and nature.

Collins, Suzanne. *Hunger Games Series.* Scholastic Press, 2008–2010. IL YA
Sixteen-year-old Katniss Everdeen accidentally becomes a contender in the annual Hunger Games, a gravely serious competition hosted by the Capitol, in which young boys and girls are pitted against each other in a televised fight to the death.

Nimmo, Jenny. *Children of the Red King (Charlie Bone).* Orchard Books, 2004– . IL 3–6.
The mysterious and magical powers of the Red King have been passed down through his descendants. These gifts—some evil and some good—turn up unexpectedly in some people who have no idea where they came from. That is what happened to Charlie Bone and to some of the children he meets behind the grim, gray walls of Bloor's Academy.

Nix, Garth. *Keys to the Kingdom.* Scholastic Press, 2005–2010. IL 3–6.
One mysterious house is the doorway to a very mysterious world, where one boy is about to venture and unlock a number of fantastical secrets!

Riordan, Rick. *Percy Jackson & the Olympians: The Complete Series.* Disney/Hyperion Books, c2005–c2009. IL 5–8
After learning that he is the son of a mortal woman and Poseidon, god of the sea, young Percy is sent to Camp Half-Blood, training camp for demigods like himself. There, Percy experiences a series of adventures, battles evil, and moves toward the prophecy that awaits him on his sixteenth birthday.

Rowling, J. K. *Harry Potter Collection: The Complete Series.* Scholastic, 2000–2009. IL 5–8
The seven books of J. K. Rowling's *Harry Potter* series follow the boy wizard through his years at Hogwarts as he tries to stop the evil Lord Voldemort with the help of his friends.

Tolkien, J. R. R. *The Hobbit; and, The Lord of the Rings.* Houghton Mifflin, c1994–c1996. IL YA
Contains the *Lord of the Rings* trilogy, and its prequel *The Hobbit*, which follows the story of a grand quest to keep the Ring of Power from falling into the hands of the evil Sauron.

Extreme Sports

Bo, Ben. *The Edge.* Lerner Sports, c1998. 138p. IL YA, Lexile: 740
A teenage gang member accused of various crimes finds redemption working and snowboarding at a ski lodge in the mountains surrounding Canada's Glacier National Park.

Deady, Kathleen W. *Extreme Mountain Biking Moves.* Capstone High-Interest Books, c2003. 32p. IL 5–8 (Non-fiction)
Discusses the sport of mountain biking, describing some of the racing and trick moves as well as safety concerns.

Doeden, Matt. *BMX Freestyle.* Capstone Press, c2005. 32p. IL 5–8, Lexile: 640 (Non-fiction)
Describes the sport of BMX freestyle, including tricks and safety information.

Edwardes, Dan. *Parkour.* Crabtree Publishing, c2009. 32p. IL 5–8, Lexile: 750 (Non-fiction)
Provides a brief overview of the history of parkour, with photographs and information on training and techniques.

Hamilton, Sue L. *BASE Jumping.* ABDO Publishing, c2010. 32p. IL 5–8 (Non-fiction)
Describes the extreme sport of BASE jumping, including brief information on its history and equipment, and photographs of jump sites.

Hamilton, Sue L. *Biking.* ABDO Publishing, c2010. 32p. IL 5–8 (Non-fiction)
A photographic introduction to extreme biking, looking at events in BMX, mountain, and ice biking, as well as road racing, and including information on bike helmets.

Hayhurst, Chris. *Bicycle Stunt Riding!: Catch Air.* Rosen Central, 2000. 64p. IL 5–8 (Non-fiction)
Describes the sport of bicycle stunt riding, including how to purchase equipment, practice stunts, ride safely, and enter competitions.

Hayhurst, Chris. *Wakeboarding!: Throw a Tantrum.* Rosen Central, 2000. 64p. IL 5–8 (Non-fiction)
Describes the history, equipment, techniques, and safety measures of wakeboarding, which is a combination of waterskiing and snowboarding.

Hobbs, Will. *Go Big or Go Home.* HarperCollins, c2008. 185p. IL 5–8, Lexile: 700
Fourteen-year-old Brady and his cousin Quinn love extreme sports, but nothing could prepare them for the aftermath of Brady's close encounter with a meteorite after it crashes into his Black Hills, South Dakota, bedroom.

Horton, Ron. *Extreme Athletes.* Lucent, Thomson/Gale, c2005. 112p. IL 5–8 (Non-fiction)
Profiles six athletes who participate in the extreme sports of tow-in surfing, rock climbing without ropes, freeskiing, paddling, BASE-jumping, and freestyle motorcross.

Masoff, Joy. *Snowboard!: Your Guide to Freeriding, Pipe & Park, Jibbing, Backcountry, Alpine, Bordercross, and More.* National Geographic, c2002. 64p. IL 5–8, Lexile: 880 (Non-fiction)
A photographic guide to snowboarding, looking at the different styles of boarding, including freeriding, pipe and park, jibbing, backcountry, alpine, and bordercross, and including definitions of terms, safety tips, pointers from professionals, and stories of legendary rides.

Extreme Sports

Maxwell, E. J. *Xtreme Sports: Cutting Edge.* Scholastic, c2003. 95p. IL 5–8, Lexile: 1020 (Non-fiction)
> Presents photographs, facts, and profiles of Tori Allen, Apolo Anton Ohno, Shaun White, and other stars of extreme sports such as surfing, rock climbing, and snowboarding.

Paulsen, Gary. *How Angel Peterson Got His Name: And Other Outrageous Tales about Extreme Sports.* Dell Yearling, 2004, c2003. 111p. IL 5–8, Lexile: 1180 (Non-fiction)
> Author Gary Paulsen relates tales from his youth in a small town in northwestern Minnesota in the late 1940s and early 1950s, such as skiing behind a souped-up car and imitating daredevil Evel Knievel.

Peterson, Christine. *Extreme Surfing.* Capstone Press, c2005. 32p. IL 5–8, Lexile: 650 (Non-fiction)
> Describes surfing and surfboards, and provides illustrated definitions of surfing terms.

Roberts, Jeremy. *Rock & Ice Climbing: Top the Tower.* Rosen Central, 2000. 63p. IL 5–8 (Non-fiction)
> Introduces the sports of rock and ice climbing, describing their history, equipment, safety tips, and outstanding performers.

Takeda, Pete. *Climb!: Your Guide to Bouldering, Sport Climbing, Trad Climbing, Ice Climbing, Alpinism, and More.* National Geographic, c2002. 64p. IL 5–8 (Non-fiction)
> An introduction and guide to climbing, including bouldering, sport climbing, trad climbing, ice climbing, and alpinism.

Series

Extreme Sports Collection. Rosen Central, 1999– . IL 5–8 (Non-fiction)
> Preteens and teens are especially drawn to extreme sports because of the risks involved and the intensity of the activities. These books emphasize safety and proper training, and provide tips on technique as well as profiles of top competitors.

Fighting School Rules

Avi. *Nothing but the Truth: A Documentary Novel.* Scholastic, c1991. 177p. IL 5–8, Lexile: NP
A ninth-grader's suspension for humming *The Star-Spangled Banner* during homeroom becomes a national news story, and leads to him and his teacher both leaving the school.

Beam, Matt. *Can You Spell Revolution?* Dutton Children's Books, c2008. 263p. IL 5–8
Five students try to overcome the boredom of Laverton Middle School by leading a revolt against dull assemblies, tyrant teachers, and the rules.

Bennett, Cherie. *A Heart Divided: A Play.* Dramatic Publishing, c2004. 75p. IL YA
When sixteen-year-old Kate, an aspiring playwright, moves from New Jersey to attend high school in the South, she becomes embroiled in a controversy about removing the school's Confederate flag symbol.

Bluestein, Jane. *High School's Not Forever.* HCI Teens, c2005. 302p. IL YA (Non-fiction)
A collection of real-life stories in which teens from across the country offer advice on how to deal with the struggles and triumphs of high school life.

Brande, Robin. *Evolution, Me & Other Freaks of Nature.* Knopf, 2009, c2007. 268p. IL YA, Lexile: 800
Mena is ostracized at church, home, and school for writing a letter of apology to a gay teen, who tried to kill himself after experiencing harassment by her fundamentalist friends. Mena struggles to find her way when new friends and school experiences force her to reconsider her beliefs.

Carter, Ally. *I'd Tell You I Love You, But Then I'd Have to Kill You.* Hyperion, c2006. 284p. IL YA, Lexile: 1000
As a sophomore at a secret spy school and the daughter of a former CIA operative, Cammie is sheltered from "normal teenage life" until she meets a local boy while on a class surveillance mission.

Castellucci, Cecil. *The Plain Janes.* Minx, c2007. IL YA (Non-fiction)
After a bombing occurs in the city, Jane and her parents move to a suburb. There, Jane befriends three outcasts—all named Jane—and starts a group called People Loving Art in Neighborhoods, which tries to enrich their community with art but instead is viewed as a threat.

Clements, Andrew. *Lunch Money.* Simon & Schuster Books for Young Readers, c2005. 222p. IL 3–6, Lexile: 840
Twelve-year-old Greg, who has always been good at money-making projects, is surprised to find himself teaming up with his lifelong rival, Maura, to create a series of comic books to sell at school.

Clements, Andrew. *No Talking.* Simon & Schuster Books for Young Readers, c2007. 146p. IL 3–6, Lexile: 820
The noisy fifth-grade boys of Laketon Elementary School challenge the equally loud fifth-grade girls to a "no talking" contest.

Cormier, Robert. *The Chocolate War.* Dell Laurel-Leaf, 2000, c1974. 263p. IL YA, Lexile: 820
A high school freshman discovers the devastating consequences of refusing to join in the school's annual fundraising drive and arousing the wrath of the school bullies.

Fighting School Rules

Crutcher, Chris. *The Sledding Hill.* Greenwillow Books, c2005. 230p. IL YA, Lexile: 1010
   Billy, recently deceased, keeps an eye on his best friend, fourteen-year-old Eddie, and helps him stand up to a conservative minister and English teacher who is orchestrating a censorship challenge.

Crutcher, Chris. *Whale Talk.* Greenwillow Books, c2001. 220p. IL YA, Lexile: 1000
   Intellectually and athletically gifted, TJ, a multiracial, adopted teenager, shuns organized sports and the gung-ho athletes at his high school—until he agrees to form a swimming team and recruits some of the school's less popular students to join it.

Doctorow, Cory. *Little Brother.* Tor, 2008. 382p. IL YA, Lexile: 900
   Interrogated for days by the Department of Homeland Security in the aftermath of a major terrorist attack on San Francisco, California, seventeen-year-old Marcus is released into what is now a police state, and decides to use his expertise in computer hacking to set things right.

Fukui, Isamu. *Truancy.* Tor, 2008. 429p. IL YA, Lexile: 1000
   In the City, where an iron-fisted Mayor's goal is perfect control through education, fifteen-year-old Tack is torn between a growing sympathy for the Truancy, an underground movement determined to bring down the system at any cost, and the desire to avenge a death caused by a Truant.

Gauthier, Gail. *Happy Kid!* G. P. Putnam's Sons, c2006. IL 5–8, Lexile: 770
   After his mother bribes him into reading a self-help book on how to form satisfying relationships and enjoy a happy life, cynical eighth-grader Kyle finds there may be more to the book than he realized.

Goobie, Beth. *Hello, Groin.* Orca Book Publishers, 2006. 271p. IL YA, Lexile: 910
   Dylan creates a display for the school library that causes much trouble for her friends, family, and schoolmates.

Green, John. *Looking for Alaska: A Novel.* Dutton, c2005. 221p. IL YA, Lexile: 930
   For sixteen-year-old Miles, his first year at Culver Creek Preparatory School in Alabama includes good friends and great pranks, but is defined by his search for answers about life and death after a fatal car crash.

Harmon, Michael B. *Brutal.* Alfred A. Knopf, c2009. 229p. IL YA, Lexile: 620
   Forced to leave Los Angeles and live in a quiet California wine town with a father she has never known, rebellious sixteen-year-old Poe Holly rails against a high school system that allows elite students special privileges and tolerates bullying of those who are different.

Hentoff, Nat. *The Day They Came to Arrest the Book: A Novel.* Dell Laurel-Leaf, 1983, c1982. 169p. IL YA, Lexile: 890
   Students and faculty at the fictional George Mason High School become embroiled in a censorship case over the novel *Huckleberry Finn.*

Howe, James. *The Misfits.* Atheneum Books for Young Readers, c2001. 274p. IL 5–8, Lexile: 960
   Four students who do not fit in at their small-town middle school decide to create a third party for the student council elections to represent all students who have ever been called names.

Fighting School Rules

Korman, Gordon. *No More Dead Dogs.* Hyperion Paperbacks for Children, 2002, c2000. 180p. IL 3–6, Lexile: 610

> Eighth-grade football hero Wallace Wallace is sentenced to detention—in his case, attending rehearsals of the school play. In spite of himself, he becomes wrapped up in the production and begins to suggest changes that improve not only the play but also his life.

Lockhart, E. *The Disreputable History of Frankie Landau-Banks: A Novel.* Disney/Hyperion Books, 2009, c2008. 345p. IL YA. Lexile: 890

> When Frankie Landau-Banks attempts to take over a secret, all-male society at her exclusive prep school, her antics with the group soon draw some unlikely attention and have unexpected consequences that could change her life forever.

Lyga, Barry. *Hero-Type.* Houghton Mifflin, 2008. 295p. IL YA, Lexile: 670

> Feeling awkward and ugly is one of several reasons why sixteen-year-old Kevin is uncomfortable with the publicity about his act of accidental heroism. When a reporter photographs him apparently being unpatriotic, though, Kevin speaks out and encourages people to think about what the symbols of freedom really mean.

Oates, Joyce Carol. *Big Mouth & Ugly Girl.* HarperTempest, 2003, c2002. 266p. IL YA, Lexile: 720

> When sixteen-year-old Matt is falsely accused of threatening to blow up his high school and his friends turn against him, an unlikely classmate comes to his aid.

Tashjian, Janet. *The Gospel According to Larry.* Dell Laurel-Leaf, 2003, c2001. 227p. IL YA, Lexile: 800

> Seventeen-year-old Josh, a loner-philosopher who wants to make a difference in the world, tries to maintain his secret identity as the author of a web site that is receiving national attention.

Thomas, Rob. *Rats Saw God.* Simon Pulse, 2007, c1996. 202p. IL YA, Lexile: 970

> In hopes of graduating, Steve York agrees to complete a hundred-page writing assignment that helps him to sort out his relationship with his famous astronaut father and the events that changed him from promising student to troubled teen.

Love Gone Bad

Brown, Jennifer. *Bitter End.* Little, Brown, 2011. 359p. IL YA
> When seventeen-year-old Alex starts dating Cole, a new boy at her high school, her two closest friends increasingly mistrust him as the relationship grows more serious.

Caletti, Deb. *Stay.* Simon Pulse, 2011. 313p. IL YA, Lexile: 700
> Clara and her father travel to a remote region of Washington state when she notices that her boyfriend, Christian, is developing obsessive behaviors. After arriving in their new home, Clara meets two brothers who captain a sailboat, a lighthouse keeper who is hiding something, and a friend of her father who knows the lighthouse keeper's secret.

Culbertson, Kim A. *Instructions for a Broken Heart.* Sourcebooks Fire, c2011. 295p. IL YA
> While on a school trip to Italy, Jessa opens one envelope each day from her best friend's care package and finds instructions designed to help her get over her recent breakup with her boyfriend.

Dessen, Sarah. *Dreamland.* Speak, 2004, c2000. 250p. IL YA, Lexile: 920
> After her older sister runs away, sixteen-year-old Caitlin decides that she needs to make a major change in her own life and begins an abusive relationship with a boy who is mysterious, brilliant, and dangerous.

Flinn, Alex. *Breathing Underwater.* HarperTempest, 2002, c2001. 263p. IL YA, Lexile: 510
> Sent to counseling for hitting his girlfriend, Caitlin, and ordered to keep a journal, sixteen-year-old Nick recounts his relationship with Caitlin, examines his controlling behavior and anger, and describes his life with his abusive father.

Giles, Gail. *Dark Song.* Little, Brown, 2010. 292p. IL YA, Lexile: 570
> After her father loses his job and she finds out that her parents have lied to her, fifteen-year-old Ames feels betrayed enough to become involved with a criminal who will stop at nothing to get what he wants.

Grace, Amanda. *But I Love Him.* Flux, c2011. 253p. IL YA
> Ann begins her senior year of high school as a happy, straight-A student and track star, but her life changes drastically when she become involved with a haunted young man named Connor and cannot seem to free herself from the abusive relationship.

Graham, Rosemary. *Stalker Girl.* Viking, 2010. 296p. IL YA, Lexile: 880
> During a difficult time in her life, when her mother and stepfather have broken up and her father cancels a trip she has been anticipating, Carly becomes obsessed with her ex-boyfriend's new girlfriend.

Kantor, Melissa. *The Breakup Bible: A Novel.* Hyperion Paperbacks, 2008, c2007. 265p. IL YA, Lexile: 980
> After a breakup with her boyfriend, school newspaper features editor Jen Lewis receives a book from her grandmother that provides basic commandments for getting over an ex and sets out to recover from the loss of the romance.

Koertge, Ronald. *Stoner & Spaz.* Candlewick Press, 2004, c2002. 169p. IL YA. Lexile: 490
> A troubled youth with cerebral palsy struggles to achieve self-acceptance with the help of a drug-addicted young woman.

Love Gone Bad

Lundgren, Jodi. *Leap.* Second Story Press, c2011. 217p. IL YA

Fifteen-year-old Natalie struggles to cope with growing up over the course of one summer as she deals with her rocky relationship with her best friend Sasha; her crush on Sasha's brother, Kevin; her confusion about her parents' divorce; and the general angst of being a teenager.

Stone, Tanya Lee. *A Bad Boy Can Be Good for a Girl.* Wendy Lamb Books, 2007, c2006. 228p. IL YA, Lexile: 780

Josie, Nicolette, and Aviva fall for the same sexy high school senior. Although each of them makes different choices, all three are changed by their experiences of love and sex.

Zevin, Gabrielle. *Memoirs of a Teenage Amnesiac.* Farrar Straus Giroux, 2007. 271p. IL YA, Lexile: 720

After a nasty fall, Naomi realizes that she has no memory of the last four years and finds herself reassessing every aspect of her life.

Online Identity

Alexovich, Aaron. *Kimmie66.* Minx, c2007. 148p. IL YA

In the twenty-third century, teen Telly Kade digs through the darkest corners of the Internet in search of the truth about her friend, Kimmie66, who left a suicide note with Telly but has been seen lurking all over the Internet.

Carey, Mike. *Confessions of a Blabbermouth.* Minx, c2007. 152p. IL YA

Tasha Flanagan uses her blog, Blabbermouth, as a weapon against her mother's new boyfriend, Jed Hazell, and his daughter when she begins to suspect they are hiding a guilty secret.

Cooper, Robbie. *Alter Ego: Digital Avatars and Their Creators.* Chris Boot, 2007. IL AD (Non-fiction)

Individuals from the United States, Asia, and Europe describe themselves and their online-game and virtual-world avatars; the book includes side-by-side images of the people and their electronic alter-egos.

Flinn, Alex. *Beastly.* HarperTeen, c2007. 304p. IL YA, Lexile: 580

In this modern retelling of "Beauty and the Beast" from the point of view of the Beast, a vain Manhattan private school student is turned into a monster and must find true love before he can return to his human form.

Kostick, Conor. *Edda.* Viking, 2011. 440p. IL YA

In the virtual world of Edda, ruler Scanthax decides he wants to invade another virtual world, embroiling the universes of Edda, Saga, and Epic in war, with only three teenagers to try to restore peace.

Kostick, Conor. *Epic.* Viking, 2007, c2004. 364p. IL YA, Lexile: 880

On New Earth, a world based on a video role-playing game, fourteen-year-old Erik persuades his friends to aid him in some unusual gambits both to save Erik's father from exile and to safeguard the futures of their families.

Kostick, Conor. *Saga.* Viking, 2008. 367p. IL YA, Lexile: 780

On Saga, a world based on a video role-playing game, fifteen-year-old Ghost lives to break rules. When the Dark Queen who controls Saga plots to enslave its people and those of New Earth, Ghost and her airboarding friends, along with Erik and his friends from Epic, try to stop her.

Mancusi, Marianne. *Gamer Girl.* Dutton Children's Books, c2008. 248p. IL YA, Lexile: 660

Struggling to fit in after her parents' divorce sends her from Boston to her grandmother's house in the country, sixteen-year-old Maddy forms a manga club at school and falls in love through an online fantasy game.

Morgan, Melissa J. *TTYL.* Grosset & Dunlap, c2005. 159p IL 5–8, Lexile: 700

Having left summer camp to return home, the girls from bunk 3C use a blog to keep one another informed of their struggles adjusting to sixth grade at their respective schools and to new situations at home.

Online Identity

Stephenson, Neal. *Snow Crash***.** Bantam Books, 2000, c1992. 440p. IL AD, Lexile: 970

Hiro Protagonist, a pizza delivery man in future America, lives an alternate life as a warrior prince in the Metaverse, where he embarks on a search-and-destroy mission for the virtual-reality villain who is trying to bring about infocalypse.

Tashjian, Janet. *The Gospel According to Larry***.** Dell Laurel-Leaf, 2003, c2001. 227p. IL YA, Lexile: 800

Seventeen-year-old Josh, a loner-philosopher who wants to make a difference in the world, tries to maintain his secret identity as the author of a website that is receiving national attention.

Pranks, Jokes, Et Cetera

Bradley, Alex. *24 Girls in 7 Days*. Dutton Books, c2005. 265p. IL YA, Lexile: 680
  Unlucky in love, teenager Jack Grammar cannot get a date to the prom until his friends play a practical joke and place a personal ad in the school online newspaper on his behalf. Now Jack has twenty-four dates and just seven days until the prom.

Cole, Brock. *The Goats*. Square Fish, 2010, c1987. 184p. IL 5–8, Lexile: 550
  Stripped and marooned on a small island by their fellow campers, a boy and a girl form an uneasy bond that grows into a deep friendship when they decide to run away and disappear without a trace.

Crutcher, Chris. *King of the Mild Frontier: An Ill-Advised Autobiography*. Greenwillow Books, c2003. 260p. IL YA, Lexile: 1180
  Chris Crutcher, author of young adult novels such as *Ironman* and *Whale Talk,* as well as short stories, describes growing up in Cascade, Idaho, and becoming a writer.

Dessen, Sarah. *The Truth about Forever*. Viking, 2004. 374p. IL YA, Lexile: 840
  In the summer following her father's death, Macy plans to work at the library and wait for her brainy boyfriend to return from camp; instead, she goes to work at a catering business, where she makes new friends and finally faces her grief.

Green, John. *Looking for Alaska*. Speak, 2005. 221p. IL YA, Lexile: 930
  For sixteen-year-old Miles, his first year at Culver Creek Preparatory School in Alabama includes good friends and great pranks, but is defined by his search for answers about life and death after a fatal car crash.

Hall, Margaret. *The Adventures of Tom Sawyer*. Stone Arch Books, c2007. 63p. IL 5-8, Lexile: 260
  A graphic-novel retelling of Mark Twain's classic story in which young Tom Sawyer and Huckleberry Finn witness a murder and are thrust into a series of dangerous situations.

Horne, Richard. *101 Things to Do before You're Old and Boring*. Walker, 2006, c2005. 202p. IL YA (Non-fiction)
  This book suggest more than one hundred adventurous or otherwise satisfying things to do at least once in life, such as dyeing one's hair, baking a cake, starting a band, and building an igloo, and provides a unique progress form for each.

Lockhart, E. *The Disreputable History of Frankie Landau-Banks: A Novel*. Disney/Hyperion Books, 2009, c2008. 345p. IL YA, Lexile: 890
  When Frankie Landau-Banks attempts to take over a secret, all-male society at her exclusive prep school, her antics with the group soon draw some unlikely attention and have unexpected consequences that could change her life forever.

Paulsen, Gary. *How Angel Peterson Got His Name: And Other Outrageous Tales about Extreme Sports*. Dell Yearling, 2004, c2003. 111p. IL 5–8, Lexile: 1180
  Author Gary Paulsen relates tales from his youth in a small town in northwestern Minnesota in the late 1940s and early 1950s, such as skiing behind a souped-up car and imitating daredevil Evel Knievel.

Pranks, Jokes, Et Cetera

Paulsen, Gary. *The Time Hackers*. Yearling, 2006, c2005. 87p. IL 3–6, Lexile: 880

When someone uses futuristic technology to play pranks on twelve-year-old Dorso Clayman, he and his best friend set off on a supposedly impossible journey through space and time trying to stop the gamesters, who are endangering the universe.

Rowling, J. K. *Harry Potter and the Order of the Phoenix*. A. A. Levine, 2003. 870p IL 5–8, Lexile: 950

Harry Potter, now a fifth-year student at Hogwarts School of Witchcraft and Wizardry, struggles with a threatening teacher, a problematic house elf, his dread of upcoming final exams, and haunting dreams that hint of his mysterious past.

Scott, Kieran. *I Was a Non-Blonde Cheerleader.* Speak, 2007, c2005. 246p. IL YA, Lexile: 750

As a brunette on the all-blonde cheerleading squad at her new Florida high school, New Jersey–born sophomore Annisa Gobrowski tries to fit in with her popular teammates without losing the friendship of Bethany, the only other non-blonde at the school, and hopes something might develop with her new, guitar-playing neighbor, who has an evil girlfriend.

Shusterman, Neal. *The Shadow Club*. Puffin, 2002. 199p. IL YA, Lexile: 760

When a junior high school boy and his friends decide to form a club of "second bests" and play anonymous tricks on their arch-rivals, the harmless pranks escalate until they become life-threatening.

Standing Up to Authority

Bauer, Joan. *Hope Was Here.* G. P. Putnam's Sons, c2000. 186p. IL YA, Lexile: 710
When sixteen-year-old Hope and the aunt who has raised her move from Brooklyn to Mulhoney, Wisconsin, to work as waitress and cook in the Welcome Stairways diner, they become involved with the diner owner's political campaign to oust the town's corrupt mayor.

Bennett, Cherie. *A Heart Divided: A Play.* Dramatic Publishing, c2004. 75p. IL YA
When sixteen-year-old Kate, an aspiring playwright, moves from New Jersey to attend high school in the South, she becomes embroiled in a controversy about removing the school's Confederate flag symbol.

Crutcher, Chris. *The Sledding Hill.* Greenwillow Books, c2005. 230p. IL YA, Lexile: 1010
Billy, recently deceased, keeps an eye on his best friend, fourteen-year-old Eddie, and helps him stand up to a conservative minister and English teacher who is orchestrating a censorship challenge.

Crutcher, Chris. *Whale Talk.* Greenwillow Books, c2001. 220p. IL YA, Lexile: 1000
Intellectually and athletically gifted, TJ, a multiracial, adopted teenager, shuns organized sports and the gung-ho athletes at his high school—until he agrees to form a swimming team and recruits some of the school's less popular students to join it.

Cushman, Karen. *The Loud Silence of Francine Green.* Clarion Books, c2006. 225p. IL 5–8, Lexile: 750
In 1949, thirteen-year-old Francine goes to Catholic school in Los Angeles, where she becomes best friends with a girl who questions authority and is frequently punished by the nuns, causing Francine to question her own values.

Doctorow, Cory. *Little Brother.* Tor, 2008. 382p. IL YA, Lexile: 900
Interrogated for days by the Department of Homeland Security in the aftermath of a major terrorist attack on San Francisco, California, seventeen-year-old Marcus is released into what is now a police state, and decides to use his expertise in computer hacking to set things right.

Garden, Nancy. *The Year They Burned the Books.* Farrar Straus Giroux, 1999. 247p. IL YA, Lexile: 760
While trying to come to terms with her own lesbian feelings, Jamie, a high -school senior and editor of the school newspaper, finds herself in the middle of a battle with a group of townspeople over the new health education curriculum.

Hiaasen, Carl. *Flush.* Alfred A. Knopf, c2005. 263p. IL 5–8, Lexile: 830
With their father jailed for sinking a river boat, Noah Underwood and his younger sister, Abbey, must gather evidence that the owner of this floating casino is emptying his bilge tanks into the protected waters around their Florida Keys home.

Hiaasen, Carl. *Hoot.* Alfred A. Knopf, c2002. 292p. IL 5–8, Lexile: 760
Roy, who is new to his small Florida community, becomes involved in another boy's attempt to save a colony of burrowing owls from a proposed construction site.

Standing Up to Authority

Hiaasen, Carl. *Scat.* Knopf, c2009. 371p. IL 5–8, Lexile: 810
Nick and Marta are both suspicious when their biology teacher, the feared Mrs. Bunny Starch, disappears, and try to uncover the truth despite the police and headmaster's insistence that nothing is wrong.

Howe, James. *The Misfits.* Atheneum Books for Young Readers, c2001. 274p. IL 5–8, Lexile: 960
Four students who do not fit in at their small-town middle school decide to create a third party for the student council elections to represent all students who have ever been called names.

Konigsburg, E. L. *The Outcasts of 19 Schuyler Place.* Atheneum Books for Young Readers, c2004. 296p. IL 5–8, Lexile: 840
Upon leaving an oppressive summer camp, twelve-year-old Margaret Rose Kane spearheads a campaign to preserve three unique towers her grand uncles have been building in their back yard for more than forty years.

Lockhart, E. *The Disreputable History of Frankie Landau-Banks: A Novel.* Disney/Hyperion Books, 2009, c2008. 345p. IL YA, Lexile: 890
When Frankie Landau-Banks attempts to take over a secret, all-male society at her exclusive prep school, her antics with the group soon draw some unlikely attention and have unexpected consequences that could change her life forever.

Lyga, Barry. *Hero-Type.* Houghton Mifflin, 2008. 295p. IL YA, Lexile: 670
Feeling awkward and ugly is one of several reasons why sixteen-year-old Kevin is uncomfortable with the publicity about his act of accidental heroism. When a reporter photographs him apparently being unpatriotic, though, Kevin speaks out and encourages people to think about what the symbols of freedom really mean.

Tashjian, Janet. *The Gospel According to Larry.* Dell Laurel-Leaf, 2003, c2001. 227p. IL YA, Lexile: 800
Seventeen-year-old Josh, a loner-philosopher who wants to make a difference in the world, tries to maintain his secret identity as the author of a website that is receiving national attention.

Vaught, Susan. *Big Fat Manifesto.* IL YA Bloomsbury, 2008. 308p. Lexile: 800
High school senior Jamie Carcaterra tries to win a scholarship by sharing her experiences as a fat girl in today's appearance-obsessed high school culture. As she opens her life up to the criticism of her classmates and the media, she begins to wonder if she is being truly honest with herself.

Series

Collins, Suzanne. *The Hunger Games Trilogy.* Scholastic Press, 2008–2010. IL YA
This series includes *The Hunger Games,* in which sixteen-year-old Katniss Everdeen becomes a contender in a gravely serious competition hosted by the Capitol, where young boys and girls are pitted against each other in a televised fight to the death; *Catching Fire,* in which Katniss and Peeta win the competition and become the faces of an impending rebellion; and *Mockingjay,* in which Katniss and her family and friends face danger because the Capitol holds her responsible for the unrest.

Standing Up to Authority

Riordan, Rick *Percy Jackson & the Olympians: The Complete Series.* Disney/Hyperion Books, c2005-c2009. IL 5-8
> After learning that he is the son of a mortal woman and Poseidon, god of the sea, young Percy is sent to Camp Half-Blood, a training camp for demigods like himself. There, he experiences a series of adventures, battles evil, and moves toward the prophecy that awaits him on his sixteenth birthday.

Technology and Ethics

Anderson, M. T. *Feed*. Candlewick Press, 2004, c2002. 299p. IL YA, Lexile: 770

In a future where most people have computer implants in their heads to control their environment, a boy meets an unusual girl who is in serious trouble.

Bachorz, Pam. *Candor*. Egmont USA, 2009. 249p. IL YA, Lexile: 350

For a fee, "model teen" Oscar Banks has been secretly—and selectively—sabotaging the subliminal messages that program the behavior of the residents of Candor, Florida. Eventually, his attraction to a rebellious new girl threatens to expose his subterfuge.

Beckett, Bernard. *Genesis*. Houghton Mifflin Harcourt, 2009. 150p. IL AD

Anaximander is a student historian applying for entrance to the Academy, the institution that governs the Republic, a closed and isolated island society established late in the twenty-first century as a refuge from worldwide plague. When she prepares a thesis on Adam Forde, a rebel who on one occasion refused to shoot a young woman approaching the island in a boat, she unwittingly reveals her own tendencies toward unconventional thought.

Doctorow, Cory. *For the Win*. Tor, 2010. 475p. IL YA, Lexile: 1070

A group of teens from around the world find themselves drawn into an online revolution arranged by a mysterious young woman known as Big Sister Nor, who hopes to challenge the status quo and change the world using her virtual connections.

Doctorow, Cory. *Little Brother*. Tor, 2008. 382p. IL YA, Lexile: 900

Interrogated for days by the Department of Homeland Security in the aftermath of a major terrorist attack on San Francisco, California, seventeen-year-old Marcus is released into what is now a police state, and decides to use his expertise in computer hacking to set things right.

Farmer, Nancy. *The House of the Scorpion*. Atheneum Books for Young Readers, c2002. 380p. IL 5–8, Lexile: 660

In a future where humans despise clones, Matt enjoys special status as the young clone of El Patron, the 142-year-old leader of a corrupt drug empire nestled between Mexico and the United States.

Fisher, Catherine. *Incarceron*. Dial Books, 2010, c2007. 442p. IL YA, Lexile: 600

To free herself from an upcoming arranged marriage, Claudia, the daughter of the Warden of Incarceron, a futuristic prison with a mind of its own, decides to help a young prisoner escape.

Hall, Teri. *The Line*. Dial Books, c2010. 219p. IL YA, Lexile: 760

Rachel thinks that she and her mother are safe working for Ms. Moore at her estate close to The Line, an invisible border of the Unified States. When Rachel has an opportunity to Cross into the forbidden zone, however, she is both frightened and intrigued.

Ishiguro, Kazuo. *Never Let Me Go*. Knopf, 2005. 288p. IL AD

Thirty-one-year-old Kathy and her old friends from Hailsham, a private school in England, are forced to face the truth about their childhood when they all come together again.

Technology and Ethics

Malley, G. R. *The Declaration*. Bloomsbury, 2007. 300p. IL YA Lexile: 930

In 2140 England, where drugs enable people to live forever and children are illegal, teenaged Anna, an obedient "Surplus" training to become a house servant, has her world view challenged when she meets Peter and discovers that her birth parents are trying to find her.

Pearson, Mary. *The Adoration of Jenna Fox*. Henry Holt, 2008. 266p. IL YA, Lexile: 570

In the not-too-distant future, when biotechnological advances have made synthetic bodies and brains possible but illegal, a seventeen-year-old girl, recovering from a serious accident and suffering from memory lapses, learns a startling secret about her existence.

Shusterman, Neal. *Unwind*. Simon & Schuster Books for Young Readers, c2007. 335p. IL YA, Lexile: 740

Three teens embark upon a cross-country journey to escape from a society that salvages body parts from children ages thirteen to eighteen.

Tashjian, Janet. *The Gospel According to Larry*. Dell Laurel-Leaf, 2003, c2001. 227p. IL YA, Lexile: 800

Seventeen-year-old Josh, a loner-philosopher who wants to make a difference in the world, tries to maintain his secret identity as the author of a website that is receiving national attention.

Westerfeld, Scott. *Uglies*. Simon Pulse, 2011, c2005. 406p. IL YA

Tally is faced with a difficult choice when her new friend Shay decides to take a chance on life on the outside rather than submit to the forced operation that turns sixteen-year-old girls into gorgeous beauties, and Tally realizes that there is a whole new side to the pretty world that she doesn't like.

Abandonment

Byars, Betsy Cromer. *The Pinballs*. Harper & Row, c1977. 136p. IL 3–6, Lexile: 600
Three lonely foster children learn to care about themselves and one another.

Cassidy, Cathy. *Dizzy: A Novel*. Puffin, 2005, c2004. 247p. IL 5–8, Lexile: 770
After an eight-year absence, Dizzy's "New Age traveler" mother suddenly shows up on her twelfth birthday and whisks her away to a series of festivals throughout Scotland in her rattletrap van.

DiCamillo, Kate. *Because of Winn-Dixie*. Candlewick Press, c2000. 185p. IL 3–6, Lexile: 610
Ten-year-old India Opal Buloni describes her first summer in the town of Naomi, Florida, and all the good things that happen to her because of her big ugly dog, Winn-Dixie.

Friel, Maeve. *Charlie's Story*. Peachtree, c1997. 121p. IL YA, Lexile: 860
After being abandoned by her mother at the age of four, living for ten years with her somewhat distracted father in Ireland, and being mercilessly bullied by her cruel classmates, Charlie Collins almost gives up on life.

Gantos, Jack. *Joey Pigza Swallowed the Key*. Farrar, Straus and Giroux, 1998. 153p. IL 5–8, Lexile: 970
To the constant disappointment of his mother and his teachers, Joey has trouble paying attention or controlling his mood swings when his prescription medications wear off and he starts getting worked up and acting wired.

Quarles, Heather. *A Door near Here*. Dell, c1998. 231p. IL YA, Lexile: 860
Four siblings struggle to maintain a semi-normal home life when their single mother's alcoholism becomes debilitating.

Smith, Hope Anita. *The Way a Door Closes*. Henry Holt, 2003. 52p. IL 3–6, Lexile: NP
A collection of poems about a thirteen-year-old boy whose father abandoned him and his family.

Voigt, Cynthia. *Dicey's Song*. Atheneum, 1982. 196p. IL 5–8, Lexile: 710
Now that the four abandoned Tillerman children are settled in with their grandmother, Dicey finds that their new beginnings require love, trust, humor, and courage.

Chasing the American Dream: Non-fiction

Blumenthal, Karen. *Let Me Play: The Story of Title IX, the Law That Changed the Future of Girls in America.* Atheneum Books for Young Readers, c2005. 152p. IL 5–8, Lexile: 1140
> Examines Title IX, the 1972 legislation that mandated schools receiving federal funds could not discriminate on the basis of gender, and focuses on the law's effects in schools, politics, sports, and the culture as a whole.

Carson, Ben. *Gifted Hands.* Zondervan, c1990. 232p. IL YA, Lexile: 950
> Captures the physician's fight to beat the odds, the secret behind his outstanding accomplishments, and what drives him to take risks.

Davis, Sampson. *We Beat the Street: How a Friendship Pact Helped Us Succeed.* Dutton Children's Books, c2005. 194p. IL 5-8, Lexile: 860
> Shares anecdotes from the childhoods, teenage years, and young adult lives of three men from Newark, New Jersey, who made a pledge to one another in high school to stay safe from drugs, gangs, and crime, and to work to become doctors—a goal they have successfully achieved.

Fleming, Candace. *Amelia Lost: The Life and Disappearance of Amelia Earhart.* Schwartz & Wade Books, c2011. 118p. IL 5–8, Lexile: 930
> Traces the life of female aviator Amelia Earhart from her childhood to her final flight, discusses the extensive search for her and her missing plane, and includes photographs, maps, handwritten notes by Amelia, and sidebars.

Govenar, Alan B. *Extraordinary Ordinary People: Five American Masters of Traditional Arts.* Candlewick Press, 2006. 85p. IL 5–8, Lexile: 930
> Through interviews and photographs, presents the art and life stories of five American masters of the traditional arts.

Helfer, Andrew. *Malcolm X: A Graphic Biography.* Hill and Wang, 2006. 102p. IL AD
> Presents a brief biography of Malcolm X in graphic novel format, describing his life from his early experiences with racism through his political and religious conversions.

Hoose, Phillip M. *Claudette Colvin: Twice Toward Justice.* Melanie Kroupa Books, 2009. 133p. IL YA, Lexile: 1000
> Presents an account of fifteen-year-old Claudette Colvin, an African American girl who refused to give up her seat to a white woman on a segregated bus in Montgomery, Alabama, nine months before Rosa Parks, and covers her role in a crucial civil rights case.

Stone, Tanya Lee. *Almost Astronauts: 13 Women Who Dared to Dream.* Candlewick Press, 2009. 133p. IL 5–8, Lexile: 980
> Profiles thirteen women who challenged social norms and government policies to prove they could be exceptional astronauts.

Taylor, Sarah Stewart. *Amelia Earhart: This Broad Ocean.* Disney/Hyperion Books, c2010. 78p. IL 5–8, Lexile: 1080
> A biographical depiction, in graphic novel format, of the life of aviator Amelia Earhart, focusing on her crossing of the Atlantic Ocean in 1928.

Autism and Asperger Syndrome

Burns, Laura J. *The Case of the Slippery Soap Star.* Sleuth Razorbill, c2005. 185p. IL 5-8
> When his mother is accused of stealing jewelry at a charity dinner, Orville and Agatha team up to find the real thief—and their prime suspect is a famous soap opera actor.

Hoopmann, Kathy. *Blue Bottle Mystery: An Asperger Adventure.* Jessica Kingsley Publishers, 2001. 96p. IL 3–6
> A boy named Ben, frustrated by his problems in school, hopes for adventure with his friend Andy when they find what looks like a genie's bottle—but Ben's life changes when he learns he has Asperger syndrome.

Hoopmann, Kathy. *Lisa and the Lacemaker: An Asperger Adventure.* Jessica Kingsley Publishers, 2002. 116p. IL 3–6
> Lisa, a girl with Asperger syndrome, discovers a series of basement rooms under her friend Ben's house and spends hours exploring the remnants of a past era.

Keating-Velasco, Joanna L. *A Is for Autism, F Is for Friend: A Kid's Book on Making Friends with a Child Who Has Autism.* Autism Asperger Publishing, c2007. 54p. IL 3–6
> This book helps middle school students better understand what autism is and encourages them to try and make friends with autistic students in the class.

Kochka. *The Boy Who Ate Stars.* Simon & Schuster Books for Young Readers, c2004. 107p. IL 5–8
> Upon moving to a new apartment, twelve-year-old Lucy befriends an autistic boy who lives upstairs. Along with her friend Theo and a pampered pooch, she takes Matthew on neighborhood adventures, hoping to open him up to the world around them.

Lamstein, Sarah. *Hunger Moon.* Front Street Books, c2004. 109p. IL 5–8
> In 1953 in Chicago, Ruth struggles to deal with her parents' constant arguing, taking care of her younger brothers, one of whom is mentally disabled, and getting along in middle school.

Lancelle, Matthew. *Sundays with Matthew: A Young Boy with Autism and an Artist Share Their Sketchbooks.* Autism Asperger Publishing, c2006. 37p. IL 3–6
> Matthew Lancelle, an eleven-year-old boy with autism, and Jeanette Lesada, his art therapist, describe their time together and explore such topics as the sea, grandmothers, and friendship in words and pictures.

Ogaz, Nancy. *Buster and the Amazing Daisy.* Jessica Kingsley, 2002. 125p. IL 3–6
> When Daisy, who is autistic, joins a mainstreamed class and trains Buster the rabbit for a pet show, she faces new challenges and makes new friends.

Robison, John Elder. *Look Me in the Eye: My Life with Asperger's.* Crown Publishers, c2007. 288p. IL AD
> John Robison recounts his struggles to fit in and communicate with others as he grew up, describing why he had so many problems relating to others and why he often turned to machines for comfort, rather than people. He also explains how his life was changed when he was diagnosed with Asperger syndrome at age forty.

Comparing and Contrasting Characters

Becker, Bonny. *A Visitor for Bear.* Candlewick Press, 2008. 56p. IL K–3, Lexile: 430
Bear's efforts to keep out visitors to his house are undermined by a very persistent mouse.

DePaola, Tomie. *Nana Upstairs & Nana Downstairs.* Puffin Books, c1973. 32p. IL K–3, Lexile: 530
Four-year-old Tommy enjoys his relationship with both his grandmother and his great-grandmother, but eventually learns to face their inevitable deaths.

Dyer, Sarah. *Clementine and Mungo.* Bloomsbury Children's Books, Distributed by Holtzbrinck Publishers, 2004. 27p. IL K–3
Clementine gives creative answers to the many questions that her younger brother Mungo asks.

Farmer, Nancy. *The House of the Scorpion.* Atheneum Books for Young Readers, c2002. 380p, IL 5–8, Lexile: 660
In a future where humans despise clones, Matt enjoys special status as the young clone of El Patron, the 142-year-old leader of a corrupt drug empire nestled between Mexico and the United States.

Henkes, Kevin. *Chester's Way.* Greenwillow Books, c1988. 32p. IL K–3, Lexile: 570
Chester and Wilson share the same exact way of doing things, until Lilly moves into the neighborhood and shows them that new ways can be just as good.

Henkes, Kevin. *Sheila Rae, the Brave.* Greenwillow Books, c1987. 32p. IL K–3, Lexile: 440
When brave Sheila Rae, who usually looks out for her sister Louise, becomes lost and scared one day, Louise comes to the rescue.

Oates, Joyce Carol. *Big Mouth & Ugly Girl.* HarperTempest, 2003, c2002. 266p. IL YA, Lexile: 720
When sixteen-year-old Matt is falsely accused of threatening to blow up his high school and his friends turn against him, an unlikely classmate comes to his aid.

Polacco, Patricia. *Pink and Say.* Philomel Books, c1994. 48p. IL K–3, Lexile: 590
Pink, a fifteen-year-old African American Union soldier, and Say, his poor white comrade, become friends as one nurses the other back to health from a battle wound and both are imprisoned at the Andersonville Civil War prison camp. Based on a true story.

Rosoff, Meg. *Jumpy Jack & Googily.* Holt, 2008. 32p. IL K–3
Jumpy Jack the snail is terrified that there are monsters around every corner, despite the reassurances of his best friend, Googily.

Seuss, Dr. *Horton Hatches the Egg.* Random House, c1968. 55p. IL K–3, Lexile: 460
A lazy bird hatching an egg wants a vacation, so she asks Horton, the elephant, to sit on her egg—which he does through all sorts of hazards until he is rewarded for doing what he said he would.

Stanley, Diane. *Saving Sweetness.* Puffin, 2001, c1996. 32p. IL K–3, Lexile: 660
The sheriff of a dusty western town rescues Sweetness, an unusually resourceful orphan, from nasty old Mrs. Sump and her terrible orphanage.

Comparing and Contrasting Characters

Series

Willems, Mo. *Elephant and Piggie Series*. Hyperion Books for Children, 2007– . IL K–3
These sweet and surprising stories are a much-needed breath of fresh air in the early reader arena. They feature the interaction between two lovable and funny characters—an optimistic, sometimes reckless pig and a cautious, pessimistic elephant. Each book has been vetted by an early learning specialist.

Conflict and Cooperation

Anderson, Laurie Halse. *Catalyst.* Viking, 2002. 232p. IL YA, Lexile: 580
Eighteen-year-old Kate, who sometimes chafes at being a preacher's daughter, finds herself losing control in her senior year as she faces difficult neighbors, the possibility that she may not be accepted by the college of her choice, and an unexpected death.

Armstrong, Jennifer. *Shattered: Stories of Children and War.* Dell Laurel-Leaf, 2003, c2002. 166p. IL 5–8, Lexile: 800
These twelve short stories describe the experiences of young children and teenagers in war, present a variety of perspectives, and provide factual notes on each conflict dramatized.

Avi. *Nothing but the Truth: A Documentary Novel.* Scholastic, 2010, c1991. 177p. IL 5–8, Lexile: NP
A ninth-grader's suspension for humming *The Star-Spangled Banner* during homeroom becomes a national news story, and leads to him and his teacher both leaving the school.

Barakat, Ibtisam. *Tasting the Sky: A Palestinian Childhood.* Farrar, Straus and Giroux, 2007. 176p. IL YA, Lexile: 870 (Non-fiction)
In this memoir, the author describes her childhood as a Palestinian refugee, discussing her family's experiences during and after the Six Day War, and the freedom she felt at learning to read and write.

Compestine, Ying Chang. *Revolution Is Not a Dinner Party: A Novel.* Holt, 2007. 249p. IL 5–8, Lexile: 740
Starting in 1972 when she is nine years old, Ling, the daughter of two doctors, struggles to make sense of the communists' Cultural Revolution, which empties stores of food, homes of appliances deemed "bourgeois," and people of laughter.

Cormier, Robert. *The Chocolate War.* Knopf, 2004, c1974. 253p. IL YA, Lexile: 820
A high school freshman discovers the devastating consequences of refusing to join in the school's annual fundraising drive and arousing the wrath of the school bullies.

Cummings, Priscilla. *Red Kayak.* Puffin Books, 2006, c2004. 209p. IL 5–8, Lexile: 800
Living near the water on Maryland's Eastern Shore, thirteen-year-old Brady and his best friends J. T. and Digger become entangled in a tragedy that tests their friendship and their ideas about right and wrong.

Curtis, Christopher Paul. *Elijah of Buxton.* Scholastic, 2009, c2007. 341p. IL 3-6, Lexile: 1070
Eleven-year-old Elijah Freeman, the first free-born child in Buxton, Canada—a haven for slaves fleeing the American South in 1859—uses his wits and skills to bring to justice the lying preacher who has stolen money that was to be used to buy a family's freedom.

Donnelly, Jennifer. *A Northern Light.* Harcourt, c2003. 389p. IL YA, Lexile: 700
In 1906, sixteen-year-old Mattie is determined to attend college and be a writer, even though that path goes against the wishes of her father and boyfriend. When she takes a job at a hotel, the death of a guest renews her determination to live her own life.

Conflict and Cooperation

Flinn, Alex. *Breathing Underwater.* HarperTempest, 2002, c2001. 263p. IL YA, Lexile: 510
  Sent to counseling for hitting his girlfriend, Caitlin, and ordered to keep a journal, sixteen-year-old Nick recounts his relationship with Caitlin, examines his controlling behavior and anger, and describes his life with his abusive father.

Gourlay, Candy. *Tall Story.* David Fickling Books, c2010. 295p. IL 5–8, Lexile: 670
  Sixteen-year-old Bernardo, who is 8 feet tall and suffers from a condition called gigantism, leaves the Philippines to live with his mother's family in London, much to the delight of his thirteen-year-old half-sister Andi, a passionate basketball player.

Kadohata, Cynthia. *Cracker!: The Best Dog in Vietnam.* Aladdin Paperbacks, 2008, c2007. 312p. IL 5–8, Lexile: 730
  A young soldier in Vietnam bonds with his bomb-sniffing German shepherd.

Kadohata, Cynthia. *Weedflower.* Atheneum Books for Young Readers, c2006. 260p. IL 5–8, Lexile: 750
  After twelve-year-old Sumiko and her Japanese American family are relocated from their flower farm in southern California to an internment camp on a Mojave Indian reservation in Arizona, she helps her family and neighbors, becomes friends with a local Indian boy, and tries to hold on to her dream of owning a flower shop.

Magoon, Kekla. *The Rock and the River.* Aladdin, 2009. 290p. IL 5–8, Lexile: 550
  In 1968 Chicago, fourteen-year-old Sam Childs is caught in a conflict between his father, who prefers a nonviolent approach to seeking civil rights for African Americans, and his older brother, who has joined the Black Panther Party.

Mikaelsen, Ben. *Touching Spirit Bear.* HarperTrophy, 2005, c2001. 289p. IL 5–8, Lexile: 670
  Fifteen-year-old Cole, trying to avoid prison, agrees to participate in a sentencing alternative based on Native American circle justice; he is sent to a remote Alaskan island, where an encounter with a huge Spirit Bear changes his life.

Naidoo, Beverley. *Out of Bounds: Seven Stories of Conflict and Hope.* HarperTrophy, 2008, c2001. 175p. IL 5–8, Lexile: 750
  This collection of seven stories by native South African Beverly Naidoo explores the theme of choice during apartheid.

Paterson, Katherine. *Bread and Roses, Too.* Clarion Books, c2006. 275p. IL 5–8, Lexile: 810
  Twelve-year-old Rosa and thirteen-year-old Jake form an unlikely friendship as they try to survive and understand the 1912 Bread and Roses strike of mill workers in Lawrence, Massachusetts.

Paulsen, Gary. *Soldier's Heart: Being the Story of the Enlistment and Due Service of the Boy Charley Goddard in the First Minnesota Volunteers: A Novel of the Civil War.* Dell Laurel-Leaf, 2000, c1998. 106p. IL YA, Lexile: 1000
  Eager to enlist in the army, fifteen-year-old Charley has a change of heart after experiencing both the physical horrors and mental anguish of Civil War combat.

Conflict and Cooperation

Rosoff, Meg. *How I Live Now.* Wendy Lamb Books, 2006, c2004. 194p. IL YA, Lexile: 1620
To get away from her pregnant stepmother in New York City, fifteen-year-old Daisy goes to England to stay with her aunt and cousins, with whom she instantly bonds. Soon, however, war breaks out and rips apart the family while devastating the land.

Smith, Roland. *Elephant Run.* Hyperion Books for Children, c2007. 318p. IL 5–8, Lexile: 750
After Nick's father and others are taken prisoner when his plantation in Burma is invaded by the Japanese in 1941, Nick and his friend Mya risk their lives to free them from the POW camp.

Spinelli, Jerry. *Milkweed: A Novel.* Knopf, 2010, c2003. 208p. IL YA, Lexile: 510
A street child, known to himself only as Stopthief, finds a welcoming community when he is taken in by a band of orphans in Warsaw ghetto—a move that helps him cope with the horrors of the Nazi regime.

Staples, Suzanne Fisher. *Under the Persimmon Tree.* Farrar, Straus and Giroux, 2005. 275p. IL YA, Lexile: 1010
A young Afghan girl, Najmah, befriends an American woman, Nusrat, in Peshawar, Pakistan, after Najmah flees her native Afghanistan during the 2001 war. Together, the pair begin a long journey to locate their missing loved ones after the war ends.

Strasser, Todd. *Give a Boy a Gun.* Simon Pulse, c2000. 208p. IL YA, Lexile: 760
Events leading up to a night of terror at a high school dance are told from the point of view of various people involved.

Strasser, Todd. *The Wave.* Dell Laurel-Leaf, c1981. 138p. IL YA, Lexile: 770
In this dramatization of an actual classroom experiment in establishing a fascist society, Laurie tries to persuade Mr. Ross to call off the experiment.

Vande Velde, Vivian. *A Coming Evil.* Houghton Mifflin, 1998. 213p. IL 5–8, Lexile: 740
Thirteen-year-old Lisette Beaucaire is resentful when her parents send her from Nazi-occupied Paris in 1940 to live with her aunt in the country. She barely has time to get bored when she learns the farm serves as a hiding place for several Jewish and Gypsy children, as well as a ghost from another time of historical conflict, who proves to be an invaluable ally.

Yep, Laurence. *Ribbons.* Putnum & Grosset Group, 1997, c1992. 179p. IL 5–8, Lexile: 710
A promising young ballet student cannot afford to continue lessons when her Chinese grandmother emigrates from Hong Kong, creating jealousy and conflict among the entire family.

Zusak, Markus. *The Book Thief.* Knopf, c2006. 552p. IL YA, Lexile: 730
Trying to make sense of the horrors of World War II, Death relates the story of Liesel—a young German girl whose book-stealing and story-telling talents help sustain her family and the Jewish man they are hiding, as well as their neighbors.

Girls Who Kick Butt

Barnes, Jennifer. *Raised by Wolves.* Egmont USA, 2010. 418p. IL YA, Lexile: 880
A girl raised by werewolves must face the horrors of her past to uncover the dark secrets that the pack has worked so hard to hide.

Burney, Claudia Mair. *The Exorsistah.* Pocket Star Books, 2010, c2008. 303p. IL YA
Seventeen-year-old Emme Vaughn, a homeless girl who can see demons, has a chance to do God's work by assisting a disgraced priest, a nun, and handsome Francis Rivers in performing exorcisms, but must first battle her personal demons, lack of discipline, and teen hormones.

Cashore, Kristin. *Graceling.* Houghton Mifflin Harcourt, 2008. 471p. IL YA, Lexile: 730
In a world where some people are born with extreme and often-feared skills called Graces, Katsa struggles for redemption from her own horrifying Grace of killing and teams up with another young fighter to save their land from a corrupt king.

Chadda, Sarwat. *Dark Goddess.* Hyperion, c2010. 376p. IL YA
A young girl who possesses dangerous powers is being hunted by werewolves; it is up to Billi SanGreal, a teenaged member of the Knights Templar, to keep the girl safe from Baba Yoga, an ancient Russian witch.

Chadda, Sarwat. *The Devil's Kiss.* Disney/Hyperion Books, c2009. 327p. IL YA, Lexile: 620
Fifteen-year-old Billi SanGreal has grown up knowing that being a member of the Knights Templar puts her in danger, but if she is to save London from catastrophe, she must make sacrifices greater than she imagined.

Gill, David Macinnis. *Soul Enchilada.* Greenwillow Books, c2009. 356p. IL YA, Lexile: 720
Eighteen-year-old Bug Smoot, having just learned that her irascible grandfather has given away both her car and her soul in a deal with the Devil, has two days to come up with a way to outsmart the Prince of Darkness and his demons.

Goodman, Alison. *Eon: Dragoneye Reborn.* Viking, 2008. 531p. IL YA, Lexile: 750
Sixteen-year-old Eon hopes to become an apprentice to one of the twelve energy dragons of good fortune and learn to be its main interpreter, but doing so will require a great deal in exchange, including keeping secret that she is a girl.

Goodman, Alison. *Eona: The Last Dragoneye.* Viking, 2011. 637p. IL YA
Eona, the first female Dragoneye in hundreds of years, joins fellow rebels Ryko and Lady Dela on a quest to find the black folio and help the young Pearl Emperor win back his throne from the evil Lord Sethon.

Lo, Malinda. *Huntress.* Little, Brown, 2011. 371p. IL YA
Seventeen-year-olds Kaede and Taisin are called to go on a dangerous and unprecedented journey to Tanlili, the city of the Fairy Queen, in an effort to restore the balance of nature in the human world.

Marriott, Zoe. *Daughter of the Flames.* Candlewick Press, 2009. 342p. IL YA
After learning that she is the sole heir to the Ruan throne, orphaned Zira, who has been trained in weaponry and martial arts as a warrior priestess, must unravel the secrets of her identity, decide her people's fate, and accept her feelings for a man who should be her enemy.

Girls Who Kick Butt

Pierce, Tamora. *Trickster's Choice*. Laurel-Leaf Books, 2008, c2003. 422p. IL 5–8, Lexile: 790
Alianne must call forth her mother's courage and her father's wit to survive on the Copper Isles in a royal court rife with political intrigue and murderous conspiracy.

Pon, Cindy. *Fury of the Phoenix*. Greenwillow Books, c2011. 362p. IL YA
Ai Ling leaves her home and family to accompany Chen Yong on his quest to find his father, haunted by the ancient evil she thought she had banished to the underworld. She must use her growing supernatural powers to save Chen Yong from the curses that follow her.

Pon, Cindy. *Silver Phoenix: Beyond the Kingdom of Xia*. Greenwillow Books, c2009. 338p. IL YA, Lexile: 760
With her father long overdue from his journey and a lecherous merchant blackmailing her into marriage, seventeen-year-old Ai Ling becomes aware of a strange power within her as she goes in search of her parent.

Rhodes, Jewell Parker. *Ninth Ward*. Little, Brown, 2010. 217p. IL 5–8, Lexile: 470
In New Orleans' Ninth Ward, twelve-year-old Lanesha, who can see spirits, and her adopted grandmother have no choice but to stay and weather the storm as Hurricane Katrina bears down upon them.

St. Crow, Lili. *Strange Angels*. Razorbill, c2009. 293p. IL YA, Lexile: 810
Sixteen-year-old Dru Anderson travels from town to town with her father, who hunts "strange" creatures. When he is turned into a zombie, Dru goes on the run with her friends Grave—freshly bitten by a werewolf—and Christophe—a half-human vampire hunter—to save herself.

Series

Cabot, Meg. *The Mediator Series*. HarperTeen, 2005– . IL YA
A girl. A guy. A new kind of ghost story! Susannah Simon is a mediator—that is, someone who can see and speak to the dead. It isn't easy being a mediator, especially when you would rather be shopping at the outlet mall or snagging your first boyfriend. But what if the ghost of a really hot guy haunts you?

Carter, Ally. *Gallagher Girls*. Disney/Hyperion, 2007–2010. IL YA
These three books feature Cammie Morgan, a secret spy school student and daughter of a former CIA operative, who uses her training to uncover information about her friends, parents, and others ,and works as part of her father's security team while he is on the campaign trail.

Collins, Suzanne. *The Hunger Games Trilogy*. Scholastic Press, 2008–2010. IL YA
This series includes *The Hunger Games,* in which sixteen-year-old Katniss Everdeen becomes a contender in a gravely serious competition hosted by the Capitol, in which young boys and girls are pitted against each other in a televised fight to the death; *Catching Fire,* in which Katniss and Peeta win the competition and become the faces of an impending rebellion; and *Mockingjay,* in which Katniss and her family and friends are in danger because the Capitol holds her responsible for the unrest.

Girls Who Kick Butt

Meyer, L. A. *Bloody Jack Series*. Harcourt, c2002– . IL YA
Reduced to begging and thievery in the streets of London, the thirteen-year-old orphan Jacky Faber disguises herself as a boy and connives her way onto a British warship set for high seas adventure in search of pirates.

Nix, Garth. *Abhorsen Trilogy.* Eos, 2003– . IL YA
This fantasy trilogy follows the magical adventures of Sabriel; her father Abhorsen, a powerful necromancer; and their ancestors and descendants in the magical Old Kingdom.

Pierce, Tamora. *Song of the Lioness Series*. Atheneum Books for Young Readers, 1983– . IL 5–8
Alanna of Trebond disguises herself as a boy to begin her journey from page to squire to knight-hood. As she masters the skills needed for battle, she must also learn to control her heart. As the first female shaman of an ancient tribe, she discovers a future worthy of her mythic past—as warrior and woman.

Mean Girls

Henkes, Kevin. *Chrysanthemum.* Greenwillow, c1991. 32p. IL K–3, Lexile: 460
Chrysanthemum loves her name—until she starts going to school and the other children begin to make fun of it.

Koss, Amy Goldman. *The Girls.* Dial Books for Young Readers, c2000. 121p. IL 5–8, Lexile: 710
Each of the girls in a middle-school clique reveals the strong, manipulative hold one member of the group exerts on the others, causing hurt and creating self-doubt among the girls.

Lester, Helen. *Hooway for Wodney Wat.* Houghton Mifflin, c1999. 32p. IL K–3, Lexile: 360
All of his classmates make fun of Rodney because he cannot pronounce his name, but it is Rodney's speech impediment that drives away the class bully.

Lovell, Patty. *Stand Tall, Molly Lou Melon.* G. P. Putnam's, c2001. 32p. IL K–3, Lexile: 560
Even when the class bully at her new school makes fun of her, Molly remembers what her grandmother told her and she feels good about herself.

Ludwig, Trudy. *My Secret Bully.* Tricycle, 2005, c2004. 32p. IL K–3
A girl confides to her mother that her best friend is treating her badly, and together they figure out what to do about it.

Madonna. *The English Roses.* Callaway, c2003. 46p. IL 3–6, Lexile: 790
Four best friends are jealous of a neighbor girl and refuse to have anything to do with her, until each has a dream in which a fairy godmother shows them what the girl's life is really like.

Marsden, Carolyn. *The Gold-Threaded Dress.* Candlewick Press, 2006, c2002. 73p. IL 3–6, Lexile: 710
When Oy and her Thai American family move to a new neighborhood, her third-grade classmates tease and exclude her because she is different.

Rodman, Mary Ann. *My Best Friend.* Viking, 2005. 30p. IL K–3, Lexile: 390
Six-year-old Lily has a best friend all picked out for play-group day, but unfortunately the differences between first graders and second graders are sometimes very large.

Whitcomb, Mary E. *Odd Velvet.* Chronicle Books, c1998. 24p. IL K–3, Lexile: 750.
Although she dresses differently from the other girls and does things that are unusual, Velvet eventually teaches her classmates that even an outsider has something to offer.

From *101 Great, Ready-to-Use Book Lists for Teens* by Nancy J. Keane. Santa Barbara, CA: Libraries Unlimited. Copyright © 2012.

Physically Different

Bauer, Joan. *Stand Tall.* Speak, 2005, c2002. 182p. IL 5–8, Lexile: 520
Tree, a twelve-year-old who is 6 feet, 3 inches tall, copes with his parents' recent divorce and his failure as an athlete by helping his grandfather, a Vietnam veteran and recent amputee, and Sophie, a new girl at school.

Bingham, Kelly L. *Shark Girl.* Candlewick Press, 2007. 276p. IL YA, Lexile: NP
After a shark attack causes the amputation of her right arm, fifteen-year-old Jane, an aspiring artist, struggles to come to terms with her loss and the changes it imposes on her day-to-day life and her plans for the future.

Blume, Judy. *Otherwise Known as Sheila the Great.* Dutton Children's Books, c1972. 138p. IL 3–6, Lexile: 590
A summer in Tarrytown, New York, is a lot of fun for ten-year-old Sheila, even though her friends make her face up to some self-truths she doesn't want to admit.

Gourlay, Candy. *Tall Story.* David Fickling Books, c2010. 295p. IL 5–8, Lexile: 670
Sixteen-year-old Bernardo, who is 8 feet tall and suffers from a condition called gigantism, leaves the Philippines to live with his mother's family in London, much to the delight of his thirteen-year-old half-sister Andi, a passionate basketball player.

Graff, Lisa. *The Thing about Georgie: A Novel.* Laura Geringer Books, c2006. 220p. IL 3–6, Lexile: 770
Georgie's dwarfism causes problems, but he could always rely on his parents, his best friend, and classmate Jeanie the Meanie's teasing—until a surprising announcement, a new boy in school, and a class project shake things up.

Hiaasen, Carl. *Hoot.* Alfred A. Knopf, c2002. 292p. IL 5–8, Lexile: 760
Roy, who is new to his small Florida community, becomes involved in another boy's attempt to save a colony of burrowing owls from a proposed construction site.

Kinney, Jeff. *Diary of a Wimpy Kid: Greg Heffley's Journal.* Amulet Books, 2007. 217p. IL 5–8, Lexile: 950
Greg records his sixth-grade experiences in a middle school where he and his best friend, Rowley—undersized weaklings amid boys who need to shave twice daily—hope just to survive. When Rowley grows more popular, however, Greg must take drastic measures to save their friendship.

Lovell, Patty. *Stand Tall, Molly Lou Melon.* G. P. Putnam's, c2001. 32p. IL K–3, Lexile: 560
Even when the class bully at her new school makes fun of her, Molly remembers what her grandmother told her and she feels good about herself.

Lupica, Mike. *Travel Team.* Philomel Books, c2004. 274p. IL 5–8, Lexile: 930
After he is cut from his travel basketball team—the very same team that his father once led to national prominence—twelve-year-old Danny Walker forms his own team of cast-offs who might have a shot at victory.

Physically Different

Nemeth, Sally. *The Heights, the Depths, and Everything in Between.* Yearling, 2008, c2006. 262p. IL 5–8, Lexile: 800
> In 1977, best friends Lucy Small, a seventh grader from Wilmington, Delaware, who is 5 feet, 10 inches tall, and Jake Little, a dwarf, try unsuccessfully to go unnoticed during their first year of junior high school.

Snyder, Zilpha Keatley. *The Treasures of Weatherby.* Atheneum Books for Young Readers, c2007. 213p. IL 3–6, Lexile: 1060
> Determined to be as strong and powerful as the first Harleigh, who built the rambling Weatherby Hall, twelve-year-old Harleigh Fourth and an equally diminutive new friend try to foil the plans of a distant relative who is seeking the long-lost Weatherby fortune.

Stroud, Jonathan. *Heroes of the Valley.* Disney/Hyperion Books, c2009. 483p. IL 5–8, Lexile: 770
> Halli Sveinsson, a mischievous young man who does not fit in with his peers and siblings, plays a trick on Ragnor that goes too far. As a consequence, he is forced to embark on a hero's quest in which he will face highway robbers, monsters, an intriguing girl, and truths about his family and the legends he grew up with.

Ylvisaker, Anne. *Little Klein.* Candlewick Press, 2007. 186p. IL 3–6, Lexile: 840
> Harold "Little" Klein is so much smaller than his three older brothers, a boisterous gang held together by big-hearted Mother Klein, that he often feels left out. But when disaster strikes, it is up to Harold and LeRoy, the stray dog he has adopted, to save the day.

Psychics

Cabot, Meg. *The Mediator.* HarperTeen, 2011. 515p. IL YA

These two stories follow the adventures of Suze Simon, a sixteen-year-old girl who can talk to the dead, as she deals with a sexy, nineteenth-century ghost named Jesse, and the troubled spirit of a murdered woman.

Chandler, Elizabeth. *The Back Door of Midnight.* Simon Pulse, 2010. 299p. IL YA, Lexile: 750

Anna struggles to maintain a sense of normalcy while staying with her eccentric aunt for the summer. When her uncle's charred body is discovered and her aunt's grief exaggerates her psychic abilities, Anna wonders who she can trust and whether her family's supernatural abilities might help her find her uncle's killer.

Dickinson, Peter. *The Gift.* Dell Laurel-Leaf, 1994, c1973. 168p. IL YA, Lexile: 960

Welsh youth Davy Price uses his gift—the ability to see into other people's minds—and finds that his family is in danger.

Duncan, Lois. *The Third Eye.* Bantam Doubleday Dell Books for Young Readers, 1991, c1984. 220p. IL YA, Lexile: 810

High school senior Karen, who worries that her psychic powers will make her seem different from other people, is frightened when a young policeman asks her to use her gift to help locate missing children.

Harper, Suzanne. *The Secret Life of Sparrow Delaney.* Greenwillow Books, 2008, c2007. 364p. IL YA, Lexile: 840

In Lily Dale, New York, a community dedicated to the religion of Spiritualism, tenth-grader Sparrow Delaney, the youngest daughter in an eccentric family of psychics, agonizes over whether to reveal her special abilities to help a friend.

Harrington, Kim. *Clarity.* Point, 2011. 246p. IL YA, Lexile: 580

Sixteen-year-old Clare Fern, a member of a family of psychics, helps the mayor and a skeptical detective solve a murder in a Cape Cod town during the height of tourist season—a crime in which her brother is a prime suspect.

Le Guin, Ursula K. *Powers.* Harcourt, c2007. 502p. IL YA, Lexile: 950

A tragedy sets Gavir, a young slave, on a dangerous road toward freedom and dealing with the powers he has hitherto kept secret, including the ability to see flashes of the future.

Matas, Carol. *Tales of a Reluctant Psychic.* Key Porter Books, c2008. 414p. IL YA

In this collection of three novels, teenage psychic Jade begins losing friends because she is different, struggles with her knowledge of a terrible future event that she may not be able to prevent, tries to gain control of the messages she is receiving in her dreams in time to help save an intended murder victim, and anticipates a visit to a university's psychic testing division while on a family vacation to Palm Springs.

Perez, Marlene. *Dead Is the New Black.* Harcourt, c2008. 190p. IL YA, Lexile: 640

Seventeen-year-old Daisy Giordano, daughter and sister of psychics, attempts to help her mother discover who is behind a series of bizarre attacks on teenage girls in their little town of Nightshade, California.

Psychics

Singleton, Linda Joy. *Don't Die Dragonfly.* Llewellyn Publications, 2004. 269p. IL YA
Sabine tries to ignore the psychic abilities that she shares with her grandmother, but when she discovers that a classmate is in real danger, she is compelled to follow her spirit guide.

Singleton, Linda Joy. *Last Dance.* Llewellyn Publications, c2005. 242p. IL YA
While trying to help her sick grandmother, Sabine and her Goth friend Thorn travel to a small California town, where they become involved in a ghostly, fifty-year-old mystery.

Singleton, Linda Joy. *Sword Play.* Llewellyn Publications, c2006. 280p. IL YA
As if being forced to return home and worrying about her grandmother's illness were not enough to deal with, a visit from Kip's ghost has Sabine checking into the circumstances of his death and discovering some facts that her former friends very much want to keep secret.

Singleton, Linda Joy. *Witch Ball.* Llewellyn Publications, c2006. 254p. IL YA
While being stalked by a mysterious Witch Ball, Sabine must contend with her growing attraction to the young handyman Dominic, her grandmother's increasing forgetfulness, and mysterious predictions that seem to come true.

Staub, Wendy Corsi. *Lily Dale: Awakening.* Walker, 2007. 228p. IL YA. Lexile: 750
When her mother dies suddenly, seventeen-year-old Calla goes to stay with her psychic grandmother in Lily Dale, a spiritualist community in western New York, where she discovers some disconcerting secrets about her practical, down-to-earth mother, and realizes that she herself may have some psychic abilities.

Vrettos, Adrienne Maria. *Sight.* Simon Pulse, 2008, c2007. 254p. IL YA, Lexile: 770
Sixteen-year-old Dylan uses her psychic abilities to help police solve crimes against children, but keeps her extracurricular activities secret from her friends at school.

Secret Societies

Barnes, Jennifer. *The Squad: Perfect Cover.* Laurel-Leaf, c2008. 275p. IL YA
High school sophomore Toby Klein enjoys computer hacking and wearing combat boots, so she thinks it is a joke when she is invited to join the cheerleading squad. Soon, however, she learns cheering is just a cover for an elite group of government operatives.

Carter, Ally. *Heist Society.* Disney Hyperion Books, c2010. 291p. IL YA, Lexile: 800
Fifteen-year-old Kat schemes her way into the best boarding school, hoping to leave the thieving antics of her family behind her. But then Hal, a former co-conspirator, appears on campus to tell Kat that a powerful mobster believes her father stole art from a priceless collection; to save him, Kat will have to recover the paintings.

Cassidy, Kay. *The Cinderella Society.* Egmont USA, 2010. 322p. IL YA, Lexile: 800
Sixteen-year-old Jess Parker fears she will never fit in at her new school, until she is invited to join the Cinderella Society, a secret sisterhood of the most popular girls in school. The group needs Jess on their side in a battle of good versus evil as they face off against the Wickeds, who are targeting innocent girls in their war against the Cinderellas.

Cormier, Robert. *The Chocolate War.* Dell Laurel-Leaf, 2000, c1974. 263p. IL YA, Lexile: 820
A high school freshman discovers the devastating consequences of refusing to join in the school's annual fundraising drive and arousing the wrath of the school bullies.

Dolby, Tom. *Secret Society.* Katherine Tegen Books, c2009. 343p. IL YA
Three Manhattan teens—Phoebe, Nick, and Lauren—are initiated into an age-old secret society that offers them the fulfillment of their wildest dreams but demands their undying loyalty. Meanwhile, Nick's friend Patch, an aspiring filmmaker, tries to document the society's activities.

Gardner, Graham. *Inventing Elliot.* Speak, 2005, c2003. 181p. IL YA, Lexile: 690
Fourteen-year-old Elliot Sutton arrives at his new high school determined that he will not become a target for teasing; however, when a group of upperclassmen called the Guardians, who are obsessed with power, try to recruit him, Elliot must make a difficult decision.

Hartinger, Brent. *Geography Club.* HarperTempest, 2004, c2003. 226p. IL YA, Lexile: 700
A group of gay and lesbian teenagers finds mutual support when they form the "Geography Club" at their high school.

Lockhart, E. *The Disreputable History of Frankie Landau-Banks.* Disney/Hyperion Books, 2009. 381p. IL YA, Lexile: 890
When Frankie Landau-Banks attempts to take over a secret, all-male society at her exclusive prep school, her antics with the group soon draw some unlikely attention and have unexpected consequences that could change her life forever.

Peterfreund, Diana. *Ascendant.* HarperTeen, c2010. 392p. IL YA, Lexile: 770
When sixteen-year-old Astrid Llewellyn, now a fully trained unicorn hunter, joins the quest to discover The Remedy at a laboratory in the French countryside, she begins to question her love for Giovanni, her loyalty to the Cloisters, and even her duty as a hunter.

Secret Societies

Peterfreund, Diana. *Rampant.* HarperTeen, 2010, c2009. 402p. IL YA, Lexile: 750

After sixteen-year-old Astrid Llewelyn survives a vicious unicorn attack, she learns that she is a descendant of the most famous unicorn hunter of all time. She also discovers that she must travel to Rome, Italy, to train in the ancient arts to carry on her family legacy and save the world from the threat posed by the reemergence of lethal unicorns.

Peterfreund, Diana. *Secret Society Girl: An Ivy League Novel.* Delta Trade Paperbacks, 2007, c2006. 296p. IL AD

College junior Amy Haskel is shocked when she is invited to join Rose & Grave, the country's most powerful and notorious secret society, and finds herself thrown into a world of high society, intrigue, and danger that threatens everything Amy has worked for.

Riordan, Rick. *The Red Pyramid.* Disney/Hyperion Books, c2010. 516p. IL 5–8, Lexile: 650

Brilliant Egyptologist Dr. Julius Kane accidentally unleashes the Egyptian god Set, who banishes the doctor to oblivion and forces his two children to embark on a dangerous journey, bringing them closer to the truth about their family and its links to a secret order that has existed since the time of the pharaohs.

Roecker, Lisa. *The Liar Society.* Sourcebooks Fire, c2011. 361p. IL YA

Kate Lowry receives an e-mail from her best friend, who died a year earlier, that makes her believe the death was not an accident. When she teams up with two classmates from her private school to uncover the truth, she realizes that some people have secrets that are so big they would kill to keep them hidden.

Rowling, J. K. *Harry Potter and the Order of the Phoenix.* A. A. Levine, 2003. 870p. IL 5–8, Lexile: 950

Harry Potter, now a fifth-year student at Hogwarts School of Witchcraft and Wizardry, struggles with a threatening teacher, a problematic house elf, his dread of upcoming final exams, and haunting dreams that hint of his mysterious past.

Stevenson, Sarah Jamila. *The Latte Rebellion.* Flux, c2011. 328p. IL YA

Asha Jamison and her best friend Carey, inspired by a racial insult, set off on a money-making trip, selling T-shirts to raise awareness for mixed-race students.

Westerfeld, Scott. *Extras.* Simon Pulse, 2007. 399p. IL YA

In an alternative civilization where the social status of each person is monitored and rated and anyone can drop from celebrity to nobody, fifteen-year-old Aya Fuse's popularity ranking is so low that her only chance of moving up is to find a good story. When she meets a group of girls who hide an explosive secret, Aya decides to expose the group—and unknowingly puts her own life in danger.

Westerfeld, Scott. *Peeps: A Novel.* Razorbill, c2005. 312p. IL YA, Lexile: 840

Cal Thompson is a carrier of a parasite that causes vampirism, and must hunt down all of the girl-friends he has unknowingly infected.

Secret Societies

Whitney, Daisy. *The Mockingbirds.* Little, Brown, 2010. 339p. IL YA, Lexile: 720

When Alex, a junior at an elite preparatory school, realizes that she may have been the victim of date rape, she confides in her roommates and sister, who convince her to seek help from a secret society, the Mockingbirds.

Series

Bray, Libba. *Gemma Doyle Trilogy.* Delacorte Press, c2003– . IL YA

After the suspicious death of her mother in 1895, sixteen-year-old Gemma returns to England, after many years in India, to attend a finishing school. There, she becomes aware of her magical powers and ability to see into the spirit world.

Westerfeld, Scott. *Midnighters.* Eos, 2004– . IL YA

Jessica Day learns that she is a member of a special group of people who were born at the stroke of midnight and can roam the town at a secret hour while others sleep—and that she must fight the evil creatures who share her power.

Werewolves

Armstrong, Kelley. *The Reckoning.* Harper, c2010. 391p. IL YA, Lexile: 600
   Fifteen-year-old Chloe, a necromancer, struggles to understand her feelings for werewolf Derek and his sorcerer brother, Simon, while seeking a way to enter the headquarters of the sinister Edison Group and rescue her aunt Lauren and her friend Rachelle.

Brin, Susannah, *The Pack.* Artesian Press, c2002. 58p. IL 5–8, Lexile: 510
   Candle Selky, a teenage member of a werewolf family, longs to live a normal human life, especially after meeting David Payne.

De Lint, Charles. *Wolf Moon.* Firebird, 2004, c1988. 245p. IL YA,
   After becoming a werewolf, Kern seeks refuge at the Inn of the Yellow Tinker. Can he guard his dreaded secret well enough to find a home there?

Dunkle, Clare B. *By These Ten Bones.* Henry Holt, 2005. 229p. IL YA
   After a mysterious young wood-carver with a horrifying secret arrives in her small Scottish town, Maddie gains his trust—and his heart—and seeks a way to save both him and her townspeople from an ancient evil.

Feasey, Steve. *Wereling.* Feiwel and Friends, 2010, c2009. 276p. IL YA, Lexile: 1050
   Fourteen-year-old Trey Laporte, having woken up one morning to the discovery that he is a werewolf, finds himself pursued by a psychopathic bloodsucker and in love with an insanely pretty girl who happens to be half-vampire.

Jinks, Catherine. *The Abused Werewolf Rescue Group.* Harcourt, 2011. 409p. IL YA
   Tobias Richard Vandevelde wakes up in a hospital with no memory of the night before, after being found unconscious in the dingo pen at Featherdale Wildlife Park, and finds out that he is a werewolf from a group of vampires.

Johnson, Christine. *Claire de Lune.* Simon Pulse, 2010. 336p. IL YA, Lexile: 690
   On her sixteenth birthday, Claire discovers strange things happening. When her mother reveals their family secret, which explains the changes, Claire feels her world, as she has known it to be, slowly slipping away.

Meyer, Stephenie. *Breaking Dawn.* Little, Brown, 2008. 756p. IL YA, Lexile: 690
   This volume continues the story of the human Bella and the vampire Edward, whose love is threatened by their difference, a werewolf named Jacob, and other outside influences.

Meyer, Stephenie. *Eclipse.* Little, Brown, 2007. 629p. IL YA, Lexile: 670
   Bella must choose between her friendship with Jacob, a werewolf, and her relationship with Edward, a vampire, but when Seattle is ravaged by a mysterious string of killings, the three of them need to decide whether their personal lives are more important than the well-being of an entire city.

Mould, Chris. *The Wooden Mile.* Roaring Brook Press, 2008, c2007. 176p. IL 5–8, Lexile: 760
   Eleven-year-old Stanley Buggle happily anticipates a long summer vacation in the house he has inherited from his great-uncle. Soon after arriving in the seemingly peaceful village of Crampton Rock, however, he discovers that along with the house he has inherited some sinister neighbors, a talking stuffed fish, and a host of mysteries surrounding his great-uncle's death.

From *101 Great, Ready-to-Use Book Lists for Teens* by Nancy J. Keane. Santa Barbara, CA: Libraries Unlimited. Copyright © 2012.

Werewolves

Perez, Marlene. *Dead Is a State of Mind.* Graphia, 2009. 175p. IL YA, Lexile: 620
When a gorgeous new student's prediction that a teacher will be murdered comes true, seventeen-year-old Daisy is determined to solve the crime, but when all signs point to the killer being a werewolf, she fears she is in over her head.

Showalter, Gena. *Unraveled.* Harlequin Teen, c2010. 572p. IL YA
Former outcast Aden Stone feels as if he is living the good life since moving to Crossroads, Oklahoma, where the three human souls living inside his head finally fit in with the town's werewolves, vampires, and other mystical beings. When Aden learns he is to be crowned Vampire King, however, he fears he will not be able to handle the responsibilities.

Smith, Cynthia Leitich. *Blessed.* Candlewick Press, 2011. 462p. IL YA
Quincie P. Morris scrambles to adjust to her new life as a teenage vampire, help Kieren—her best friend, her true love, and a hybrid werewolf—clear his name of murder charges, prevent a vampire from bringing about the end of the world, and maintain her dead parents' restaurant. When Zachary, her newly hired waiter, reveals his true nature—and a flaming sword—Quincie takes off with him to put an end to the bloodshed and save the world.

Smith, Cynthia Leitich. *Tantalize.* Candlewick Press, 2007. 310p. IL YA, Lexile: 760
When multiple murders in Austin, Texas, threaten the grand reopening of her family's vampire-themed restaurant, seventeen-year-old Quincie, an orphan, worries that her best friend-turned-love-interest, Kieren, a werewolf-in-training, may be the prime suspect.

Stiefvater, Maggie. *Forever.* Scholastic Press, 2011. 390p, IL YA
As the werewolves are hunted by those intent on destroying them, Sam and Grace risk everything to be together.

Stiefvater, Maggie. *Linger.* Scholastic Press, 2010. 362p. IL YA, Lexile: 800
Grace and Sam struggle to keep their relationship together, while Grace lies to her parents and keeps a secret from them and Sam copes with his werewolf past.

Vande Velde, Vivian. *Companions of the Night.* Magic Carpet Books/Harcourt, 2002, c1995. 212p. IL YA, Lexile: 870
When sixteen-year-old Kerry Nowicki helps a young man escape from a group of men who claim he is a vampire, she finds herself faced with some bizarre and dangerous choices.

Series

Feasey, Steve. *Wereling Series.* Feiwel & Friends, c2009– . IL YA
Fourteen-year-old Trey Laporte, having woken up one morning to the discovery that he is a werewolf, finds himself pursued by a psychopathic bloodsucker and in love with an insanely pretty girl who happens to be half-vampire.

Global Warming

Bastedo, Jamie. *Sila's Revenge.* Red Deer Press, c2010. 320p. IL 3–6
Eighteen-year-old Ashley Anowiak and her drumming group, the Dream Drummers, are invited by a wealthy eccentric, Jack Masters, to fly to Australia where they believe they will be a part in an ecological project. All too soon, they learn that the former environmentalist is working on a cataclysmic plan that will destroy the entire planet.

Bertagna, Julie. *Exodus.* Walker, 2008, c2002. 345p. IL YA, Lexile: 870
In the year 2100, as the island of Wing is about to be covered by water, fifteen-year-old Mara discovers the existence of New World sky cities that are safe from the storms and rising waters, and convinces her people to travel to one of these cities to save themselves.

Gutman, Dan. *Roberto & Me.* Harper, c2010. 180p. IL 5–8, Lexile: 580
Stosh travels back to 1969 to try to prevent the untimely death of Roberto Clemente, a legendary baseball player and humanitarian. Upon his return to the present, he meets his own great-grandson, who takes him into the future; what he finds there is more shocking than anything he has encountered in his travels to the past.

Lloyd, Saci. *The Carbon Diaries 2015.* Holiday House, 2009, c2008. 330p. IL YA, Lexile: 690
In 2015, when England becomes the first nation to introduce carbon dioxide rationing in a drastic bid to combat climate change, sixteen-year-old Laura documents the first year of rationing as her family spirals out of control.

Patterson, James. *The Final Warning.* Little, Brown and Co., 2008. 256p. IL YA, Lexile: 720
While on a mission to Antarctica to save the world from global warming, fourteen-year-old Maximum Ride and the other members of the Flock—a band of genetically modified children who can fly—are pursued by their creator, the Uber-Director, who wants to auction them off to the highest bidder.

Weyn, Suzanne. *Empty.* Scholastic Press, 2010. 183p. IL 5–8, Lexile: 790
When, just ten years in the future, oil supplies run out and global warming leads to devastating storms, senior high school classmates Tom, Niki, Gwen, Hector, and Brock realize that the world as they know it is ending and lead the way to a more environmentally friendly society.

Hunting and Fishing

Adamson, Thomas K. *Deer Hunting.* Capstone Press, c2011. 32p. IL 3–6 (Non-fiction)
Describes some of the skills and tools needed for deer hunting, covering equipment, guns, ammunition, safety, and other topics.

Beard, Daniel Carter. *The American Boy's Handy Book.* Derrydale Press, 2001. 391p. IL 5–8 (Non-fiction)
An 1890 manual of past-times that includes instructions for making kites, fishing poles, a blow gun, boats, and theatrical costumes, and for raising dogs, stuffing animals, stocking an aquarium, and camping.

James, M. R. *Bowhunting Equipment & Skills.* Creative Publishing International, c1997. 128p. IL AD (Non-fiction)
A photo-illustrated guide to bow hunting that covers equipment choices and maintenance, skills, and tuning.

Frahm, Randy. *Deer Hunting.* Capstone Press, c2008. 48p. IL 5–8, Lexile: 790 (Non-fiction)
Describes the equipment and techniques associated with deer hunting, including proper clothing and safety issues.

Hopkins, Ellen. *Freshwater Fishing.* Capstone Press, c2008. 48p. IL 5–8, Lexile: 840 (Non-fiction)
Describes the equipment, skills, conservation issues, and safety concerns of freshwater fishing.

Junger, Sebastian. *The Perfect Storm: A True Story of Men against the Sea.* Norton, c1997. 227p. IL AD (Non-fiction)
Uses interviews, memoirs, radio conversations, and technical research to recreate the last days of the crew of the *Andrea Gail,* a fishing boat that was lost in a storm off the coast of Nova Scotia in October 1991.

Kaminsky, Peter. *Fishing for Dummies.* Wiley Publishing, c2011. 364p. IL AD (Non-fiction)
A guide to fishing providing an overview of the sport; discussing bait, tackle, rods, reels, gear, clothing, and food; and offering advice on how to catch fish.

Lawrence, H. Lea. *The Ultimate Guide to Small Game and Varmint Hunting: How to Hunt Squirrels, Rabbits, Woodchucks, Coyotes, Foxes, and Other Game Animals.* Lyons Press, c2002. 252p. IL AD (Non-fiction)
A guide to small game hunting that provides tips for hunting specific types of small animals, plus detailed natural histories of every important small-game species and advice on guns, ammunition, and optics for different species.

MacRae, Sloan. *Deer Hunting.* PowerKids Press, 2011. 32p. IL 3–6 (Non-fiction)
Describes the equipment and techniques associated with deer hunting, including proper clothing and safety issues.

Paulsen, Gary. *Father Water, Mother Woods: Essays on Fishing and Hunting in the North Woods.*
Bantam Doubleday Dell Books for Young Readers, 1996, c1994. 177p. IL YA (Non-fiction)
Takes the reader through the seasons, from the incredible taste of a spring fish fresh from the smokehouse, to the first sight of the first deer, to the peace of winter days spent dreaming by the stove in a fishhouse on the ice. Shows fishing and hunting as pleasure, art, companionship, and sources of life's deepest lessons.

Hunting and Fishing

Piven, Joshua. *The Complete Worst-Case Scenario Survival Handbook.* Chronicle Books, c2007. 507p. IL AD (Non-fiction)
> Presents instructions for surviving everything from taking a car trip with family to being buried alive, drawing from the eleven versions of the *Worst-Case Scenario Survival Handbook.* All of the books are available on a searchable CD-ROM.

Rutter, Michael. *Fly Fishing Made Easy: A Manual for Beginners with Tips for the Experienced.* Falcon Guides, c2007. 222p. IL AD (Non-fiction)
> An introduction to fly fishing that discusses casting, types of flies, recommended gear, and the characteristics of several different fish, including trout, salmon, and bass.

Slade, Suzanne. *Let's Go Fishing.* PowerKids Press, 2007. 32p. IL 3–6 (Non-fiction)
> An introduction to the sport of fishing, discussing where people fish, the gear and bait they use, fishing techniques, and the different types of fishing and fish.

Spencer, Jim. *Guide to Trapping.* Stackpole Books, c2007. 202p. IL AD (Non-fiction)
> A guide to trapping animals, including raccoons, muskrats, beavers, coyotes, and foxes, with advice on trap styles and techniques for each, scouting locations, and preparing and marketing pelts.

Weber, Susan Bartlett. *Opening Day.* Tilbury House, c2007. 32p. IL 3–6, Lexile: 530 (Non-fiction)
> Sam, whose mother is a vegetarian, joins his friend, Eric, on opening day so he can form his own opinion about hunting. Includes facts about deer habits, tracking, and hunting.

Wilson, Patrick. *Trapping, Fishing, and Plant Food.* Mason Crest Publishers, 2003. 64p. IL AD (Non-fiction)
> Explains how the Special Forces live, eat, and survive in the wilderness, describing how to set traps to catch small animals, which fish can be caught with improvised line and bait, which plant food is edible, and how to spot poisonous flora and fungi.

Series

Complete Guide to Fishing. Mason Crest Publishers, c2003– . (Non-fiction)
> A stunning series for both beginners and seasoned fisherman! Myriad topics are covered, from the anatomy of the fish to flyfishing to effective tackle accessories to rod building and even cooking the perfect fish.

Edge Books: The Great Outdoors. Capstone Press, c2004– . (Non-fiction)
> Readers learn about the equipment needed, the techniques to employ, and the safety and conservation measures that will ensure a great adventure in the wilderness.

Remembering September 11, 2001

Curtiss, A. B. *The Little Chapel That Stood.* OldCastle Publishing, c2003. 33p. IL K–3 (Non-fiction)
The story of how St. Paul's Chapel, which was located across the street from the Twin Towers of the World Trade Center, survived the September 11, 2001, collapse of the buildings and then served as a service depot for rescuers.

Deedy, Carmen Agra. *14 Cows for America.* Peachtree, c2009. 38p. IL K–3 (Non-fiction)
An illustrated tale of a gift of fourteen cows given by the Maasai people of Kenya to the United States as a gesture of comfort and friendship in the wake of the attacks of September 11, 2001.

Dwyer, Jim. *102 Minutes: The Untold Story of the Fight to Survive inside the Twin Towers.* Times Books, 2005. 322p. IL AD (Non-fiction)
The story of the men and women who saved themselves and others in the final minutes before the World Trade Towers collapsed on September 11, 2001, including testimony from workers in the buildings, police and fire personnel, a construction manager, and a window washer.

Gerstein, Mordicai. *The Man Who Walked between the Towers.* Roaring Brook Press, c2003. 40p. IL K–3, Lexile: 480 (Non-fiction)
A lyrical evocation of Philippe Petit's 1974 tightrope walk between the World Trade Center towers.

Jacobson, Sid. *The 9/11 Report: A Graphic Adaptation.* Hill and Wang, 2006. 133p. IL AD (Non-fiction)
A graphic novel adaptation of *The 9/11 Commission Report,* the results of the investigation of the September 11, 2001, terrorist attacks on the United States.

Kalman, Maira. *Fireboat: The Heroic Adventures of the John J. Harvey.* G. P. Putnam's Sons, c2002. 42p. IL K–3, Lexile: 280 (Non-fiction)
A fireboat, launched in 1931, is retired after many years of fighting fires along the Hudson River, but is saved from being scrapped and then called into service again on September 11, 2001.

Levithan, David. *Love Is the Higher Law.* Alfred A. Knopf, c2009. 167p. IL YA, Lexile: 920
Three New York City teens express their reactions to the bombing of the World Trade Center on September 11, 2001, and its impact on their lives and the world.

Longman, Jere. *Among the Heroes: United Flight 93 and the Passengers and Crew Who Fought Back.* Perennial, 2003. 296p. IL AD (Non-fiction)
This chronicle of the events surrounding the hijacking and crash of United Flight 93 on September 11, 2001, focuses on the passengers' efforts to overtake the hijackers and prevent the plane from being used as a weapon against an American landmark.

McCann, Colum. *Let the Great World Spin: A Novel.* Random House, c2009. 349p. IL AD
Philippe Petit's illicit 1974 high-wire walk between the World Trade Center towers is the touchstone for stories of the people down below, including an Irish monk living in the Bronx projects, a Park Avenue mother in mourning for her son who died in Vietnam, and a heroin-addicted hooker.

Remembering September 11, 2001

Meminger, Neesha. *Shine, Coconut Moon.* Margaret K. McElderry Books, 2010, c2009. 247p. IL YA, Lexile: 740

In the days and weeks following the terrorist attacks on September 11, 2001, Samar, who is of Punjabi heritage but has been raised with no knowledge of her past by her single mother, strives to learn about her family's history and get in touch with the grandparents her mother shuns.

Osborne, Mary Pope. *New York's Bravest.* Dragonfly Books, 2002. 32p. IL K–3, Lexile: 350

The story of the heroic deeds of the legendary New York firefighter, Mose Humphreys.

Roth, Susan L. *It's Still a Dog's New York: A Book of Healing.* National Geographic Society, c2001. 32p. IL K–3

Pepper and Rover, two New York City dogs, feel miserable after the tragedy of September 11, 2001, but both dogs manage to recover and enjoy life again.

Senzai, N. H. *Shooting Kabul.* Simon & Schuster Books for Young Readers, c2010. 262p. IL 3–6, Lexile: 800

Escaping from Taliban-controlled Afghanistan in the summer of 2001, eleven-year-old Fadi and his family immigrate to the San Francisco Bay Area, where Fadi schemes to return to the Pakistani refugee camp where his little sister was accidentally left behind.

Spiegelman, Art. *In the Shadow of No Towers.* Pantheon Books, c2004. IL AD (Non-fiction)

On ten large-scale pages, Pulitzer Prize–winning cartoonist Art Spiegelman shares his experiences and thoughts on the day the World Trade Center collapsed and the aftermath of the tragedy.

Winter, Jeanette. *September Roses.* Farrar Straus Giroux, 2004. 33p. IL K–3

Two sisters find a good use for the roses they have grown when their plane from South Africa is delayed by a storm, causing them to miss a flower show in New York City.

Part 3

Books about Self

Tattoos and Body Modification

Alagna, Magdalena. *Everything You Need to Know about the Dangers of Cosmetic Surgery.* Rosen Publishing Group, 2002. 64p. IL YA, Lexile: 900 (Non-Fiction)
Provides information on the negative side effects of cosmetic surgery and discusses how they can be avoided.

Anderson, M. T. *Feed.* Candlewick Press, 2004, c2002. 299p. IL YA, Lexile: 770
In a future where most people have computer implants in their heads to control their environment, a boy meets an unusual girl who is in serious trouble.

Cefrey, Holly. *Cloning and Genetic Engineering.* Children's Press, c2002. 48p. IL YA, Lexile: 790 (Non-Fiction)
Introduces cloning and genetic engineering, exploring the technology and social issues involved and looking toward what the future might bring as it becomes possible to duplicate even human DNA.

Farmer, Nancy. *The House of the Scorpion.* Atheneum Books for Young Readers, c2002. 380p. IL 5–8, Lexile: 660
In a future where humans despise clones, Matt enjoys special status as the young clone of El Patron, the 142-year-old leader of a corrupt drug empire nestled between Mexico and the United States.

Halam, Ann. *Dr. Franklin's Island.* Dell Laurel-Leaf, 2003, c2002. 245p. IL YA, Lexile: 690
When their plane crashes over the Pacific Ocean, three science students are left stranded on a tropical island and then imprisoned by a doctor who is performing horrifying experiments on humans involving the transfer of animal genes.

Hughes, Monica. *The Keeper of the Isis Light.* Aladdin Paperbacks, c1980. 232p. IL 5–8, Lexile: 820
Sixteen-year-old Olwen, who lives alone on the planet Isis with her faithful robot, falls in love with an arrival from Earth and complications ensue.

Miller, Jean-Chris. *The Body Art Book: A Complete, Illustrated Guide to Tattoos, Piercings, and Other Body Modifications.* Berkley, 2004. 127p. IL AD (Non-Fiction)
Presents a history of body art; explains how to get safe and well-produced tattoos, piercings, scars, brands, and other body modifications; discusses procedures and aftercare; and provides an extensive national directory of body art studios.

Oates, Joyce Carol. *The Tattooed Girl: A Novel.* Harper Perennial, 2006, c2003. 307p. IL AD
An author famous for a novel about his Jewish grandparents' lives during the Holocaust is diagnosed with a debilitating nerve disease and hires a troubled, abused young woman as his assistant, unaware that she and her boyfriend are anti-Semitic.

Patterson, James. *Angel: A Maximum Ride Novel.* Little, Brown, 2011. 291p. IL YA, Lexile: 700
Heartbroken after her best friend and soul mate Fang leaves her flock, Maximum Ride begins to believe the evil scientists who are trying to convince her that she needs to save the world, and that Dylan, the newest member of her flock, is her perfect mate.

Tattoos and Body Modification

Polhemus, Ted. *Hot Bodies, Cool Styles: New Techniques in Self-Adornment.* Thames & Hudson, 2004. 176p. IL AD (Non-Fiction)
Photographs and text describe the latest trends in self-adornment, exploring how body adornment has become central to human nature, helping people express their beliefs, religion, hobbies, ethnicity, and more.

Shelley, Mary Wollstonecraft. *Frankenstein.* Oxford University Press, 2010. 276p. IL YA, Lexile: 940
Victor Frankenstein has discovered the secret of generating life from lifeless matter, and has created a monster being by using this terrible power.

Thompson, Kate. *Fourth World.* Bloomsbury, 2005. 330p. IL YA, Lexile: 880
Fifteen-year-old Christie and his older stepbrother, Danny, travel to the home and mysterious laboratory of the elder boy's scientist mother, where they learn a shocking truth about the nature of her experiments.

Westerfeld, Scott. *Uglies Series.* Simon Pulse, c2005– . IL YA
Tally is faced with a difficult choice when her new friend Shay decides to risk life on the outside rather than submit to the forced operation that turns sixteen-year-old girls into gorgeous beauties; she realizes that there is a whole new side to the pretty world that she doesn't like.

Bromance

Alexie, Sherman. *The Absolutely True Diary of a Part-time Indian*. Little, Brown, 2007. 229p. IL YA, Lexile: 600

Budding cartoonist Junior leaves his troubled school on the Spokane Indian Reservation to attend an all-white farm town school, where the only other Native American is the school mascot.

Almond, David. *Clay*. Delacorte Press, c2006. 247p. IL YA, Lexile: 490

The developing relationship between teenager Davie and a mysterious new boy in town morphs into something darker and more sinister when Davie learns firsthand of the boy's supernatural powers.

Almond, David. *Kit's Wilderness*. Delacorte Press, 2000. 229p. IL YA, Lexile: 470

Thirteen-year-old Kit goes to live with his grandfather in the decaying coal mining town of Stoneygate, England, and finds both the old man and the town haunted by ghosts of the past.

Boyne, John. *The Boy in the Striped Pajamas: A Fable*. David Fickling Books, 2006. 215p. IL YA, Lexile: 1080

Bored and lonely after his family moves from Berlin to a place called "Out-With" in 1942, Bruno, the son of a Nazi officer, befriends a boy in striped pajamas who lives behind a wire fence.

Bradbury, Jennifer. *Shift*. Atheneum Books for Young Readers, c2008. 245p. IL YA, Lexile: 770

When best friends Chris and Win go on a cross-country bicycle trek the summer after graduating and only one of the pair returns, the FBI wants to know what happened.

Goldman, Steven. *Two Parties, One Tux, and a Very Short Film about the Grapes of Wrath*. IL YA Bloomsbury, 2008. 307p. Lexile: 770

Mitch, a shy and awkward high school junior, negotiates the difficult social situations he encounters, both with girls and with his best friend David, after David reveals to him that he is gay.

Green, John. *An Abundance of Katherines*. Dutton Books, c2006. 227p. IL YA, Lexile: 890

Having been recently dumped for the nineteenth time by a girl named Katherine, recent high school graduate and former child prodigy Colin sets off on a road trip with his best friend to try to find some new direction in life while also trying to create a mathematical formula to explain his relationships.

Green, John. *Paper Towns*. Dutton Books, c2008. 305p. IL YA, Lexile: 850

One month before graduating from his Central Florida high school, Quentin "Q" Jacobsen basks in the predictable boredom of his life until the beautiful and exciting Margo Roth Spiegelman, Q's neighbor and classmate, takes him on a midnight adventure and then mysteriously disappears.

Hinton, S. E. *The Outsiders*. Viking Press, 1967. 188p. IL YA, Lexile: 750

The struggle of three brothers to stay together after their parent's death and their quest for identity among the conflicting values of their adolescent society.

Jenkins, A. M. *Repossessed*. HarperTeen, c2007. 218p. IL YA, Lexile: 700

A fallen angel, tired of being unappreciated while doing his pointless, demeaning job, leaves Hell, enters the body of a seventeen-year-old boy, and tries to experience the full range of human feelings before being caught and punished. Meanwhile, the boy's family and friends puzzle over his changed behavior.

Bromance

Kluger, Steve. *My Most Excellent Year: A Novel of Love, Mary Poppins, & Fenway Park.* Dial Books, c2008. 403p. IL YA, Lexile: 1030

Three teenagers in Boston narrate their experiences of a year of new friendships, first loves, and coming into their own.

Lyga, Barry. *Hero-Type.* Houghton Mifflin, 2008. 295p. IL YA, Lexile: 670

Feeling awkward and ugly is one of several reasons why sixteen-year-old Kevin is uncomfortable with the publicity about his act of accidental heroism. When a reporter photographs him apparently being unpatriotic, however, Kevin speaks out and encourages people to think about what the symbols of freedom really mean.

Pena, Matt de la. *Mexican Whiteboy.* Delacorte Press, c2008. 249p. IL YA, Lexile: 680

Danny, who is tall and skinny but has a talent for pitching a fastball, cannot seem to fit in at school in San Diego, where his combined Mexican and white heritage causes people to judge him before he even speaks.

Volponi, Paul. *Black and White.* Viking, 2005. 185p. IL YA, Lexile: 710

Two star high school basketball players—one black and one white—experience the justice system differently after committing a crime together and getting caught.

Voorhees, Coert. *The Brothers Torres.* Disney/Hyperion Books, c2008. 316p. IL YA, Lexile: 780

Sophomore Frankie finally finds the courage to ask his long-term friend, Julianne, to the homecoming dance, which ultimately leads to a face-off between a tough senior whose family owns most of their small, New Mexico town, and Frankie's soccer-star older brother and his gang-member friends.

Choices

Alexie, Sherman. *The Absolutely True Diary of a Part-time Indian*. Little, Brown, 2007. 229p. IL YA, Lexile: 600

> Budding cartoonist Junior leaves his troubled school on the Spokane Indian Reservation to attend an all-white farm town school, where the only other Native American is the school mascot.

Anderson, Laurie Halse. *Twisted*. IL YA Viking, 2007. 250p. Lexile: 680

> After finally getting noticed by someone other than school bullies and his ever-angry father, seventeen-year-old Tyler enjoys his tough new reputation and the attentions of a popular girl, but when life starts to go bad again, he must choose between transforming himself or giving in to his destructive thoughts.

Asher, Jay. *Thirteen Reasons Why: A Novel*. Razorbill, c2007. 288p. IL YA, Lexile: 550

> High school student Clay Jenkins receives a box in the mail containing seven cassette tapes recorded by his crush, Hannah Baker, who committed suicide. He spends a bewildering and heart-breaking night crisscrossing their town, listening to Hannah's voice recounting the events leading up to her death.

Blundell, Judy. *What I Saw and How I Lied*. Scholastic Press, 2008. 284p. IL YA, Lexile: 620

> In 1947, with her jovial stepfather Joe back from the war and family life returning to normal, teen-age Evie, smitten by the handsome young ex-GI who seems to have a secret hold on Joe, finds her-self caught in a complicated web of lies whose devastating outcome changes both her life and that of her family forever.

Bodeen, S. A. *The Compound*. Feiwel and Friends, 2008. 248p. IL YA, Lexile: 570

> Fifteen-year-old Eli, locked inside a radiation-proof compound built by his father to keep them safe following a nuclear attack, begins to question his future, as well as his father's grip on sanity as the family's situation steadily disintegrates over the course of six years.

Collins, Suzanne. *The Hunger Games*. Scholastic Press, 2008. 374p. IL YA, Lexile: 810

> Sixteen-year-old Katniss Everdeen accidentally becomes a contender in the annual Hunger Games, a gravely serious competition hosted by the Capitol, in which young boys and girls are pitted against each other in a televised fight to the death.

Connor, Leslie. *Waiting for Normal*. Katherine Tegen Books, c2008. 290p. IL 5–8, Lexile: 570

> Twelve-year-old Addie tries to cope with her mother's erratic behavior and being separated from her beloved stepfather and half-sisters when she and her mother go to live in a small trailer by the railroad tracks on the outskirts of Schenectady, New York.

Coy, John. *Crackback*. Scholastic Press, 2005. 201p. IL YA, Lexile: 490

> Miles barely remembers when football was fun after being sidelined by a new coach, constantly criticized by his father, and pressured by his best friend to take performance-enhancing drugs.

Deuker, Carl. *Painting the Black*. Avon, 1999, c1997. 248p. IL YA, Lexile: 670

> When star athlete Josh Daniels moves in across the street, Ryan Ward doesn't realize how much his life will change during his senior year at Seattle's Crown Hill High.

Choices

Deuker, Carl. *Runner.* Houghton Mifflin, 2005. 216p. IL YA, Lexile: 670
Living with his alcoholic father on a broken-down sailboat on Puget Sound has been hard on seventeen-year-old Chance Taylor, but when his love of running leads to a high-paying job, he quickly learns that the money is not worth the risk.

Ellis, Ann Dee. *This Is What I Did.* Little, Brown, 2009, c2007. 157p. IL YA, Lexile: 550
Bullied because of an incident in his past, eighth-grader Logan is unhappy at his new school and has difficulty relating to others—until he meets a quirky girl and a counselor who believe in him.

Fleischman, Paul. *Whirligig.* Square Fish, 2010, c1998. 133p. IL YA, Lexile: 760
While traveling to each corner of the country to build a whirligig in memory of the girl whose death he caused, sixteen-year-old Brian finds forgiveness and atonement.

Forman, Gayle. *If I Stay: A Novel.* Dutton Books, c2009. 201p. IL YA, Lexile: 830
While in a coma following an automobile accident that killed her parents and younger brother, seventeen-year-old Mia, a gifted cellist, weighs whether to live with her grief or join her family in death.

Koja, Kathe. *Headlong.* Farrar, Straus and Giroux, 2008. 195p. IL YA, Lexile: 920
High school sophomore Lily opens herself to new possibilities when, despite others' warnings, she becomes friends with "ghetto girl" Hazel, a new student at the private Vaughn School, which Lily, following in her elitist mother's footsteps, has attended since preschool.

Korman, Gordon. *The Juvie Three.* Hyperion, c2008. 249p. IL YA, Lexile: 730
Gecko, Arjay, and Terence—all in trouble with the law—must find a way to keep their halfway house open to stay out of juvenile detention.

Mikaelsen, Ben. *Touching Spirit Bear.* HarperCollins, c2001. 241p. IL 5–8, Lexile: 670
After his anger erupts into violence, fifteen year-old Cole, to avoid going to prison, agrees to participate in a sentencing alternative based on the Native American circle justice. He is sent to a remote Alaskan island, where an encounter with a huge Spirit Bear changes his life.

Monninger, Joseph. *Baby.* Front Street, c2007. 173p. IL YA, Lexile: 580
Fifteen-year-old Baby's last chance at foster care is with the Potters. While she likes the family and enjoys learning to race their sled dogs, she feels she should go back on the streets with her boyfriend if she cannot find the mother who has deserted her again.

Myers, Walter Dean. *Street Love.* Amistad/HarperTeen, 2007, c2006. 134p. IL YA, Lexile: NP
A story in free verse in which Damien, a seventeen-year-old from Harlem, takes a bold step to ensure that he and his new love, Junice, will not be separated.

Nelson, Blake. *Paranoid Park.* Speak, 2008, c2006. 180p. IL YA
A sixteen-year-old Portland, Oregon, skateboarder, whose parents are going through a difficult divorce, is engulfed by guilt and confusion when he accidentally kills a security guard at a train yard.

Choices

Perkins, Mitali. *Secret Keeper.* Delacorte Press, c2009. 225p. IL YA, Lexile: 800
In 1974, when her father leaves New Delhi, India, to seek a job in New York, Ashi, a tomboy at the advanced age of sixteen, feels thwarted in the home of her extended family in Calcutta where she, her mother, and sister must stay. When her father dies before he can send for them, the family must remain with their relatives and observe the old-fashioned traditions that Ashi hates.

Shusterman, Neal. *Unwind.* Simon & Schuster Books for Young Readers, c2007. 335p. IL YA, Lexile: 740
Three teens embark upon a cross-country journey to escape from a society that salvages body parts from children ages thirteen to eighteen.

Smith, Roland. *Peak.* Harcourt, c2007. 246p. IL YA, Lexile: 760
A fourteen-year-old boy attempts to be the youngest person to reach the top of Mount Everest.

Wallace, Rich. *One Good Punch.* A. Knopf, c2007. 114p. IL YA, Lexile: 790
Eighteen-year-old Michael Kerrigan, writer of obituaries for the *Scranton Observer* and captain of the track team, is ready for the most important season of his life—until the police find four joints in his school locker, and he is faced with a choice that could change everything.

Civic Ideals

Bauer, Joan. *Hope Was Here.* Speak, c2000. 186p. IL YA, Lexile: 710

When sixteen-year-old Hope and the aunt who has raised her move from Brooklyn to Mulhoney, Wisconsin, to work as waitress and cook in the Welcome Stairways diner, they become involved with the diner owner's political campaign to oust the town's corrupt mayor.

Bennett, Cherie. *A Heart Divided: A Play.* Dramatic Publishing, c2004. 75p. IL YA

When sixteen-year-old Kate, an aspiring playwright, moves from New Jersey to attend high school in the South, she becomes embroiled in a controversy about removing the school's Confederate flag symbol.

Carvell, Marlene. *Who Will Tell My Brother?* Hyperion Paperbacks for Children, 2004, c2002. 150p. IL 5–8, Lexile: NP

During his lonely crusade to remove offensive mascots from his high school, a Native American teenager learns more about his heritage, his ancestors, and his place in the world.

Crutcher, Chris. *The Sledding Hill.* HarperTempest, 2006, c2005. 230p. IL YA, Lexile: 1010

Billy, recently deceased, keeps an eye on his best friend, fourteen-year-old Eddie, and helps him stand up to a conservative minister and English teacher who is orchestrating a censorship challenge.

D'Adamo, Francesco. *Iqbal: A Novel.* Aladdin Paperbacks, 2005, c2003. 120p. IL 3–6, Lexile: 730

This fictionalized account tells the story of the Pakistani child who escaped from bondage in a carpet factory and went on to help liberate other children like him before being gunned down at the age of thirteen.

Fleischman, Paul. *Seedfolks.* HarperTrophy, 1999, c1997. 69p. IL 5–8, Lexile: 710

One by one, a number of people of varying ages and backgrounds transform a trash-filled, inner-city lot into a productive and beautiful garden; in doing so, the gardeners are themselves transformed.

Garden, Nancy. *The Year They Burned the Books.* Farrar Straus Giroux, 1999. 247p. IL YA, Lexile: 760

While trying to come to terms with her own lesbian feelings, Jamie, a high school senior and editor of the school newspaper, finds herself in the middle of a battle with a group of townspeople over the new health education curriculum.

Hartinger, Brent. *Geography Club.* HarperTempest, 2004, c2003. 226p. IL YA, Lexile: 700

A group of gay and lesbian teenagers finds mutual support when they form the "Geography Club" at their high school.

Hiaasen, Carl. *Hoot.* Alfred A. Knopf, c2002. 292p. IL 5–8, Lexile: 760

Roy, who is new to his small Florida community, becomes involved in another boy's attempt to save a colony of burrowing owls from a proposed construction site.

Hyde, Catherine Ryan. *Pay It Forward: A Novel.* Simon & Schuster, c1999. 311p. IL AD, Lexile: 630

A young boy who believes in the goodness of human nature sets out to change the world with his seemingly simple plan, but he soon learns that some people are not willing to help him.

Civic Ideals

Konigsburg, E. L. *The Outcasts of 19 Schuyler Place.* Atheneum Books for Young Readers, c2004. 296p. IL 5–8, Lexile: 840
>	After leaving an oppressive summer camp, twelve-year-old Margaret Rose Kane spearheads a campaign to preserve the three unique towers her grand uncles have been building in their back yard for more than forty years.

Mikaelsen, Ben. *Petey.* Disney/Hyperion Books, c1998. 280p. IL 5–8
>	In 1922, Petey, who has cerebral palsy, is misdiagnosed as an idiot and institutionalized; sixty years later, still in the institution, he befriends a boy and shares with him the joy of life.

Nye, Naomi Shihab. *Going Going.* Greenwillow Books, c2005. 232p. IL YA, Lexile: 820
>	Florrie, a sixteen-year-old living in San Antonio, Texas, leads her friends and a new boyfriend in a campaign that supports small businesses and protests the effects of chain stores.

Schmidt, Gary, D. *The Wednesday Wars.* Clarion Books, c2007. 264p. IL 5–8, Lexile: 990
>	During the 1967 school year, on Wednesday afternoons when all his classmates go to either Catechism or Hebrew school, seventh-grader Holling Hoodhood stays in Mrs. Baker's classroom. There, they read the plays of William Shakespeare and Holling learns valuable lessons about the world he lives in.

Sharenow, Robert. *My Mother the Cheerleader: A Novel.* Laura Geringer Books/HarperTeen, 2009, c2007. 288p. IL YA, Lexile: 820
>	Thirteen-year-old Louise uncovers secrets about her family and her neighborhood during the violent protests over school desegregation in 1960 New Orleans.

Spinelli, Jerry. *Maniac Magee: A Novel.* Little, Brown, c1990. 184p. IL 3–6, Lexile: 820
>	After his parents die, Jeffrey Lionel Magee's life becomes legendary, as he accomplishes athletic and other feats that awe his contemporaries.

Tashjian, Janet. *The Gospel According to Larry.* Dell Laurel-Leaf, 2003, c2001. 227p. IL YA, Lexile: 800
>	Seventeen-year-old Josh, a loner-philosopher who wants to make a difference in the world, tries to maintain his secret identity as the author of a website that is receiving national attention.

Thomas, Rob. *Doing Time: Notes from the Undergrad.* Simon & Schuster Books for Young Readers, c1997. 184p. IL YA, Lexile: 800
>	These ten stories describe the experiences of students at the fictional Robert E. Lee High School as they set out to fulfill the graduation requirement to perform two hundred hours of community service.

Winerip, Michael. *Adam Canfield of the Slash.* Candlewick Press, 2005. 326p. IL 3–6, Lexile: 830
>	While serving as co-editors of their school newspaper, middle schoolers Adam and Jennifer uncover fraud and corruption in their school and in the city's government.

Coming of Age: Non-fiction

Akbar, Said Hyder. *Come Back to Afghanistan: A California Teenager's Story.* 2005. 339p. IL YA
  Presents the author's first-hand account and observations of living in Afghanistan when his father is appointed President Hamid Karzai's chief spokesman.

Allison, Anthony. *Hear These Voices: Youth at the Edge of the Millennium.* Dutton Children's Books, 1999. 169p. IL YA, Lexile: 960
  Presents case studies of teenagers living with homelessness, prostitution, alcoholism, and neighborhood violence, along with interviews with staff members from organizations committed to helping teenagers in crisis.

Am I Blue?: Coming Out from the Silence. HarperTrophy, c1994. 273p. IL YA, Lexile: 760
  A collection of short stories about homosexuality by such authors as Bruce Coville, M. E. Kerr, William Sleator, and Jane Yolen.

Beah, Ishmael. *A Long Way Gone: Memoirs of a Boy Soldier.* Farrar Straus and Giroux, 2007. 229p. IL AD, Lexile: 920
  Ishmael Beah describes his experiences after he was driven from his home by war in Sierra Leone and picked up by the government army at the age of thirteen; he served as a soldier for three years before being removed from fighting by UNICEF and eventually moving to the United States.

Conway, Jill K. *The Road from Coorain.* Vintage Books, 1990. 238p IL AD
  Conway's memoir recalls her journey into adulthood from a 30,000-acre sheep ranch in Coorain, Australia, to America, where she became the first woman president of Smith College.

Guys Write for Guys Read. Viking, 2005. 272p. IL YA Lexile: 920
  A collection of short stories, drawings, poems, and memoirs from well-known writers of "guy" fiction, written by boys, for boys. Includes pieces by Daniel Pinkwater, Neil Gaiman, Will Hobbs, Stephen King, and Gary Paulsen, among others.

Houston, Jeanne Wakatsuki. *Farewell to Manzanar: A True Story of Japanese American Experience during and after the World War II Internment.* Houghton Mifflin, 2002, c1973. 188p. IL YA, Lexile: 1040
  Biography of Jeanne Wakatsuki Houston describing her experience of living at the Manzanar internment camp during World War II and explaining how it has influenced her life.

Levine, Stephanie Wellen. *Mystics, Mavericks, and Merrymakers: An Intimate Journey among Hasidic Girls.* New York University Press, c2003. 255p. IL AD
  The author draws from her experiences in the Lubavitch community of Crown Heights, Brooklyn, to examine the lives of Hasidic girls ages thirteen to twenty-three, discussing their hopes, thoughts, values, and feelings about religious life.

McCourt, Frank. *Angela's Ashes: A Memoir.* Scribner, c1996. 363p. IL YA, Lexile: 1110
  The author chronicles his impoverished childhood in Limerick, Ireland, in the 1930s and 1940s, describing his father's alcoholism and talent for storytelling; the challenges and tragedies his mother faced, including the loss of three children; and his early experiences in the Catholic church. The account balances painful memories with humor.

Coming of Age: Non-fiction

War Is—: Soldiers, Survivors, and Storytellers Talk about War. Candlewick Press, 2008. 200p. IL YA
A collection of essays, memoirs, letters, and fiction that present opposing viewpoints on the nature of war by such contributors as Mark Twain, Bob Dylan, and Ernie Pyle.

What Are You?: Voices of Mixed-Race Young People. Holt, 1999. 273p IL YA, Lexile: 900
Many young people of racially mixed backgrounds discuss their feelings about family relationships, prejudice, dating, personal identity, and other issues.

Cultural Development

Abelove, Joan. *Go and Come Back.* Puffin Books, 2000, 1998. 176p. IL YA, Lexile: 620
Alicia, a young tribeswoman living in a village in the Amazonian jungle of Peru, tells about the two American women anthropologists who arrive to study her people's way of life.

Bagdasarian, Adam. *Forgotten Fire.* Dell Laurel-Leaf, 2002, c2000. 272p. IL YA, Lexile: 1050
This story describes how Vahan Kenderian survived the Turkish massacre of the Armenians in 1915.

Chang, Pang-Mei Natasha. *Bound Feet & Western Dress.* Anchor Books, 1997, c1996. 215p IL AD (Non-fiction)
This story describes the experience of the author's great-aunt Chang Yu-i, a woman who challenged Chinese tradition by refusing to have her feet bound, marrying and divorcing preeminent poet Hsu Chih-mo, and running the Shanghai Women's Savings Bank during the 1930s.

Ellis, Deborah. *The Breadwinner.* House of Anansi, 2001, c2000. 170p. IL 5–8, Lexile: 630
Conscious of the strict limitations imposed by the Taliban rulers of Kabul, Afghanistan, on women's freedom and behavior, eleven-year-old Parvana disguises herself as a boy to earn money so that her family can survive after her father's arrest.

Hautzig, Esther Rudomin. *The Endless Steppe: Growing up in Siberia.* HarperTrophy, 1987, c1968. 243p. IL YA, Lexile: 940
The author recounts her five years of hardship and trials spent in Siberia, after she and her family were arrested in Poland by the Russians as political enemies during World War II.

Ho, Minfong. *The Clay Marble.* Farrar Straus Giroux, 1993, c1991. 163p. IL 5–8, Lexile: 860
In the late 1970s, twelve-year-old Dara enters a refugee camp in war-torn Cambodia and becomes separated from her family.

Jiang, Ji-li. *Red Scarf Girl: A Memoir of the Cultural Revolution.* Collins/HarperTeen, 2008, c1997. 285p. IL 5–8, Lexile: 780 (Non-fiction)
The author tells about the happy life she led in China up until she was twelve years old, when her family became a target of the Cultural Revolution; she discusses the choice she had to make between denouncing her father and breaking with her family, or refusing to speak against him and losing her future in the Communist Party.

Joseph, Lynn. *The Color of My Words.* Joanna Cotler Books, 2002, c2000. 138p. IL 3–6, Lexile: 840
When life gets difficult for Ana Rosa, a twelve-year-old would-be writer living in a small village in the Dominican Republic, she can depend on her older brother to make her feel better—until the life-changing events on her thirteenth birthday.

Namioka, Lensey. *April and the Dragon Lady.* Harcourt, c1994. 214p. IL YA, Lexile: 710
Feeling confined by the traditional Chinese family attitudes exhibited by her strong-willed, manipulative grandmother, sixteen-year-old April Chen fights for her independence.

Cultural Development

Namioka, Lensey. *Ties That Bind, Ties That Break: A Novel.* Dell Laurel-Leaf, 2000, c1999. 154p. IL YA, Lexile: 830

Ailin's life takes a different turn when she defies the traditions of upper-class Chinese society by refusing to have her feet bound.

Ryan, Pam Munoz. *Esperanza Rising.* Scholastic, 2001, c2000. 262p. IL 5–8, Lexile: 750

Esperanza and her mother are forced to leave their life of wealth and privilege in Mexico to work in the labor camps of Southern California, where they must adapt to the harsh circumstances facing Mexican farm workers on the eve of the Great Depression.

Soto, Gary. *Pacific Crossing.* Harcourt, 1992. 134p. IL 5–8, Lexile: 750

Fourteen-year-old Mexican American Lincoln Mendoza spends a summer with a host family in Japan, encountering new experiences and making new friends.

Staples, Suzanne Fisher. *Haveli.* Dell Laurel-Leaf, 2002, c1993. 320p. IL YA, Lexile: 1030

Having given in to the ways of her people in Pakistan and married the rich older man to whom she was pledged against her will, Shabanu is now the victim of his family's blood feud and the malice of his other wives.

Staples, Suzanne Fisher. *Under the Persimmon Tree.* Farrar, Straus and Giroux, 2005. 275p. IL YA, Lexile: 1010

A young Afghan girl, Najmah, befriends an American woman, Nusrat, in Peshawar, Pakistan, after Najmah flees her native Afghanistan during the 2001 war; together they begin a long journey to locate their missing loved ones after the war ends.

Ung, Loung. *First They Killed My Father: A Daughter of Cambodia Remembers.* Harper Perennial, 2006, c2000. 238p. IL YA, Lexile: 920 (Non-fiction)

Loung Ung, one of seven children of a high-ranking government official in Phnom Penh, tells of her experiences after her family was forced to flee from Pol Pot's Khmer Rouge army, discusses her training as a child soldier in a work camp for orphans, and describes how her surviving siblings were eventually reunited.

Voices from the Fields: Children of Migrant Farmworkers Tell Their Stories. Little, Brown, c1993. 96p. IL 5–8, Lexile: 850 (Non-fiction)

Photographs, poems, and interviews with children reveal the hardships and hopes of Mexican American migrant farm workers and their families.

Yumoto, Kazumi. *The Friends.* Farrar, Straus and Giroux, 2005, c1992. 169p. IL 5–8, Lexile: 710

Curious about death, three sixth-grade boys decide to spy on an old man while waiting for him to die, but they end up becoming his friends.

Differing Belief Systems

Abdel-Fattah, Randa. *Does My Head Look Big in This?* Orchard Books, 2007, c2005. 360p. IL YA, Lexile: 850
> Year eleven at an exclusive prep school in the suburbs of Melbourne, Australia, would be tough enough, but it is further complicated for Amal when she decides to wear the hijab, the Muslim head scarf, full-time as a badge of her faith—without losing either her identity or her sense of style.

Abdel-Fattah, Randa. *Ten Things I Hate about Me.* Orchard Books, 2009, c2006. 297p. IL YA, Lexile: 720
> Lebanese Australian Jamilah, known in school as Jamie, hides her heritage from her classmates and tries to pass by dyeing her hair blonde and wearing blue-tinted contact lenses, until her conflicted feelings become too much for her to bear.

Cooper, Susan. *Greenwitch.* Margaret K. McElderry Books, 1997, c1974. 147p. IL 5–8, Lexile: 830
> Jane's invitation to witness the making of the Greenwitch begins a series of sinister events in which she and her two brothers help the Old Ones recover the grail stolen by the Dark.

Desai Hidier, Tanuja. *Born Confused.* Scholastic Press, 2002. 413p. IL 5–8, Lexile: 890
> As Dimple Lala turns seventeen, she realizes that life is about to become more complex as her best friend starts pulling away and her parents try to find a suitable boyfriend for Dimple, despite the fact that she is not interested in romance.

Dhami, Narinder. *Bindi Babes.* Yearling, 2005, c2003. 184p. IL 3–6, Lexile: 660
> Three Indian British sisters team up to marry off their traditional, nosy aunt and get her out of the house.

Ellis, Deborah. *The Breadwinner Trilogy.* Groundwood Books/House of Anansi Press, 2009. 439p. IL 3–6
> This collection of three novels looks at conditions in Afghanistan under the control of the Taliban through the experiences of Parvana and Shauzia, two young girls who must disguise themselves as boys so that they can move about freely and help their families and the people of their country.

Farmer, Nancy. *A Girl Named Disaster.* Orchard Books, c1996. 309p. IL 5–8, Lexile: 730
> While journeying to Zimbabwe, eleven-year-old Nhamo struggles to escape drowning and starvation, and in so doing comes close to the luminous world of the African spirits.

Gilmore, Rachna. *Lights for Gita.* Tilbury House, 1994. 24p. IL K–3, Lexile: 600
> Just moved from India, Gita looks forward to her favorite holiday, Divali, but things are so different in her new home that she wonders if she will ever adjust to her new life.

Green, John. *An Abundance of Katherines.* Dutton Books, c2006. 227p. IL YA, Lexile: 890
> Having been recently dumped for the nineteenth time by a girl named Katherine, recent high school graduate and former child prodigy Colin sets off on a road trip with his best friend to try to find some new direction in life while also trying to create a mathematical formula to explain his relationships.

Differing Belief Systems

Hayes, Rosemary. *Mixing It.* Frances Lincoln Children's Books, 2007. 185p. IL YA
The lives of two young people in England—Fatimah, a devout Muslim, and Steve, a white, nonreligious boy—are changed when a press photo taken of them after a terrorist attack makes it appear that they are a couple and that Fatimah saved him and let her Muslim friend die.

Khan, Rukhsana. *Many Windows: Six Kids, Five Faiths, One Community.* Napoleon, c2008. 84p. IL 3–6, RL 3.4
A collection of stories told by six children from different religious faiths, including a brief introduction to the five faiths.

Khan, Rukhsana. *Wanting Mor.* Groundwood Books/House of Anansi Press, 2009. 190p. IL YA
Jameela must depend on memories of her beloved mother Mor to sustain her when her stepmother abandons her in a busy market in Afghanistan and she ends up in an orphanage run by the same army that killed many of her family members.

Koja, Kathe. *Buddha Boy.* Farrar, Straus and Giroux, 2003. 117p. IL 5–8, Lexile: 1090
Justin spends time with Jinsen, the unusual and artistic new student whom the school bullies torment and call Buddha Boy. Eventually, he makes choices that affect Jinsen, himself, and the entire school.

Konigsburg, E. L. *About the B'nai Bagels.* Aladdin Paperbacks, 2008, c1969. 181p. IL 3–6
Mark Setzer tells about his troubles in general, and in particular about his misfortunes on the Little League team managed by his mother and coached by his brother.

Krishnaswami, Uma. *Naming Maya.* Farrar Straus Giroux, 2004. 178p. IL 5–8, Lexile: 770
When Maya accompanies her mother to India to sell her grandfather's house, she uncovers family history relating to her parents' divorce and learns more about herself and her relationship with her mother.

Kuijer, Guus. *The Book of Everything: A Novel.* A. A. Levine Books, 2006, c2004. 101p. IL 3–6, Lexile: 530
Nine-year-old Thomas receives encouragement from many sources, including candid talks with Jesus, to help him tolerate the strict family life dictated by his deeply religious father.

Laird, Elizabeth. *Crusade.* Macmillan Children's, 2008, c2007. 389p. IL 5–8
Young Adam eagerly joins the Crusade to reclaim the Holy Land in the service of a local knight, while a doctor's apprentice in the camp of Sultan Saladin hopes to avoid engaging in conflict with the invading crusaders.

Laird, Elizabeth. *A Little Piece of Ground.* Haymarket Books, 2006. 216p. IL YA, Lexile: 830
During the Israeli occupation of Ramallah in the West Bank of Palestine, twelve-year-old Karim and his friends create a secret place for themselves where they can momentarily forget the horrors of war.

Lanagan, Margo. *Tender Morsels.* Alfred A. Knopf, c2008. 436p. IL YA, Lexile: 950
A young woman who has endured unspeakable cruelties is magically granted a safe haven apart from the real world and allowed to raise her two daughters in this alternate reality—at least until the barrier between her imagined world and the real one begins to break down.

Differing Belief Systems

Littman, Sarah. *Confessions of a Closet Catholic.* Puffin Books, 2006, c2005. 193p. IL 5–8, Lexile: 930

To become more like her best friend, eleven-year-old Justine decides to give up Judaism to become Catholic. After her beloved, religious grandmother dies, however, she realizes that she needs to seek her own way of being Jewish.

Medearis, Angela Shelf. *Seven Spools of Thread: A Kwanzaa Story.* Albert Whitman & Co., 2000. 40p. IL 3–6, Lexile: 430

When they are given the seemingly impossible task of turning thread into gold, the seven Ashanti brothers put aside their differences, learn to get along, and embody the principles of Kwanzaa. The book includes information on Kwanzaa, West African cloth weaving, and instructions for making a belt.

Meminger, Neesha. *Shine, Coconut Moon.* Margaret K. McElderry Books, 2010, c2009. 247p. IL YA, Lexile: 740

In the days and weeks following the terrorist attacks on September 11, 2001, Samar, who is of Punjabi heritage but has been raised with no knowledge of her past by her single mother, strives to learn about her family's history and get in touch with the grandparents her mother shuns.

Muth, Jon J. *Zen Shorts.* Scholastic Press, 2005. 40p. IL K–3, Lexile: 540

When Stillwater the bear moves into the neighborhood, the stories he tells to three siblings teach them to look at the world in new ways.

Nye, Naomi Shihab. *Habibi.* Simon Pulse, 1999, c1997. 271p. IL YA, Lexile: 850

Fourteen-year-old Liyana Abboud, her younger brother, and her parents move from St. Louis to a new home between Jerusalem and the Palestinian village where her father was born, where they face many changes and must deal with the tensions between Jews and Palestinians.

Ostow, Micol. *So Punk Rock (And Other Ways to Disappoint Your Mother): A Novel.* Flux, c2009. 246p. IL YA, Lexile: 760

Four suburban New Jersey students from the Leo R. Gittleman Jewish Day School form a rock band that becomes inexplicably popular, leading to feelings of exhilaration, friction, confrontation, and soul-searching among the group's members.

Perkins, Mitali. *Monsoon Summer.* Random House Children's Books, 2006, c2004. 257p. IL YA, Lexile: 750

Secretly in love with her best friend and business partner Steve, fifteen-year-old Jazz must spend the summer away from him when her family goes to India during that country's rainy season to help set up a clinic.

Perry, M. LaVora. *Taneesha Never Disparaging.* Wisdom Publications, c2008. 202p. IL 3–6

Taneesha must learn to make peace with herself and with others after she is teased because of her choice of friends and her Buddhist religion.

Pratchett, Terry. *The Bromeliad Trilogy.* HarperCollins, c1998. 502p. IL 5–8

After generations of existing in the human-sized world, a group of 4-inch-high gnomes discover their true nature and origin, with the help of a black square called the Thing.

Differing Belief Systems

Provoost, Anne. *In the Shadow of the Ark.* A. A. Levine, 2004. 368p. IL YA
>Re Jana, a young healer and masseuse, believes that Noach's son Ham, the married object of her affection, will save her and her family if his father's terrifying predictions about a great flood sent from God come true.

Reinhardt, Dana. *A Brief Chapter in My Impossible Life.* Wendy Lamb Books, c2007. 228p. IL YA, Lexile: 910
>Sixteen-year-old atheist Simone Turner-Bloom's life changes in unexpected ways when her parents convince her to make contact with her biological mother, an agnostic from a Jewish family who is losing her battle with cancer.

Rosofsky, Iris. *Miriam.* Harper & Row, c1988. 188p. IL YA
>A young Jewish girl must learn to reconcile her family's—and her own—orthodoxy with her need for independence and her desire to fit in with the rapidly changing outside world.

Stork, Francisco X. *Marcelo in the Real World.* Arthur A. Levine Books, 2009. 312p. IL YA, Lexile: 700
>Marcelo Sandoval, a seventeen-year-old boy on the high-functioning end of the autistic spectrum, faces new challenges, including romance and injustice, when he goes to work for his father in the mailroom of a corporate law firm.

Wilson, Leslie. *Saving Rafael.* Andersen Press, 2009. 410p. IL YA
>Fifteen-year-old Jenny, who has been friends with her Jewish neighbor Rafael since they were young children, goes to great lengths to save him when the Nazis take over Berlin.

Healthy Eating

Barron, Rex. *Showdown at the Food Pyramid.* G. P. Putnam's Sons, c2004. 27p. IL K–3
When snack foods take over the food pyramid and make it collapse, members of the various food groups have to work together using the Great Food Guide to rebuild it.

Carle, Megan. *Teens Cook: How to Cook What You Want to Eat.* Ten Speed Press, c2004. 146p. IL YA (Non-fiction)
This collection of seventy-five quick and easy recipes for teens includes information on ingredients, along with general cooking tips and shortcuts.

Cobb, Vicki. *Junk Food.* Millbrook Press, c2006. 48p. IL 3–6 (Non-fiction)
An introduction to the science behind the making and packaging of junk food, including popcorn, chocolate, corn chips, and other snacks.

D'Amico, Joan. *The Healthy Body Cookbook: Over 50 Fun Activities and Delicious Recipes for Kids.* Wiley, c1999. 184p. IL 3–6 (Non-fiction)
Discusses the various parts of the human body and what to eat to keep them healthy. Includes recipes that contain nutrients important for the heart, muscles, teeth, skin, nerves, and other parts of the body.

Hollyer, Beatrice. *Let's Eat!: What Children Eat around the World.* Henry Holt and Co., 2004, c2003. 41p. IL 3–6 (Non-fiction)
This children's book on the traditional foods around the world, including those eaten in Thailand, South Africa, Mexico, France, and India, provides a number of recipes.

Kalman, Bobbie. *Super Snacks.* Crabtree Publishing, 2003. 32p. IL 3–6 (Non-fiction)
Explores why and how to have delicious and healthy snacks through nutrition facts and easy recipes for nourishing foods.

Katzen, Mollie. *Honest Pretzels: And 64 Other Amazing Recipes for Cooks Ages 8 & Up.* Tricycle Press, c1999. 177p. IL 3–6 (Non-fiction)
This cookbook provides step-by-step instructions for sixty-five easy-to-prepare recipes, arranged in such categories as breakfast specials, soups, desserts, and snacks.

Kohl, MaryAnn F. *Snacktivities!: 50 Edible Activities for Parents and Children.* Robins Lane Press, c2001. 102p. IL AD (Non-fiction)
This cookbook provides step-by-step instructions for fifty creative snack activities—such as "Trees in Snow" and "Erupting Lava Apple"—designed for young children and parents to do together.

Krizmanic, Judy. *The Teen's Vegetarian Cookbook.* Puffin, 1999. 186p. IL YA (Non-fiction)
Recipes for all types of vegetarian dishes are accompanied by information and advice on vegetarian diet and quotes from teenage vegetarians.

Lagasse, Emeril. *Emeril's There's a Chef in My Soup!: Recipes for the Kid in Everyone.* HarperCollins, c2002. 242p. IL 3–6 (Non-fiction)
World-famous chef Emeril Lagasse shares some of his favorite recipes that children can make, as well as tips for the whole family on how to have fun and be safe in the kitchen.

Healthy Eating

McFarland, Lyn Rossiter. *Mouse Went out to Get a Snack.* Farrar Straus Giroux, 2005. IL K–3, Lexile: 9032p.

> A hungry mouse finds a tableful of delectable morsels in quantities that illustrate counting from one to ten.

Miller, Edward. *The Monster Health Book: A Guide to Eating Healthy, Being Active, & Feeling Great for Monsters & Kids!* Holiday House, c2006. 40p. IL 3–6, Lexile: 880 (Non-fiction)

> This illustrated guide to health and nutrition provides information on the food pyramid, the five food groups, and tips and suggestions related to eating right, getting enough sleep, and finding ways to exercise.

Ray, Rachael. *Cooking Rocks!: Rachael Ray 30-Minute Meals for Kids.* Lake Isle Press, Distributed by National Book Network (NBN), c2004. 224p. IL 3–6 (Non-fiction)

> This cookbook for kids contains recipes they can make for themselves, including kitchen basics, beverages, snacks, and subs.

Shanley, Ellen L. *Fueling the Teen Machine.* Bull Publishing, c2011. 279p. IL YA (Non-fiction)

> Provides teenagers and their parents with healthy eating and nutrition guidelines, discussing how teens can eat healthy meals and snacks, how parents can identify eating disorders, and how both can evaluate diet plans.

Individuality

Anderson, Laurie Halse. *Speak.* Speak, 2006, c1999. 197p. IL YA, Lexile: 690
A traumatic event near the end of the summer has a devastating effect on Melinda's freshman year in high school. The most recent edition includes bonus material and a new foreword by the author.

Castellucci, Cecil. *Beige.* Candlewick Press, 2007. 307p. IL YA, Lexile: 540
Katy, a quiet French Canadian teenager, reluctantly leaves Montreal to spend time with her estranged father, an aging Los Angeles punk rock legend.

Cushman, Karen. *The Loud Silence of Francine Green.* Clarion Books, c2006. 225p. IL 5–8, Lexile: 750
In 1949, thirteen-year-old Francine goes to Catholic school in Los Angeles. There, she becomes best friends with a girl who questions authority and is frequently punished by the nuns, causing Francine to question her own values.

Donnelly, Jennifer. *A Northern Light.* Harcourt, c2003. 389p. IL YA, Lexile: 700
In 1906, sixteen-year-old Mattie is determined to attend college and be a writer despite the wishes of her father and boyfriend. When she takes a job at a hotel, the death of a guest renews her determination to live her own life.

Harrar, George. *Not as Crazy as I Seem.* Houghton Mifflin, 2003. 202p. IL 5–8
When fifteen-year-old Devon enters a new prestigious prep school at the midyear point, he is plagued by compulsions such as the need to sort things into groups of four.

Koja, Kathe. *The Blue Mirror.* Farrar, Straus and Giroux, 2004. 119p. IL YA, Lexile: 1130
Seventeen-year-old loner Maggy Klass, who frequently seeks refuge from her alcoholic mother's apartment by sitting and drawing in a local cafe, becomes involved in a destructive relationship with a charismatic homeless youth named Cole.

Mackler, Carolyn. *The Earth, My Butt, and Other Big Round Things.* Candlewick Press, 2003. 246p. IL YA, Lexile: 790
Feeling as if she does not fit in with the other members of her family, who are all thin, brilliant, and good-looking, fifteen-year-old Virginia tries to deal with her self-image, her first physical relationship, and her disillusionment with some of the people closest to her.

Murdock, Catherine Gilbert. *Dairy Queen.* Houghton Mifflin, 2006. 274p. IL YA, Lexile: 990
After spending her summer running the family farm and training the quarterback for her school's rival football team, sixteen-year-old D. J. decides to go out for the sport herself, not anticipating the reactions of those around her.

Peters, Julie Anne. *Define "Normal": A Novel.* Little, Brown, 2003, c2000. 196p. IL 5–8, Lexile: 350
When she agrees to meet with Jasmine as a peer counselor at their middle school, Antonia never dreams that this girl with the black lipstick and pierced eyebrow will end up helping her deal with the serious problems she faces at home and become a good friend.

Individuality

Spinelli, Jerry. *Love, Stargirl.* Knopf, c2007. 274p. IL 5–8, Lexile: 610
   Still moping months after being dumped by her Arizona boyfriend Leo, fifteen-year-old Stargirl, a home-schooled free spirit, writes "the world's longest letter" to Leo, describing her new life in Pennsylvania.

Strasser, Todd. *The Wave.* Dell Laurel-Leaf, c1981. 138p. IL YA, Lexile: 770
   In this account of an actual classroom experiment in establishing a fascist society, Laurie tries to persuade Mr. Ross to call off the experiment.

Tolan, Stephanie S. *Surviving the Applewhites.* HarperTrophy, 2004, c2002. 216p. IL 5–8, Lexile: 820
   Jake, a budding juvenile delinquent, is sent for home schooling to the arty and eccentric Applewhite family's Creative Academy, where he discovers talents and interests he never knew he had.

Inner Conflict

Achebe, Chinua. *Things Fall Apart.* Knopf, 1992. 181p. IL AD, Lexile: 890
Set in an Ibo village in Nigeria, the novel recreates pre-Christian tribal life and shows how the coming of the white man led to the breaking up of the old ways.

Almond, David. *Kit's Wilderness.* Delacorte Press, 2000. 229p. IL YA, Lexile: 470
When thirteen-year-old Kit goes to live with his grandfather in the decaying coal mining town of Stoneygate, England, he finds both the old man and the town haunted by ghosts of the past.

Anderson, Laurie Halse. *Catalyst.* Viking, 2002. 232p. IL YA, Lexile: 580
Eighteen-year-old Kate, who sometimes chafes at being a preacher's daughter, finds herself losing control in her senior year as she faces difficult neighbors, the possibility that she may not be accepted by the college of her choice, and an unexpected death.

Anderson, Laurie Halse. *Speak.* Farrar Straus Giroux, 1999. 197p. IL YA, Lexile: 690
A traumatic event near the end of the summer has a devastating effect on Melinda's freshman year in high school.

Bechard, Margaret. *Hanging on to Max.* Simon Pulse, 2003. 204p. IL YA, Lexile: 420
When his girlfriend decides to give their baby away, seventeen-year-old Sam is determined to keep the child and raise him alone.

Black, Holly. *Tithe: A Modern Faerie Tale.* Simon & Schuster, c2002. 310p. IL YA, Lexile: 750
Sixteen-year-old Kaye, who has been visited by faeries since childhood, discovers that she is a magical faerie creature with a special destiny.

Butler, Octavia E. *Kindred.* Beacon Press, 1988, c1979. 264p. IL YA
A young African American woman is mysteriously sent back in time, which inspires her irresistible curiosity about her family's past.

Card, Orson Scott. *Ender's Game.* TOR, 2006, c1991. 226p. IL AD, Lexile: 780
Young Ender Wiggin may prove to be the military genius Earth needs to fight a desperate battle against a deadly alien race that will determine the future of the human race.

Cooney, Caroline B. *Code Orange.* Laurel-Leaf Books, 2007, c2005. 200p. IL YA, Lexile: 850
While conducting research for a school paper on smallpox, Mitty finds an envelope containing 100-year-old smallpox scabs and fears that he has infected himself and all of New York City.

Crutcher, Chris. *Ironman.* HarperTempest, 2004, c1995. 279p. IL YA, Lexile: 980
While training for a triathlon, seventeen-year-old Bo attends an anger management group at school, which leads him to examine his relationship with his father.

Crutcher, Chris. *Staying Fat for Sarah Byrnes.* Mac Lib Re, 1993. 303p. IL YA
The daily class discussions about the nature of man, the existence of God, abortion, organized religion, suicide, and other contemporary issues serve as a backdrop for a high school senior's attempt to answer a friend's dramatic cry for help.

Inner Conflict

Dessen, Sarah. *Dreamland.* Speak, 2004, c2000. 250p. IL YA, Lexile: 920

After her older sister runs away, sixteen-year-old Caitlin decides that she needs to make a major change in her own life and begins an abusive relationship with a boy who is mysterious, brilliant, and dangerous.

Dessen, Sarah. *Someone like You.* Viking, 1998. 281p. IL YA, Lexile: 820

Halley's junior year of high school includes the death of her best friend Scarlett's boyfriend, the discovery that Scarlett is pregnant, and Halley's own first serious relationship.

Draper, Sharon M. *The Battle of Jericho.* Atheneum Books for Young Readers, c2003. 297p. IL YA, Lexile: 700

A high school junior and his cousin suffer the ramifications of joining what seems to be a "reputable" school club.

Draper, Sharon M. *Double Dutch.* Atheneum Books for Young Readers, c2002. 183p. IL 5–8, Lexile: 760

Three eighth-grade friends, preparing for the International Double Dutch Championship jump rope competition in their home town of Cincinnati, Ohio, must cope with Randy's missing father, Delia's inability to read, and Yo Yo's encounter with the class bullies.

Efaw, Amy. *Battle Dress.* Speak, c2000. 290p. IL YA, Lexile: 650

As a newly arrived freshman at West Point, seventeen-year-old Andi finds herself gaining both confidence and self-esteem as she struggles to get through the grueling six weeks of new cadet training known as the Beast.

Flake, Sharon. *Bang!* Jump at the Sun/Hyperion Paperbacks for Children, 2007, c2005. 298p. IL YA, Lexile: 590

Two years after the shooting death of thirteen-year-old Mann's little brother, Mann's father—who believes his son died because he made him too "soft"—takes Mann and his friend camping and abandons them in an attempt to make them tough.

Flake, Sharon. *Begging for Change.* Jump at the Sun/Hyperion Paperbacks for Children, 2007, c2004. 248p. IL 5–8, Lexile: 1060

Raspberry steals money from a friend to get her mother out of a tough situation, and must now face the consequences of her action and her fear of going down the same path as her drug-addicted father.

Flinn, Alex. *Breathing Underwater.* HarperTempest, 2002, c2001. 263p. IL YA, Lexile: 510

Sent to counseling for hitting his girlfriend, Caitlin, and ordered to keep a journal, sixteen-year-old Nick recounts his relationship with Caitlin, examines his controlling behavior and anger, and describes living with his abusive father.

Gaines, Ernest J. *In My Father's House.* Vintage Books, 1992. 214p. IL YA

A minister and civil rights leader in a small, rural African American community is suddenly confronted with events from his past that threaten to destroy the life he has built.

Inner Conflict

Goobie, Beth. *The Lottery.* Orca Book Publishers, 2002. 264p. IL YA
Fifteen-year-old Sally Hanson, chosen as the latest victim of the Shadow Council, the secret club that controls school life, finds the strength to stand up to the bullies with the help of her brother and other special friends.

Green, John. *Looking for Alaska: A Novel.* Dutton, c2005. 221p. IL YA, Lexile: 930
For sixteen-year-old Miles, his first year at Culver Creek Preparatory School in Alabama includes good friends and great pranks, but is defined by the search for answers about life and death after a fatal car crash.

Hosseini, Khaled. *The Kite Runner.* Riverhead Books, 2003. 324p. IL AD, Lexile: 840
Amir, haunted by his betrayal of Hassan, the son of his father's servant and a childhood friend, returns to Kabul as an adult after he learns Hassan has been killed, in an attempt to redeem himself by rescuing Hassan's son from a life of slavery to a Taliban official.

Johnson, Angela. *The First Part Last.* Simon & Schuster Books for Young Readers, c2003. 131p. IL YA, Lexile: 790
Bobby's carefree teenage life changes forever when he becomes a father and must care for his adored baby daughter.

Johnson, Maureen. *The Key to the Golden Firebird: A Novel.* HarperTrophy, 2005, c2004. 297p. IL YA, Lexile: 740
As three teenaged sisters struggle to cope with their father's sudden death, they find they must reexamine friendships, lifelong dreams, and their relationships with one another and their father.

Kelly, Nora. *My Sister's Keeper.* Poisoned Pen Press, 2000, c1992. 221p. IL AD
Gillian Adams investigates attacks on the Feminist Union at the university where she teaches.

Klause, Annette Curtis. *Blood and Chocolate.* Delacorte Press, 2007, c1997. 264p. IL YA, Lexile: 720
Having fallen for a human boy, a beautiful teenage werewolf must battle both her packmates and the fear of the townspeople to decide where she belongs and with whom.

Koertge, Ronald. *Stoner & Spaz.* Candlewick Press, 2004, c2002. 169p. IL YA, Lexile: 490
A troubled youth with cerebral palsy struggles toward self-acceptance with the help of a drug-addicted young woman.

Koja, Kathe. *Talk.* Square Fish, 2008, c2005. 139p. IL YA, Lexile: 940
Kit auditions for a controversial school play and discovers his talent for acting; however, both he and his costar face crises in their views of themselves and in their close relationships.

L'Engle, Madeleine. *Many Waters.* Farrar, Straus, Giroux, 1986. 310p. IL 5–8, Lexile: 700
The fifteen-year-old Murry twins, Sandy and Dennys, are accidentally sent back to a strange Biblical time period, in which mythical beasts roam the desert and a man named Noah is building a boat in preparation for a great flood.

Mackler, Carolyn. *Vegan Virgin Valentine.* Candlewick Press, 2004. 228p. IL YA, Lexile: 840
Mara's niece, who is only one year younger, moves in, creating conflict between the two teenagers because of their opposing personalities.

Inner Conflict

McKinley, Robin. *Beauty: A Retelling of the Story of Beauty & the Beast.* HarperCollins, c1978. 247p. IL YA, Lexile: 970
 Kind Beauty grows to love the Beast, at whose castle she is compelled to stay. Through her love, she releases him from the spell that had turned him from a handsome prince into an ugly beast.

McKinley, Robin. *The Hero and the Crown.* Greenwillow, c1985. 246p. IL 5–8, Lexile: 1120
 Aerin, with the guidance of the wizard Luthe and the help of the blue sword, wins the birthright due her as the daughter of the Damarian king and a witchwoman of the mysterious, demon-haunted North.

Na, An. *A Step from Heaven.* Speak, 2002, c2001. 160p. IL 5–8, Lexile: 670
 A young Korean girl and her family find it difficult to learn English and adjust to life in America.

Naylor, Phyllis Reynolds. *The Fear Place.* Aladdin Paperbacks, 1996. 118p. IL 5–8, Lexile: 810
 When he and his older brother Gordon are left camping alone in the Rocky Mountains, twelve-year-old Doug faces his fear of heights and his feelings about Gordon—with the help of a cougar.

Nixon, Joan Lowery. *Caught in the Act.* Bantam Doubleday Dell Books for Young Readers, 1996, c1988. 150p. IL 5–8, Lexile: 800
 Eleven-year-old Michael Patrick Kelly, a native of New York City, is sent to a foster home—a Missouri farm populated by a sadistic owner, a bullying son, and a number of secrets, one of which may be murder.

Nolan, Han. *Born Blue.* Harcourt, 2003, c2001. 284p. IL YA, Lexile: 920
 Janie was four years old when she nearly drowned due to her mother's neglect. Through an unhappy foster home experience, and years of feeling that she is unwanted, she keeps alive her dream of someday being a famous singer.

Nolan, Han. *Dancing on the Edge.* Harcourt, 2007, c1997. 244p. IL YA, Lexile: 850
 A young girl from a dysfunctional family creates for herself an alternative world, which nearly results in her death but ultimately leads her to reality.

Oates, Joyce Carol. *Freaky Green Eyes.* HarperTempest, c2003. 341p. IL YA, Lexile: 810
 Fourteen-year-old Frankie relates the events of the year leading up to her mother's mysterious disappearance and her own struggle to discover and accept the truth about her parents' relationship.

Plum-Ucci, Carol. *The Body of Christopher Creed.* Harcourt, Inc., c2000. 259 p. IL YA, Lexile: 720
 Sixteen-year-old Torey Adams embarks on a path of terror and pain when he sets out to investigate the disappearance of Christopher Creed, a weird kid who vanished from his small hometown of Steepleton, leaving behind only a cryptic e-mail message as a clue to what happened to him.

Soto, Gary. *Buried Onions.* Harcourt Brace, c1997. 149p. IL YA, Lexile: 850
 When nineteen-year-old Eddie drops out of college, he struggles to find a place for himself as a Mexican American living in a violence-infested neighborhood of Fresno, California.

Spinner, Stephanie. *Quicksilver.* Laurel-Leaf, 2006, c2005. 229p. IL YA, Lexile: 770
 The stories of the Trojan War, Persephone and Demeter, Perseus, Odysseus, and others are recounted from the perspective of Zeus's son and messenger, Hermes.

Inner Conflict

Staples, Suzanne Fisher. *Shabanu: Daughter of the Wind.* Dell Laurel-Leaf, 2003, c1989. 240p. IL YA, Lexile: 970

Eleven-year old Shabanu, the daughter of a nomad in the Cholistan Desert of present-day Pakistan, is pledged in marriage to an older man whose money will bring prestige to the family. She must either accept the decision, as is the custom, or risk the consequences of defying her father's wishes.

Trueman, Terry. *Stuck in Neutral.* HarperTempest, 2001, c2000. 114p. IL 5–8, Lexile: 820

Fourteen-year-old Shawn McDaniel, who suffers from severe cerebral palsy and relies on others to help him, relates his perceptions of his life, his family, and his condition, especially as he believes his father is planning to kill him.

Westerfeld, Scott. *Uglies.* Simon Pulse, c2005. 406p. IL YA

Tally is faced with a difficult choice when her new friend Shay decides to risk life on the outside rather than submit to the forced operation that turns sixteen-year-old girls into gorgeous beauties; she soon realizes that there is a whole new side to the pretty world that she doesn't like.

Lack of Self-Confidence

Halpern, Julie. *Into the Wild Nerd Yonder.* Feiwel and Friends, 2009. 247p. IL YA
When high school sophomore Jessie's long-term best friend transforms herself into a punk and goes after Jessie's would-be boyfriend, Jessie decides to visit "the wild nerd yonder" and seek true friends among classmates who play Dungeons and Dragons.

Headley, Justina Chen. *North of Beautiful.* Little, Brown, 2009. 373p. IL YA, Lexile: 850
Terra, a sensitive, artistic high school senior born with a facial port-wine stain, struggles with issues of inner and outer beauty with the help of her Goth classmate Jacob.

Jones, Patrick. *Things Change.* Walker, 2006, c2004. 216p. IL YA, Lexile: 710
Sixteen-year-old Johanna, one of the best students in her class, develops a passionate attachment for troubled seventeen-year-old Paul and finds her plans for the future changing in unexpected ways.

Mackler, Carolyn. *The Earth, My Butt, and Other Big Round Things.* Candlewick Press, 2003. 246p. IL YA, Lexile: 790
Feeling as if she does not fit in with the other members of her family, who are all thin, brilliant, and good-looking, fifteen-year-old Virginia tries to deal with her self-image, her first physical relationship, and her disillusionment with some of the people closest to her.

Olson, Gretchen. *Call Me Hope: A Novel.* Little, Brown and Company Books for Young Readers, 2008, c2007. 272p. IL 3–6, Lexile: 780
In Oregon, eleven-year-old Hope tries to cope with her mother's verbal abuse by devising survival strategies for herself based on a history unit about the Holocaust. Meanwhile, she works toward buying a pair of purple hiking boots by helping at a second-hand shop.

Supplee, Suzanne. *Artichoke's Heart.* Dutton Books, c2008. 276p IL YA, Lexile: 780
When she is almost sixteen years old, Rosemary decides she is sick of being overweight, mocked at school and at Heavenly Hair (her mother's beauty salon), and feeling out of control. As she slowly loses weight, she realizes that she is able to cope with her mother's cancer, having a boyfriend for the first time, and discovering that other people's lives are not as perfect as they seem from the outside.

Telgemeier, Raina. *Smile.* Graphix, 2010. 213p. IL 3–6
The author relates, in graphic form, her experiences after she injured her two front teeth and had to have surgeries and wear embarrassing braces and headgear, all while also dealing with the trials and tribulations of middle school.

Westerfeld, Scott. *Uglies.* Simon Pulse, 2005. 406p. IL YA
Tally is faced with a difficult choice when her new friend Shay decides to risk life on the outside rather than submit to the forced operation that turns sixteen-year-old girls into gorgeous beauties; she soon realizes that there is a whole new side to the pretty world that she doesn't like.

Wiseman, Rosalind. *Boys, Girls, and Other Hazardous Materials.* Putnam's, c2010. 282p. IL YA, Lexile: 660
Transferring to a new high school, freshman Charlotte "Charlie" Healey faces tough choices as she tries to shed her "mean girl" image.

Materialism

Anderson, M. T. *Feed.* Candlewick Press, 2004, c2002, 299p. IL YA, Lexile: 770
In a future where most people have computer implants in their heads to control their environment, a boy meets an unusual girl who is in serious trouble.

Koja, Kathe. *Buddha Boy.* Farrar, Straus and Giroux, 2003. 117p. IL 5–8, Lexile: 1090
Justin spends time with Jinsen, the unusual and artistic new student whom the school bullies torment and call Buddha Boy; eventually, he makes choices that affect Jinsen, himself, and the entire school.

Menzel, Peter. *Material World: A Global Family Portrait.* Sierra Club Books, 1995. 255p. IL YA (Non-fiction)
A photo-journey through the homes and lives of 30 families, revealing culture and economic levels around the world.

Nye, Naomi Shihab. *Going Going.* Greenwillow Books, c2005. 232p. IL YA, Lexile: 820
Florrie, a sixteen-year-old living in San Antonio, Texas, leads her friends and a new boyfriend in a campaign that supports small businesses and protests the effects of chain stores.

Tashjian, Janet. *The Gospel According to Larry.* Dell Laurel-Leaf, 2003, c2001. 227p. IL YA, Lexile: 800
Seventeen-year-old Josh, a loner-philosopher who wants to make a difference in the world, tries to maintain his secret identity as the author of a website that is receiving national attention.

Tashjian, Janet. *Vote for Larry.* Holt, c2004. 224p. IL YA, Lexile: 810
Not yet eighteen years old, Josh—also known as Larry—Larry, comes out of hiding and returns to public life, this time to run for president as an advocate for issues of concern to youth and to encourage voter turnout.

Westerfeld, Scott. *So Yesterday: A Novel.* Razorbill, c2004. 225p. IL YA, Lexile: 770
Hunter Braque, a New York City teenager who is paid by corporations to spot what is "cool," combines his analytical skills with girlfriend Jen's creative talents to find a missing person and thwart a conspiracy directed at the heart of consumer culture.

Part 4

Setting

Crossing the Border

Andreas, Peter. *Border Games: Policing the U.S.–Mexico Divide.* Cornell University Press, c2009. 180p. IL AD (Non-fiction)

    The author explores the ways in which border control has changed in recent years, and explains why the sharp escalation in law enforcement at the United States–Mexico border provides a political mechanism for coping with the unintended consequences of past policy choices.

Arellano, Gustavo. *Ask a Mexican!* Scribner, 2008, c2007. 256p. IL AD (Non-fiction)

    Columnist Gustavo Arellano shares some of the often irreverent and sometimes serious questions that he has answered in his syndicated column, which explores various aspects of Mexican culture.

Beatty, Patricia. *Lupita Manana.* HarperTrophy, 2000, c1981. 190p. IL 5–8, Lexile: 760

    To help her poverty-stricken family, 13-year-old Lupita enters California as an illegal alien and starts to work while constantly on the watch for "la migra."

Buss, Fran Leeper. *Journey of the Sparrows.* Puffin, 2002. 155p. IL 5–8, Lexile: 760

    Maria and her brother and sister, Salvadoran refugees, are smuggled into the United States in crates and try to eke out a living in Chicago with the help of a sympathetic family.

Canales, Viola. *The Tequila Worm.* Wendy Lamb, c2005. 199p. IL YA, Lexile: 830

    Sofia finds that her experiences as a scholarship student at an Episcopal boarding school in Austin only strengthen her ties to her family in the barrio community of McAllen, Texas.

Cisneros, Sandra. *Caramelo, or, Puro Cuento: A Novel.* Alfred A. Knopf, 2002. 443p. IL AD

    Celaya "Lala" Reyes, traveling from Chicago to Mexico City each summer, draws together stories of her Mexican American family of shawl-makers, including her papa and Awful Grandmother.

Cisneros, Sandra. *The House on Mango Street.* A. A. Knopf, 1998., 134p. IL YA, Lexile: 870

    A young girl living in a Hispanic neighborhood in Chicago ponders the advantages and disadvantages of her environment and evaluates her relationships with family and friends.

Farmer, Nancy. *The House of the Scorpion.* Atheneum Books for Young Readers, c2002. 380p. IL 5–8, Lexile: 660

    In a future where humans despise clones, Matt enjoys special status as the young clone of El Patron, the 142-year-old leader of a corrupt drug empire nestled between Mexico and the United States.

Fehrenbach, T. R. *Lone Star: A History of Texas and the Texans.* Da Capo Press, 2000. 767p. IL YA

    The author traces the history of Texas from prehistory through the twentieth century, discussing the people, politics, and events that have shaped the Lone Star State.

Fullerton, Alma. *Libertad.* Fitzhenry & Whiteside, c2008. 215p. IL 5–8

    After their mother dies, Libertad and his younger brother Julio leave their home near the Guatemala City dump and perform as street musicians along the Rio Grande River while hoping to cross the border into the United States and locate their father.

Garcia, Alma M. *The Mexican Americans.* Greenwood Press, 2002. 220p. IL YA (Non-fiction)

    An overview of the history and experiences of Mexican Americans, covering the history of Mexico–U.S. relations and Mexican immigration, Mexican and Mexican American culture, and such topics as changing gender relations, political identity, and naturalization policies.

Crossing the Border

Grande, Reyna. *Across a Hundred Mountains: A Novel.* Washington Square Press, 2007, c2006. 266p. IL AD
> Juana, abandoned when her mother is jailed, heads for the United States in search of her father, who left years earlier to find work. Along the way, she meets a young prostitute who plays a major role in the course of the rest of her life.

Gutierrez, David G. *Between Two Worlds: Mexican Immigrants in the United States.* Rowman, 1996. 271p. IL AD (Non-fiction)
> This collection of eleven essays deals with both the historical and contemporary aspects of Mexican emigration to the United States.

Jimenez, Francisco. *Breaking Through.* Houghton Mifflin, c2001. 195p. IL 5–8, Lexile: 750
> Having come from Mexico to California ten years ago, fourteen-year-old Francisco is still working in the fields but fighting to improve his life and complete his education.

Jimenez, Francisco. *The Circuit: Stories from the Life of a Migrant Child.* Houghton Mifflin, 1999, c1997. 116p. IL 5–8, Lexile: 880
> This exploration focuses on a migrant family's experiences moving through labor camps and facing poverty and impermanence, and discusses how they endure through faith, hope, and back-breaking work.

Lachtman, Ofelia Dumas. *The Girl from Playa Blanca.* Pinata Books, 1995. 259p. IL YA
> When Elena and her little brother, Carlos, leave their Mexican seaside village to search for their immigrant father in Los Angeles, they encounter intrigue, crime, mystery, friendship, and love.

Martinez, Ruben. *Crossing Over: A Mexican Family on the Migrant Trail.* Picador USA, 2002, c2001. 330p. IL AD (Non-fiction)
> This account chronicles the experiences of one Mexican family who attempted to cross the U.S.–Mexico border.

McCarthy, Cormac. *All the Pretty Horses.* Knopf, c1992. 301p IL AD, Lexile: 940
> John Grady Cole is too young to be given charge of the family ranch and is cut off from the only life he has ever imagined wanting.

Mikaelsen, Ben. *Red Midnight.* HarperTrophy/Rayo, 2003, c2002. 212p. IL 5–8, Lexile: 690
> After soldiers kill his family, twelve-year-old Santiago and his four-year-old sister flee Guatemala in a kayak and try to reach the United States.

Mikaelsen, Ben. *Sparrow Hawk Red.* Hyperion Books for Children, c1993. 185p. IL 5–8, Lexile: 620
> Thirteen-year-old Ricky, the Mexican American son of a former Drug Enforcement Agency employee, tries to avenge his mother's murder by crossing over into Mexico to steal a high-tech radar plane from drug smugglers.

Nazario, Sonia. *Enrique's Journey.* Random House Trade Paperbacks, 2006. 299p. IL AD, Lexile: 830 (Non-fiction)
> The issues of family and illegal immigration are addressed through the story of a young boy's dangerous journey from Honduras to the United States in search of his mother, who left him and his sibling behind to make a better life for her family.

Crossing the Border

Quinones, Sam. *Antonio's Gun and Delfino's Dream: True Tales of Mexican Migration.* University of New Mexico Press, 2007. 318p. IL AD (Non-fiction)
This collection of true stories recounts the experiences of Mexican immigrants struggling to cope with life in the United States, examining how the experiences of immigrants in various regions differ.

Resau, Laura. *Red Glass.* Delacorte Press, c2007. 275p. IL 5–8, Lexile: 800
Sixteen-year-old Sophie has been frail and delicate since her premature birth. She discovers her true strength during a journey through Mexico, where the six-year-old orphan her family hopes to adopt was born, and to Guatemala, where her would-be boyfriend hopes to find his mother and plans to settle.

Rodriguez, Gregory. *Mongrels, Bastards, Orphans, and Vagabonds: Mexican Immigration and the Future of Race in America.* Vintage Books, 2008, c2007. 317p. IL AD (Non-fiction)
This non-fiction account traces the history of Mexican immigration into the United States, and examines the long-term cultural and political influences that Mexican Americans have on the nation.

Rodriguez, Luis J. *Always Running: La Vida Loca, Gang Days in L.A.* Simon & Schuster, 2005. 262p. IL AD, Lexile: 830 (Non-fiction)
The author recounts his childhood while growing up in poverty in Los Angeles, his encounters with racism in school and on the streets, and his struggle to overcome prejudice, drugs, and violence.

Ryan, Pam Munoz. *Becoming Naomi Leon.* Scholastic, 2004. 246p. IL 5–8, Lexile: 830
When Naomi's absent mother resurfaces to claim her, Naomi runs away to Mexico with her great-grandmother and younger brother in search of her father.

Ryan, Pam Munoz. *Esperanza Rising.* Scholastic, 2000. 262p. IL 5–8, Lexile: 750
Esperanza and her mother are forced to leave their life of wealth and privilege in Mexico and work in the labor camps of Southern California, where they must adapt to the harsh circumstances facing Mexican farm workers on the eve of the Great Depression.

Saldana, Rene. *The Jumping Tree: A Novel.* Dell Laurel-Leaf, 2002, c2001. 181p. IL 5–8, Lexile: 770
Rey, a Mexican American living with his close-knit family in a Texas town near the Mexican border, describes his transition from boy to young man.

Soto, Gary. *Living up the Street: Narrative Recollections.* Bantam Doubleday Dell Books for Young Readers, 1992, c1985. 167p. IL YA, Lexile: 1140 (Non-fiction)
The author describes his experiences growing up as a Mexican American in Fresno, California.

Taylor, Theodore. *The Maldonado Miracle.* Harcourt, 2003. 167p. IL 5–8, Lexile: 710
A twelve-year-old Mexican crosses the border illegally to join his father in California.

Urrea, Luis Alberto. *Across the Wire: Life and Hard Times on the Mexican Border.* Anchor Books, 1993. 190p. IL YA (Non-fiction)
This study considers what life is like for those refugees living on the Mexican side of the U.S. border.

Crossing the Border

Urrea, Luis Alberto. *Into the Beautiful North: A Novel.* Little, Brown, 2009. 342p. IL AD
Nineteen-year-old Nayeli becomes very aware of the lack of men in Tres Camarones after watching the movie *The Magnificent Seven* at a local theater, and comes up with a plan to travel to the United States—specifically, Illinois—and recruit a group of men to return with her to Mexico to protect and repopulate her remote village.

Villareal, Ray. *Alamo Wars.* Pinata Books, c2008. 187p. IL 5–8, Lexile: 650
When a Texas school puts on an original play about the Alamo, the students and teachers confront modern conflicts about history, identity, and the meaning of courage.

Genocide

Bagdasarian, Adam. *Forgotten Fire.* Dell Laurel-Leaf, 2002, c2000. 272p. IL YA, Lexile: 1050
This story describes how Vahan Kenderian survived the Turkish massacre of the Armenians in 1915.

Balakian, Peter. *The Burning Tigris: The Armenian Genocide and America's Response.* Perennial, 2004, c2003. 483p. IL AD (Non-fiction)
This study focuses on the Armenian genocide, which began in the 1890s when Sultan Abdul Hamid II ordered the massacre of Armenians, and occurred a second time in 1915 at the hands of the Ottoman Turks. It discusses the American response to the crisis and its implications for genocides in the twenty-first century.

Deng, Benson. *They Poured Fire on Us from the Sky: The True Story of Three Lost Boys from Sudan.* Public Affairs, c2005. IL AD (Non-fiction)
The author presents the stories of three young men, who, as children in the late 1980s, were forced from their homes by war in the Sudan and traveled, along with thousands of other boys, nearly one thousand miles in search of refuge, surviving hunger, illness, and human and animal predators.

Filipovic, Zlata. *Zlata's Diary: A Child's Life in Sarajevo.* Penguin Books, 2006, c1994. 197p. IL 5–8 (Non-fiction)
This diary was written by a thirteen-year-old girl living in Sarajevo; it was begun just before her eleventh birthday, when there was still peace in her homeland.

Frank, Anne. *The Diary of a Young Girl.* Bantam Books, 1993, c1952. 283p. IL YA, Lexile: 1080 (Non-fiction)
A thirteen-year-old Dutch Jewish girl records her impressions of the two years she and seven others spent hiding from the Nazis before they were discovered and taken to concentration camps. The most recent edition includes entries previously omitted from earlier versions.

Ilibagiza, Immaculee. *Left to Tell: Discovering God amidst the Rwandan Holocaust.* Hay House, c2006. 215p. IL AD (Non-fiction)
Immaculee Ilibagiza, who endured the murder of her family as a result of genocide in Rwanda in 1994, describes how she was able to later forgive those who had killed them.

Jansen, Hanna. *Over a Thousand Hills I Walk with You.* Carolrhoda, 2006. 342p. IL YA, Lexile: 790
Jeanne, the only member of her family not murdered in the Rwandan genocide, struggles to start a new life without her family, while coping with the violent memories that haunt her.

Jungersen, Christian. *The Exception: A Novel.* Nan A. Talese/Doubleday, c2006. 502p. IL AD
Four women working for a nonprofit organization in Copenhagen believe they are being stalked by Mirko Zigic, a Serbian war criminal about whom they are gathering information. When they begin receiving death threats, their relationship is tested by suspicion and fear.

Lowry, Lois. *Number the Stars.* Houghton Mifflin, c1989. 137p. IL 5–8
In 1943, during the German occupation of Denmark, ten-year-old Annemarie learns how to be brave and courageous when she helps shelter her Jewish friend from the Nazis.

Genocide

Mikaelsen, Ben. *Red Midnight.* HarperTrophy/Rayo, 2003, c2002. 212p. IL 5–8, Lexile: 690
　　After soldiers kill his family, twelve-year-old Santiago and his four-year-old sister flee Guatemala in a kayak and try to reach the United States.

Rusesabagina, Paul. *An Ordinary Man: An Autobiography.* Penguin Books, 2007, c2006. 207p. IL AD, Lexile: 1060 (Non-fiction)
　　Paul Rusesabagina recounts the story of his life, describing what it was like to grow up on a small farm in Rwanda, how he became the first Rwandan general manager of a Belgian-owned hotel, and how he helped his fellow countrymen during the 1994 Rwandan genocide.

Spinelli, Jerry. *Milkweed: A Novel.* Laurel-Leaf, 2005, c2003. 208p. IL YA, Lexile: 510
　　This story follows a young Jewish orphan in the Warsaw ghetto during World War II, as he slowly understands the horrible reality that surrounds him and attempts to steal goods to help others survive.

Stassen, Jean-Philippe. *Deogratias: A Tale of Rwanda.* First Second, 2006. 79p. IL YA (Non-fiction)
　　This graphic novel describes the Tutsi genocide in Rwanda in 1994 through the eyes of a boy named Deogratias, a Hutu, who is in love with Benigne, a Tutsi.

Ung, Loung. *First They Killed My Father: A Daughter of Cambodia Remembers.* Harper Perennial, 2006, c2000. 238p. IL YA, Lexile: 920 (Non-fiction)
　　Loung Ung, one of seven children of a high-ranking government official in Phnom Penh, tells of her experiences after her family was forced to flee from Pol Pot's Khmer Rouge army, including her training as a child soldier in a work camp for orphans, and how her surviving siblings were eventually reunited.

Ung, Loung. *Lucky Child: A Daughter of Cambodia Reunites with the Sister She Left Behind.* Harper Perennial, 2006, c2005. 268p. IL AD (Non-fiction)
　　Loung Ung recounts her struggles to adapt to life in America after arriving in 1980 as a ten-year-old Cambodian refugee.

Zusak, Markus. *The Book Thief.* Knopf, c2006. 552p. IL YA, Lexile: 730
　　Trying to make sense of the horrors of World War II, Death relates the story of Liesel—a young German girl whose book-stealing and story-telling talents help sustain her family and the Jewish man they are hiding, as well as their neighbors.

Global Transformation

Cohen, Marina. *Changing Cultural Landscapes: How Are People and Their Communities Affected by Migration and Settlement?* Crabtree Pub., c2010. 48p. IL 5–8, Lexile: 1200 (Non-fiction)
    Explores how migration and settlement influence culture, and provides historical examples.

Growing up Ethnic in America: Contemporary Fiction about Learning to Be American. Penguin Books, 1999. 347p. IL YA, Lexile: 910
    Contains thirty-five short fiction stories in which the authors explore issues of race and ethnicity in America.

Hale, Shannon. *River Secrets.* Bloomsbury, 2008, c2006. 290p. IL YA, Lexile: 860
    Young Razo travels from Bayern to Tira at war's end as part of a diplomatic corps, but mysterious events in the Tiran capital fuel simmering suspicions and anger, and Razo must find out who is responsible before it is too late and he becomes trapped in an enemy land.

Homelessness

Carey, Janet Lee. *The Double Life of Zoe Flynn.* Atheneum Books for Young Readers, c2004. 233p. IL 3–6, Lexile: 770
> When Zoe's family has to live in their van for months after moving from California to Oregon so her father can find work, Zoe tries to keep her sixth-grade classmates from discovering that she is homeless.

Carlson, Natalie Savage. *The Family under the Bridge.* HarperCollins, c1986, c1958. 99p. IL 3–6, Lexile: 680
> An old tramp, adopted by three fatherless children when their mother hides them under a bridge on the Seine, finds a home for the mother and children and a job for himself.

Carmi, Giora. *A Circle of Friends.* Star Bright Books, c2003. 32p. IL K–3
> When a boy anonymously shares his snack with a homeless man, he begins a cycle of good will.

Connor, Leslie. *Waiting for Normal.* Katherine Tegen Books, c2008. 290p. IL 5–8, Lexile: 570
> Twelve-year-old Addie tries to cope with her mother's erratic behavior and being separated from her beloved stepfather and half-sisters when she and her mother go to live in a small trailer by the railroad tracks on the outskirts of Schenectady, New York.

Curtis, Christopher Paul. *Bud, Not Buddy.* Delacorte Press, c1999. 245p. IL 5–8, Lexile: 950
> Ten-year-old Bud, a motherless boy living in Flint, Michigan, during the Great Depression, escapes a bad foster home and sets out in search of the man whom he believes to be his father—the renowned bandleader, H. E. Calloway of Grand Rapids.

Draper, Sharon M. *Double Dutch.* Atheneum Books for Young Readers, c2002. 183p. IL 5–8, Lexile: 760
> Three eighth-grade friends, preparing for the International Double Dutch Championship jump rope competition in their home town of Cincinnati, Ohio, cope with Randy's missing father, Delia's inability to read, and Yo Yo's encounter with the class bullies.

Farmer, Nancy. *A Girl Named Disaster.* Orchard Books, c1996. 309p. IL 5–8. Lexile: 730
> While journeying to Zimbabwe, eleven-year-old Nhamo struggles to escape drowning and starvation and in so doing comes close to the luminous world of the African spirits.

Flake, Sharon. *Begging for Change.* Jump at the Sun/Hyperion Paperbacks for Children, 2007, c2004. 248p. IL 5–8, Lexile: 1060
> When Raspberry steals money from a friend to get her mother out of a tough situation, she now face the consequences of her action and her fear of going down the same path as her drug-addicted father.

Flake, Sharon. *Money Hungry.* Jump at the Sun/Hyperion Paperbacks for Children, 2007, c2001. 188p. IL 5–8, Lexile: 650
> All thirteen-year-old Raspberry can think about is making money so that she and her mother never have to worry about living on the streets again.

Gates, Doris. *Blue Willow.* Puffin Books, 1976, c1940. 172p. IL 3–6, Lexile: 920
> A little girl, who wants most of all to have a real home and to go to a regular school, hopes that the valley where her family has stopped, which so resembles the pattern on her treasured blue willow plate, will be their permanent home.

Homelessness

Giff, Patricia Reilly. *Nory Ryan's Song.* Dell Yearling, 2003, c2000. 148p. IL 5–8, Lexile: 600
When a terrible blight attacks Ireland's potato crop in 1845, twelve-year-old Nory Ryan's courage and ingenuity help her family and neighbors survive.

Hesse, Karen. *Brooklyn Bridge.* Square Fish, c2011. 229p. IL 5–8, Lexile: 680
Fourteen-year-old Joseph Michtom's life takes a dramatic turn when, in 1903 Brooklyn, his parents turn their apartment into a factory for making teddy bears. Meanwhile, Joseph wonders whether he will ever see the glitter of Coney Island.

Holman, Felice. *Slake's Limbo.* Aladdin Paperbacks, 1986, c1974. 117p. IL YA, Lexile: 960
Thirteen-year-old Aremis Slake, hounded by his fears and misfortunes, flees into New York City's subway tunnels, never again—he believes—to emerge.

Leal, Ann Haywood. *Also Known as Harper.* Henry Holt, 2009. 246p. IL 5–8, Lexile: 800
Writing poetry helps fifth-grader Harper Lee Morgan cope with her father's abscnce, her family's eviction, and her need to skip school to care for her brother while their mother works. Things look even brighter when she befriends a mute girl and a kindly disabled woman.

Myers, Walter Dean. *Darnell Rock Reporting.* Dell, 1996, c1994. 135p. IL 5–8, Lexile: 710
Thirteen-year-old Darnell's twin sister and the other members of the Corner Crew have doubts about his work on the school newspaper, but the article he writes about a homeless man changes his attitude about school.

O'Connor, Barbara. *How to Steal a Dog: A Novel.* Farrar, Straus and Giroux, 2007. 170p, IL 3–6, Lexile: 700
Living in the family car in a small North Carolina town after her father leaves his wife and children virtually penniless, Georgina is desperate to improve her family's situation. Unwilling to accept her overworked mother's calls for patience, she persuades her younger brother to help her in an elaborate scheme to get money by stealing a dog and then claiming the reward that the owners are bound to offer.

Paterson, Katherine. *The Same Stuff as Stars.* Clarion Books, c2002. 242p. IL 5–8, Lexile: 670
When Angel's self-absorbed mother leaves her and her younger brother with their poor great-grandmother, the eleven-year-old girl worries not only about her mother, her brother, her imprisoned father, and the frail old woman, but also about a mysterious man who begins sharing with her the wonder of the stars.

Quick, Matthew. *Sorta like a Rock Star: A Novel.* Little, Brown, 2010. 355p. IL YA, Lexile: 1030
Amber Appleton, who lives in a school bus with her mother, refuses to give in to despair and continues visiting the elderly at a nursing home, teaching English to Korean women, and caring for a Vietnam veteran and his dog. A fatal tragedy, however, may prove to be one burden too many for the seventeen-year-old girl.

Rapp, Adam. *33 Snowfish.* Candlewick Press, 2003. 179p. IL YA, Lexile: 1050
A homeless boy, running from the police with a fifteen-year-old, drug-addicted prostitute; her boyfriend, who just killed his own parents; and a baby, gets the chance to make a better life for himself.

Homelessness

Ryan, Pam Munoz. *Esperanza Rising.* Scholastic, 2000. 262p. IL 5–8, Lexile: 750
Esperanza and her mother are forced to leave their life of wealth and privilege in Mexico to go work in the labor camps of Southern California, where they must adapt to the harsh circumstances facing Mexican farm workers on the eve of the Great Depression.

Spinelli, Jerry. *Maniac Magee: A Novel.* Little, Brown, c1990. 184p. IL 3–6. Lexile: 820
After his parents die, Jeffrey Lionel Magee's life becomes legendary, as he accomplishes athletic and other feats that awe his contemporaries.

Strasser, Todd. *Can't Get There from Here.* Simon & Schuster Books for Young Readers, c2004. 198p. IL YA, Lexile: 620
Tired of being hungry, cold, and dirty from living on the streets of New York City with a tribe of other homeless teenagers who are dying, one by one, a girl named Maybe ponders her future and longs for someone to care about her.

Van Draanen, Wendelin. *Runaway.* Knopf, c2006. 250p. IL 5–8, Lexile: 740
After running away from her fifth foster home, Holly, a twelve-year-old orphan, travels across the country, keeping a journal of her experiences and struggle to survive.

Voigt, Cynthia. *Homecoming.* Atheneum Books for Young Readers, c1981. 312p. IL 5–8, Lexile: 630
Abandoned by their mother, four children begin a search for a home and an identity.

Parallel Worlds

Barker, Clive. *Abarat.* Joanna Cotler Books, 2004, c2002. 431p. IL YA, Lexile: 760
Candy Quackenbush of Chickentown, Minnesota, journeys to the Abarat, an archipelago filled with strange wonders, where it is revealed to her that she has been there before, and that it is her responsibility to save the mysterious place from threatening evil forces.

Chabon, Michael. *Summerland.* Disney/Hyperion Books, 2011, c2002. 500p. IL 5–8
The ferishers—little creatures who ensure perfect weather for Summerland—recruit Ethan Feld—one of history's worst baseball players—to help them in their struggle to save Summerland, and ultimately the world, from giants, goblins, and other legendary, terrible creatures.

Collins, Suzanne. *Gregor the Overlander.* Scholastic, c2003. 311p. IL 3–6, Lexile: 630
When eleven-year-old Gregor and his two-year-old sister are pulled into a strange underground world, they trigger an epic battle involving humans, bats, rats, cockroaches, and spiders while on a quest foretold by an ancient prophecy.

Gaiman, Neil. *Coraline.* HarperCollins, c2002. 162p. IL 5–8, Lexile: 740
Looking for excitement, Coraline ventures through a mysterious door into a world that is similar to, yet disturbingly different from her own, and where she must challenge a gruesome entity to save herself, her parents, and the souls of three others.

Key, Alexander. *The Forgotten Door.* Scholastic, c1965. 140p. IL 3–6, Lexile: 720
After falling through a forgotten door and ending up on the strange planet Earth, Jon is befriended by a family and soon realizes his presence has put their lives in danger. He must find the secret passage again quickly, or he may never get home.

L'Engle, Madeleine. *A Wrinkle in Time*. Farrar, Straus and Giroux, 1999, c1962. 203p. IL 5–8, Lexile: 740
Three extraterrestrial beings take Meg and her friends to another world.

Nix, Garth. *Mister Monday.* Scholastic, c2003. 361p. IL 3–6, Lexile: 800
Arthur Penhaligon, who is destined to die at a young age, is saved by a key shaped like the minute hand of a clock. His survival invokes the wrath of the mysterious Mister Monday, who will stop at nothing to get the key back, and Arthur is forced into a desperate quest to unravel the secrets of the key and discover his true fate.

Yolen, Jane. *The Devil's Arithmetic.* Puffin Books, 1990, c1988. 170p. IL 5–8, Lexile: 730
Hannah resents the traditions of her Jewish heritage until time travel places her in the middle of a small Jewish village in Nazi-occupied Poland.

Series

Hoffman, Mary. *Stravaganza.* Bloomsbury, 2008– . IL YA
Seventeen-year-old Matt, painfully dyslexic and insecure, discovers that he can travel between worlds after being transported to Talia, where he joins Luciano and other Stravaganti in trying to prevent the di Chimici family's breakthrough into our world.

Parallel Worlds

MacHale, D. J. *Pendragon*. Aladdin Paperbacks, 2002–2004. IL 5–8
   Fourteen-year-old Bobby Pendragon is apprenticed to his Uncle Press, a Traveler responsible for solving interdimensional conflict. Bobby soon finds he must travel from one territory to another to stop an evil enemy named Saint Dane.

Pullman, Philip. *His Dark Materials*. Knopf, 2002– . IL 5–8
   This trilogy of fantasy novels by a British writer, Philip Pullman, follows the coming of age of two children, Lyra Belacqua and Will Parry, as they wander through a series of parallel universes.

Supernatural/Paranormal ("Beyond Twilight")

List by: Donna Zecha, Hopkinton Middle/High School, New Hampshire

Books for Older Teens

Bick, Ilsa J. *Draw the Dark*. Carolrhoda Lab, c2010. 338p. IL YA, Lexile: 790
Seventeen-year-old Christian Cage lives with his uncle in Winter, Wisconsin, where his nightmares, visions, and strange paintings draw him into a mystery involving German prisoners of war, a mysterious corpse, and Winter's last surviving Jew.

Billingsley, Franny. *Chime*. Dial Books, c2011. 361p. IL YA.
In the early twentieth century in Swampsea, seventeen-year-old Briony, who can see the spirits that haunt the marshes around their town, feels responsible for her twin sister's horrible injury—until a young man enters their lives and exposes secrets that even Briony does not know about.

Bray, Libba. *A Great and Terrible Beauty*. Delacorte Press, c2003. 403p. IL YA, Lexile: 760
After the suspicious death of her mother in 1895, sixteen-year-old Gemma returns to England, after many years in India, to attend a finishing school. There, she becomes aware of her magical powers and ability to see into the spirit world.
Sequels: *Rebel Angels; The Sweet Far Thing*

Clare, Cassandra. *City of Bones*. M. K. McElderry Books, c2007. 485p. IL YA, Lexile: 740
Suddenly able to see demons and the Darkhunters who are dedicated to returning them to their own dimension, fifteen-year-old Clary Fray is drawn into this bizarre world when her mother disappears and Clary herself is almost killed by a monster.
Sequels: *City of Ashes; City of Glass; City of Fallen Angels*

Clare, Cassandra. *Clockwork Angel*. M. K. McElderry Books, c2010. 479p. IL YA, Lexile: 780
In this prequel to *Mortal Instruments* series, sixteen-year-old Tessa Gray travels to England in search of her brother, only to be abducted by the Dark Sisters, residents of London's Downworld, home to the city's supernatural folk. She becomes the object of much attention—both good and bad—when it is discovered she has the power to transform at will into another person.

Cremer, Andrea. *Nightshade*. Philomel Books, c2010. 454p. IL YA
Calla and Ren have been raised knowing it is their destiny to mate with each other and rule over their shape-shifting wolf pack. When a human boy arrives and vies for Calla's heart, she is faced with a decision that could change her whole world.

Fantaskey, Beth. *Jessica's Guide to Dating on the Dark Side*. Harcourt, c2009. 354p. IL YA, Lexile: 770
Seventeen-year-old Jessica, who was adopted and raised in Pennsylvania, learns that she is descended from a royal line of Romanian vampires and that she is betrothed to a vampire prince, who poses as a foreign exchange student while courting her.

Supernatural/Paranormal ("Beyond Twilight")

Fitzpatrick, Becca. *Hush, Hush*. Simon & Schuster Books for Young Readers, c2009. 391p. IL YA, Lexile: 640

High school sophomore Nora has always been very cautious in her relationships, but when Patch, who has a dark side she can sense, enrolls at her school, she is mysteriously and strongly drawn to him, despite warnings from her best friend, the school counselor, and her own instincts.
Sequels: *Crescendo; Silence* (publication date: October 2011)

Garcia, Kami, & Stohl, Margaret. *Beautiful Creatures*. Little, Brown, c2009. 563p. IL YA, Lexile: 670

In a small South Carolina town, where it seems little has changed since the Civil War, sixteen-year-old Ethan is powerfully drawn to Lena, a new classmate with whom he shares a psychic connection and whose family hides a dark secret that may be revealed on her sixteenth birthday.
Sequel: *Beautiful Darkness*

Jones, Carrie. *Need*. Bloomsbury, c2009. 306p. IL YA, Lexile: 510

Depressed after the death of her stepfather, high school junior Zara goes to live with her grandmother in a small Maine town. Her new friends tell Zara the strange man she keeps seeing there may be a pixie king, and that only "were" creatures can stop him from taking souls.

Kate, Lauren. *Fallen*. Delacorte Press, c2009. 452p. IL YA, Lexile: 830

Suspected in the death of her boyfriend, seventeen-year-old Luce is sent to a Savannah, Georgia, reform school, where she meets two intriguing boys and learns the truth about the strange shadows that have always haunted her.
Sequels: *Torment; Passion*

Keaton, Kelly, *Darkness Becomes Her.* Simon Pulse, c2011. 273p. IL YA, Lexile: 770

In post-apocalyptic New Orleans, now a sanctuary for supernatural beings, a hardened teenager on the run searches for the truth about her monstrous heritage and discovers a curse that could reignite an ancient war between gods and monsters.

Kostova, Elizabeth. *The Historian*. Little, Brown, c2005. 642p. IL AD

Late one night, exploring her father's library, a young woman finds an ancient book and a cache of yellowing letters. The letters, which are all addressed to "My dear and unfortunate successor," plunge her into a world she never dreamed of—a labyrinth where the secrets of her father's past and her mother's mysterious fate connect to an inconceivable evil hidden in the depths of history. It is a quest for the truth about Vlad the Impaler, the medieval ruler whose barbarous reign formed the basis of the legend of Dracula.

McBride, Lish. *Hold Me Closer, Necromancer*. Henry Holt, c2010. 342p. IL YA, Lexile: 650

Sam LaCroix, a Seattle fast-food worker and college dropout, discovers that he is a necromancer, part of a world of harbingers, werewolves, and satyrs—and one dangerous necromancer who sees Sam as a threat to his lucrative business of raising the dead.

Plum-Ucci, Carol. *Fire Will Fall*. Harcourt, c2010. 485p. IL YA, Lexile: 810

Moved to a mansion in the South Jersey Pine Barrens, four teenagers, trying to recover from being poisoned by terrorists, struggle with health issues, personal demons, and supernatural events, as operatives try to track down the terror cell.

Supernatural/Paranormal ("Beyond Twilight")

Scott, Inara. *The Candidates*. Hyperion, c2010. 293p. IL YA, Lexile: 740
Fifteen-year-old Dancia is recruited by a boarding school for teenagers with special abilities, where she makes friends for the first time, is attracted to a popular junior, and becomes involved with a dangerous classmate.

Stiefvater, Maggie. *Shiver.* Scholastic, c2009. 392p. IL YA, Lexile: 740
Throughout all the years she has watched the wolves in the woods behind her house, Grace has been particularly drawn to an unusual yellow-eyed wolf, which, in its turn, has been watching her with increasing intensity.
Sequels: ***Linger; Forever***

Refugees and Resettlement

Almagor, Gila. *Under the Domim Tree*. Simon & Schuster Books for Young Readers, 1995. 164p. IL YA, Lexile: 750

> The author chronicles the joys and troubles experienced by a group of teenagers, mostly Holocaust survivors, living at an Israeli youth settlement in 1953.

Applegate, Katherine. *Home of the Brave*. Feiwel And Friends, 2007. 249p. IL 5–8, Lexile: NP

> Kek, an African refugee, is confronted by many strange things at the Minneapolis home of his aunt and cousin, as well as in his fifth-grade classroom. He longs for his missing mother, but finds comfort in the company of a cow and her owner.

Bat-Ami, Miriam. *Two Suns in the Sky*. Puffin Books, 2001, c1999. 223p. IL YA, Lexile: 550

> In 1944, an upstate New York teenager named Christine meets and falls in love with Adam, a Yugoslavian Jew living in a refugee camp, despite their parents' conviction that they do not belong together.

Burg, Ann E. *All the Broken Pieces: A Novel in Verse*. Scholastic Press, 2009. 218p. IL 5–8, Lexile: 680

> Two years after being airlifted out of Vietnam in 1975, Matt Pin is haunted by the terrible secret he left behind. Now, in his loving adoptive home in the United States, a series of profound events forces him to confront his past.

Burg, Ann E. *Rebekkah's Journey: A World War II Refugee Story*. Sleeping Bear Press, c2006. 48p. IL 3–6

> After eluding capture by the Nazis, seven-year-old Rebekkah and her mother are brought from Italy to the United States to begin a new life.

Flood, Bo. *Warriors in the Crossfire*. Front Street, c2010. 142p. IL 5–8, Lexile: 560

> Joseph, living on the island of Saipan during World War II, learns what it means to be a warrior as he and his family struggle to survive in the face of impending invasion.

Fullerton, Alma. *Libertad*. Fitzhenry & Whiteside, c2008. 215p. IL 5–8

> After their mother dies, Libertad and his younger brother Julio leave their home near the Guatemala City dump and perform as street musicians along the Rio Grande River while hoping to cross the border into the United States and locate their father.

Hesse, Karen. *Aleutian Sparrow*. Aladdin Paperbacks, 2005, c2003. 156p. IL 5–8, Lexile: NP

> An Aleutian Islander recounts her suffering during World War II in American internment camps designed to "protect" the population from the invading Japanese.

Kadohata, Cynthia. *A Million Shades of Gray*. Atheneum Books for Young Readers, c2010. 216p. IL 5–8, Lexile: 700

> A boy takes refuge in the jungle with his elephant when the Viet Cong launch an attack on his village in the aftermath of the Vietnam War.

Kadohata, Cynthia. *Weedflower*. Atheneum Books for Young Readers, c2006. 260p. IL 5–8, Lexile: 750

> After twelve-year-old Sumiko and her Japanese American family are relocated from their flower farm in southern California to an internment camp on a Mojave Indian reservation in Arizona,

Refugees and Resettlement

she helps her family and neighbors, becomes friends with a local Indian boy, and tries to hold on to her dream of owning a flower shop.

Kurtz, Jane. *The Storyteller's Beads.* Harcourt Brace, c1998. 154p. IL 3–6, Lexile: 750
During the political strife and famine of the 1980s, two Ethiopian girls—one Christian and the other Jewish and blind—struggle to overcome many difficulties, including their prejudices about each other, as they make the dangerous journey out of Ethiopia.

Levitin, Sonia. *The Return.* Fawcett Juniper, c1987. 181p. IL 5–8, Lexile: 720
Desta and the other members of her Falasha family, who are Jews suffering from discrimination in Ethiopia, finally flee the country and attempt the dangerous journey to Israel.

Lieurance, Suzanne. *The Lucky Baseball: My Story in a Japanese-American Internment Camp.*
Enslow Publishers, c2010. 160p. IL 3–6
In 1942, after the Japanese bomb Pearl Harbor, twelve-year-old Harry Yakamoto and his family are forced to move to an internment camp, where they must learn to survive in the desert of California under the watchful eyes of armed guards. The book includes a section about the treatment of Japanese Americans during World War II.

Lobel, Anita. *No Pretty Pictures: A Child of War.* Collins, 2008, c1998. 239p. IL 5–8, Lexile: 750
(Non-fiction)
The author, who is a well-known illustrator of children's books, describes her experiences as a Polish Jew during World War II and her years in Sweden after the war's end.

Magorian, Michelle. *Good Night, Mr. Tom.* HarperTrophy, 1986, c1981. 318p. IL 5–8, Lexile: 760
A battered child learns to embrace life when he is adopted by an old man in the English countryside during World War II.

Manivong, Laura. *Escaping the Tiger.* Harper, 2010. 216p. IL YA, Lexile: 750
In 1982, twelve-year-old Vonlai, his parents, and his sister Dalah escape from Laos to a Thai refugee camp, where they spend four long years struggling to survive in hopes of one day reaching America.

Mazer, Norma Fox. *Good Night, Maman.* Houghton Mifflin Harcourt, c1999. 185p IL 5–8, Lexile: 510
After spending years fleeing from the Nazis in war-torn Europe, twelve-year-old Karin Levi and her older brother Marc find a new home in a refugee camp in Oswego, New York.

Paterson, Katherine. *The Day of the Pelican.* Clarion Books, 2009. 145p. IL 5–8, Lexile: 770
In 1998, when the hostilities in Kosovo escalate, thirteen-year-old Meli's life as an ethnic Albanian changes forever after her brother escapes his Serbian captors; her entire family is forced to flee from one refugee camp to another until they are able to immigrate to America.

Pellegrino, Marge. *Journey of Dreams.* Frances Lincoln Children's Books, 2009. 250p. IL 5–8,
Lexile: 740
Tomasa and her family struggle during a time of war in Guatemala before setting out on a journey to find Mama and Carlos, who have gone into hiding. They brave various dangers before eventually making their way to the United States.

Refugees and Resettlement

Robinson, Anthony. *Hamzat's Journey: A Refugee Diary.* Frances Lincoln Children's Books, 2010, c2009. 29p. IL 3–6 (Non-fiction)

Hamzat, a boy born in Chechnya in 1993, tells about his life in a time of war, and explains how he and his family came to live in England after he stepped on a landmine and had to have his leg amputated.

Shea, Pegi Deitz. *Tangled Threads: A Hmong Girl's Story.* Clarion Books, c2003. 236p. IL 5–8, Lexile: 630

After ten years in a refugee camp in Thailand, thirteen-year-old Mai Yang travels to Providence, Rhode Island, where her Americanized cousins introduce her to pizza, shopping, and beer, while her grandmother and new friends keep her connected to her Hmong heritage.

Smith, Icy. *Half Spoon of Rice: A Survival Story of the Cambodian Genocide.* East West Discovery Press, 2010. 42p. IL 5–8

Nine-year-old Nat and his family are forced from their home in Cambodia on April 17, 1975, marched for many days, separated from one another, and forced to work in the rice fields, where Nat concentrates on survival. The book includes historical notes and photographs documenting the Cambodian genocide.

Williams, Mary. *Brothers in Hope: The Story of the Lost Boys of Sudan.* Lee & Low, c2005. 38p. IL 3–6, Lexile: 670

Eight-year-old Garang, orphaned by a civil war in Sudan, finds the inner strength needed to lead other boys as they trek hundreds of miles seeking safety in Ethiopia, and then Kenya, before being offered sanctuary in the United States many years later.

Road Trip

Avi. *The True Confessions of Charlotte Doyle*. Avon, 1997, c1990. 229p. IL 5–8, Lexile: 740
Thirteen-year-old Charlotte Doyle, the only passenger on a voyage from England to America in 1832, must take serious matters into her own hands when she learns that the captain has murderous intentions.

Bauer, Joan. *Hope Was Here*. G. P. Putnam's Sons, c2000. 186p. IL YA, Lexile: 710
When sixteen-year-old Hope and the aunt who has raised her move from Brooklyn to Mulhoney, Wisconsin, to work as waitress and cook in the Welcome Stairways diner, they become involved with the diner owner's political campaign to oust the town's corrupt mayor.

Bauer, Joan. *Rules of the Road*. Putman's, 1998. 201p. IL YA, Lexile: 850
Sixteen-year-old Jenna gets a job driving the elderly owner of a chain of successful shoe stores from Chicago to Texas to confront the son who is trying to force her to retire. Along the way, Jenna hones her talents as a saleswoman and finds the strength to face her alcoholic father.

Bradbury, Jennifer. *Shift*. Atheneum Books for Young Readers, c2008. 245p. IL YA, Lexile: 770
When best friends Chris and Win go on a cross-country bicycle trek the summer after graduating and only one of the pair returns, the FBI wants to know what happened.

Bray, Libba. *Going Bovine*. Delacorte Press, c2009. 480p. IL YA, Lexile: 680
Cameron Smith, a disaffected sixteen-year-old diagnosed with mad cow disease, sets off on a road trip with a death-obsessed, video-gaming dwarf he meets in the hospital in an attempt to find a cure for his illness.

Caletti, Deb. *Honey, Baby, Sweetheart*. Simon Pulse, 2008, c2004. 308p. IL YA, Lexile: 900
In the summer of her junior year, sixteen-year-old Ruby McQueen and her mother, both nursing broken hearts, set out on a journey to reunite an elderly woman with her long-lost love. In the process, the pair learns many things about "the real ties that bind" people to one another.

Cooney, Caroline B. *Hit the Road*. Delacorte Press, c2006. 183p. IL YA, Lexile: 790
Sixteen-year-old Brittany acts as chauffeur for her grandmother and three other eighty-something women going to what is supposedly their college reunion, on a long drive that involves lies, theft, and kidnappings.

Creech, Sharon. *Walk Two Moons*. HarperCollins, c1994. 280p. IL 5–8, Lexile: 770
After her mother leaves home suddenly, thirteen-year-old Sal and her grandparents take a car trip retracing her mother's route. Along the way, Sal recounts the story of her friend Phoebe, whose mother also left her family.

Creech, Sharon. *The Wanderer*. Joanna Cotler Books, 2002, c2000. 305p. IL 3–6, Lexile: 830
Thirteen-year-old Sophie and her cousin Cody record their transatlantic crossing aboard the *Wanderer*, a forty-five-foot sailboat on which they, along with uncles and another cousin, are en route to visit their grandfather in England.

Fleischman, Paul. *Whirligig*. Square Fish, 1998. 133p. IL YA, Lexile: 760
While traveling to each corner of the country to build a whirligig in memory of the girl whose death he caused, sixteen-year-old Brian finds forgiveness and atonement.

Road Trip

Green, John. *An Abundance of Katherines.* Dutton Books, c2006. 227p. IL YA, Lexile: 890
Having been recently dumped for the nineteenth time by a girl named Katherine, recent high school graduate and former child prodigy Colin sets off on a road trip with his best friend to try to find some new direction in life while also trying to create a mathematical formula to explain his relationships.

Green, John. *Paper Towns.* Dutton Books, c2008. 305p. IL YA, Lexile: 850
One month before graduating from his Central Florida high school, Quentin "Q" Jacobsen basks in the predictable boredom of his life—until the beautiful and exciting Margo Roth Spiegelman, Q's neighbor and classmate, takes him on a midnight adventure and then mysteriously disappears.

High, Linda Oatman. *Sister Slam and the Poetic Motormouth Roadtrip.* Bloomsbury, c2004. 256p. IL YA
In this novel told in slam verse, best friends and aspiring poets Laura and Twig embark on a road trip after graduating from high school. The pair travel from Pennsylvania to New York City to compete at slam poetry events.

Hyde, Catherine Ryan. *Becoming Chloe.* Alfred A. Knopf, c2006. 215p. IL YA, Lexile: 600
A gay teenage boy and a fragile teenage girl meet while living on the streets of New York City and eventually decide to take a road trip across America to discover whether the world is a beautiful place.

Johnson, Maureen. *13 Little Blue Envelopes.* HarperCollins, c2005. 317p. IL YA, Lexile: 770
When seventeen-year-old Ginny receives a packet of mysterious envelopes from her favorite aunt, she leaves New Jersey to criss-cross Europe on a sort of scavenger hunt that transforms her life.

Kerouac, Jack. *On the Road.* Viking, 2007. 307p. IL AD
This fiftieth anniversary edition of Jack Kerouac's thinly fictionalized autobiography chronicles his cross-country adventure across North America on a quest for self-knowledge as experienced by his alter-ego, Sal Paradise, and Sal's friend Dean Moriarty—Kerouac's real-life friend Neal Cassady.

Kingsolver, Barbara. *The Bean Trees: A Novel.* HarperFlamingo, 1998. 261p. IL YA, Lexile: 900
Taylor, a poor Kentuckian, makes her way west with an abandoned baby girl and stops in Tucson. There, she finds friends and discovers resources in apparently empty places.

Law, Ingrid. *Savvy.* Dial Books for Young Readers, Walton Media, c2008. 342p. IL 5–8, Lexile: 1070
On her thirteenth birthday, Mibs Beaumont receives a revelation about her "savvy"—a magical power unique to each member of her family—just as her father is injured in a terrible accident.

Lowry, Brigid. *Guitar Highway Rose.* St. Martin's Griffin, 2005, c1997. 196p. IL YA
Two fifteen-year-olds, Rosie and Asher, upset over the various unhappy circumstances of their lives in the Australian city of Perth, decide to run away.

Mackler, Carolyn. *Guyaholic.* Candlewick Press, 2007. 176p. IL YA
Vivienne Valentine, known as V to her friends, has a history of hooking up with a new guy every few days, but her latest boyfriend, Sam, seems to be different from her past relationships. When

Road Trip

---

her feelings start to scare her, V makes a stupid mistake that destroys their relationship and sends her on a cross-country journey of self-discovery.

Marchetta, Melina. *Jellicoe Road*. HarperTeen, 2008, 2006. 419p. IL YA, Lexile: 820
Abandoned by her drug-addicted mother at the age of eleven, high school student Taylor Markham struggles with her identity and family history at a boarding school in Australia.

Myracle, Lauren. *How to Be Bad*. HarperTeen, 2009, c2008. 325p. IL YA, Lexile: 630
Told in alternating voices, Jesse, Vicks, and Mel, hoping to leave all their worries and woes behind, escape their small town by taking a road trip to Miami.

Naylor, Phyllis Reynolds. *Sang Spell*. Simon Pulse, 2002, c1998. 212p. IL 5–8, Lexile: 880
When his mother is killed in an automobile accident, high school student Josh decides to hitchhike across country. While on his journey, he finds himself trapped in a mysterious village somewhere in the Appalachian Mountains, among a group of people who call themselves Melungeons.

Nelson, R. A. *Breathe My Name*. Razorbill, c2007. 314p. IL YA, Lexile: 560
Since her adoption, seventeen-year-old Frances has lived a quiet suburban life. Soon after she begins falling for the new boy at school, however, she receives a summons from her mentally ill birth mother, who has just been released—after serving eleven years in prison for smothering Frances's younger sisters—and still wants to kill Frances.

Paulsen, Gary. *The Car*. Harcourt, 2006, c1994. 182p. IL YA, Lexile: 900
A teenager left on his own travels west in a kit car he built himself. Along the way, he picks up two Vietnam veterans, who take him on an eye-opening journey.

Pearson, Mary. *The Miles Between*. Holt, 2009. 266p. IL YA, Lexile: 650
Seventeen-year-old Destiny keeps a painful childhood secret all to herself—until she and three classmates from her exclusive boarding school take off on an unauthorized road trip in search of "one fair day."

Pena, Matt de la. *We Were Here*. Delacorte Press, c2009. 357p. IL YA, Lexile: 770
After a judge sentences Miguel to spend a year in a group home and write in a journal, he makes plans to escape the youth detention center and go to Mexico, where he can put his past behind him.

Shaw, Tucker. *Confessions of a Backup Dancer*. Simon Pulse, 2004. 265p. IL YA, Lexile: 990
Kelly Kimbal lands a job as a back-up dancer for pop diva Darcy Barnes, but is soon fired by Darcy's overbearing mother—until Darcy develops the courage to tell her mother off and bring Kelly back into the show.

Wittlinger, Ellen. *Zigzag*. Simon & Schuster Books for Young Readers, c2003. 264p. IL YA, Lexile: 730
A high-school junior makes a trip with her aunt and two cousins, discovering places she did not know existed and strengths she did not know she had.

Road Trip

Wolf, Allan. *Zane's Trace.* Candlewick Press, 2007. 177p. IL YA, Lexile: NP
Believing he has killed his grandfather, Zane Guesswind heads for his mother's Zanesville, Ohio, grave to kill himself, driving the 1969 Plymouth Barracuda his long-gone father left behind. Along the way to his destination, assorted characters help Zane discover who he really is.

Yansky, Brian. *My Road Trip to the Pretty Girl Capital of the World.* Cricket Books, 2003. 178p. IL YA
In 1979, when his life in Mansfield, Iowa, seems to fall apart, seventeen-year-old Simon takes his father's car and sets out for Texas, looking for his birth parents and picking up a man claiming to be Elvis, two bums, and an abused young wife along the way.

Sci-Fi/Futuristic

List by: Donna Zecha, Hopkinton Middle/High School, New Hampshire

Books for Ages 12 and Up

Bacigalupi, Paolo. *Ship Breaker.* Little, Brown, c2010. 326p. IL YA, Lexile: 690
In a futuristic world, teenaged Nailer scavenges copper wiring from grounded oil tankers for a living. When he finds a beached clipper ship with a girl in the wreckage, he has to decide whether he should strip the ship for its wealth or rescue the girl.

Bodeen, S. A. *The Compound.* Feiwel & Friends, c2008. 248p. IL YA, Lexile: 570
Eli and his family have lived in the Compound for six years. The world they knew is gone, and Eli's father built the Compound to keep them safe. Now they can't get out—because he won't let them leave.

Bodeen, S. A. *The Gardener.* Feiwel and Friends, c2010. 233p. IL YA, Lexile: 620
When high school sophomore Mason finds a beautiful but catatonic girl in the nursing home where his mother works, the discovery leads him to revelations about a series of disturbing human experiments that have a connection to his own life.

Clayton, Emma. *The Roar.* Chicken House, c2008. 496p. IL 3–6, Lexile: 910
Twelve-year-old twins, Mika and Ellie, live in a future behind a wall, safe from the plague animals beyond—or so they have been told. When one of them disappears, and the other takes part in a virtual reality game, they begin to discover that their concrete world is built on lies. Determined to find each other again, they go in search of the truth. As a strange sound in their heads grows into a roar, they find out that children and the planet have never mattered more.

Collins, Suzanne. *The Hunger Games*. Scholastic, c2008. 374p. IL YA, Lexile: 810
In a future North America, where the rulers of Panem maintain control through an annual televised survival competition pitting young people from each of the twelve districts against one another, sixteen-year-old Katniss's skills are put to the test when she voluntarily takes her younger sister's place.
Sequels: *Catching Fire; Mockingjay*

Dashner, James. *The Maze Runner.* Delacorte Press, c2009. 375p. IL YA, Lexile: 770
Sixteen-year-old Thomas wakes up with no memory in the middle of a maze and realizes he must work with the community in which he finds himself if he is to escape.
Sequel: *The Scorch Trials*

DiTerlizzi, Tony. *The Search for WondLa.* Simon & Schuster, c2010. 477p. IL 5–8, Lexile: 760
Living in isolation with a robot on what appears to be an alien world populated with bizarre life forms, a twelve-year-old human girl called Eva Nine sets out on a journey to find others like her. The book features "augmented reality" pages, in which readers with a webcam can access additional information about Eva Nine's world.

Sci-Fi/Futuristic

Falkner, Brian. *Brain Jack.* Random House, c2009. 347p. IL YA, Lexile: 810

In a near-future New York City, fourteen-year-old computer genius Sam Wilson manages to hack into the AT&T network and sets off a chain of events that have profound effects on human activity throughout the world.

Grant, Michael. *Gone.* HarperTeen, c2008. 558p. IL YA, Lexile: 620

In a small town on the coast of California, everyone older than the age of fourteen suddenly disappears, setting up a battle between the remaining town residents and the students from a local private school, as well as between those who have "The Power" and are able to perform supernatural feats and those who do not.

Sequels: *Hunger;Lies; Plague*

Haddix, Margaret Peterson. *Found.* Simon & Schuster, c2008. 314p. IL 5–8, Lexile: 750

When thirteen-year-olds Jonah and Chip, who are both adopted, learn they were discovered on a plane that appeared out of nowhere, full of babies with no adults on board, they realize that they have uncovered a mystery involving time travel and two opposing forces, each trying to repair the fabric of time.

Sequels: *Sent; Sabotaged*

Kostick, Conor. *Epic.* Viking, 2007, c2004. 364p. IL YA, Lexile: 880

On New Earth, a world based on a video role-playing game, fourteen-year-old Erik persuades his friends to aid him in some unusual gambits to save Erik's father from exile and safeguard the futures of their families.

Sequels: *Saga; Edda*

Malley, Gemma. *The Declaration.* Bloomsbury, c2007. 320p. IL YA, Lexile: 930

Anna is the child of parents who refused to sign the Declaration, which forbids people to have children. She must now choose between breaking the law or facing certain death.

Sequels: *The Resistance; The Legacy*

Patneaude, David. *Epitaph Road.* Egmont USA, c2010. 266p. IL YA, Lexile: 720

In 2097, men are a small and controlled minority in a utopian world ruled by women. In this setting, fourteen-year-old Kellen must fight to save his father from an outbreak of the virus that killed ninety-seven percent of the male population thirty years earlier.

Patterson, James. *Maximum Ride: The Angel Experiment.* Little, Brown, c2005. 422p. IL YA, Lexile: 700

After the mutant Erasers abduct the youngest member of their group, the "bird kids," who are the result of genetic experimentation, take off in pursuit and find themselves struggling to understand their own origins and purpose.

Sequels: *Maximum Ride: School's out Forever; Saving the World and Other Extreme Sports; The Final Warning: A Maximum Ride Novel; Max: A Maximum Ride Novel; Fang: A Maximum Ride Novel; Angel: A Maximum Ride Novel*

Sci-Fi/Futuristic

Pfeffer, Susan Beth. *Life as We Knew It.* Harcourt, c2006. 337p. IL YA, Lexile: 770

Through her journal entries, sixteen-year-old Miranda describes her family's struggle to survive after a meteor hits the moon, causing worldwide tsunamis, earthquakes, and volcanic eruptions. Sequels: *The Dead and the Gone; This World We Live in*

Reichs, Kathy. *Virals.* Razorbill, c2010. 454p. IL YA, Lexile: 480

Tory Brennan and her friends are exposed to a canine parvovirus when they rescue a dog from a medical testing facility. They soon realize they have heightened senses, which they use to solve a cold case involving murder.

Shusterman, Neal. *Unwind.* Simon & Schuster, c2007. 335p. IL YA, Lexile: 740

In a future world where youths between the ages of thirteen and eighteen can have their lives "unwound" and their body parts harvested for use by others, three teens go to extreme lengths to uphold their beliefs—and, perhaps, save their own lives.

Westerfeld, Scott. *Leviathan.* Simon Pulse, c2009. 440p. IL YA, Lexile: 790

Part historical fiction and part science fiction, this novel set in an alternate 1914 Europe focuses on fifteen-year-old Austrian Prince Alek, who is on the run from the Clanker Powers, which are attempting to take over the globe using mechanical machinery. Alek forms an uneasy alliance with Deryn, who, disguised as a boy to join the British Air Service, is learning to fly genetically engineered beasts. Sequel: *Behemoth*

Books for Older Teens

Doctorow, Cory. *Little Brother.* Tor Teen, c2008. 380p. IL YA, Lexile: 900

After being interrogated for days by the Department of Homeland Security in the aftermath of a major terrorist attack on San Francisco, California, seventeen-year-old Marcus, released into what is now a police state, decides to use his expertise in computer hacking to set things right.

Fisher, Catherine. *Incarceron.* Hodder Children's Books, c2007. 458p. IL YA, Lexile: 600

To free herself from an upcoming arranged marriage, Claudia, the daughter of the Warden of Incarceron, a futuristic prison with a mind of its own, decides to help a young prisoner escape. Sequel: *Sapphique*

Gill, David Macinnis. *Black Hole Sun.* Greenwillow Books, c2010. 340p. IL YA, Lexile: 610

On the planet Mars, sixteen-year-old Durango and his crew of mercenaries are hired by the settlers of a mining community to protect their most valuable resource from a feral band of marauders.

Ness, Patrick. *The Knife of Never Letting Go.* Candlewick Press, c2008. 479p. IL YA, Lexile: 860

Todd and Viola are pursued by power-hungry Prentiss and mad minister Aaron as they set out across New World, searching for answers about their colony's true past and seeking a way to warn the ship bringing settlers from Old World. Sequels: *The Ask and the Answer; Monsters of Men*

Sci-Fi/Futuristic

Oliver, Lauren. *Delirium*. Harper, c2011. 441p. IL YA.
Lena looks forward to receiving the government-mandated cure that prevents the delirium of love and leads to a safe, predictable, and happy life—until ninety-five days before her eighteenth birthday and her treatment, when she falls in love.

Pearson, Mary E. *The Adoration of Jenna Fox*. Henry Holt, c2008. 266p. IL YA, Lexile: 570
In the not-too-distant future, when biotechnological advances have made synthetic bodies and brains possible but illegal, a seventeen-year-old girl, recovering from a serious accident and suffering from memory lapses, learns a startling secret about her existence.

Reeve, Philip. *Fever Crumb*. Scholastic Press, c2010. 325p. IL YA, Lexile: 1000
Foundling Fever Crumb has been raised as an engineer, even though females in the future London, England, are not believed capable of rational thought. At age fourteen, she leaves her sheltered world and begins to learn startling truths about her past while facing dangers in the present.

Revis, Beth. *Across the Universe*. Razorbill, c2011. 398p. IL YA.
Amy, having been cryogenically frozen and placed onboard a spaceship that was supposed to land on a distant planet three hundred years in the future, is unplugged fifty years too early. She finds herself stuck inside an enclosed world ruled by a tyrannical leader and his rebellious teenage heir, and confused about who to trust and why someone is trying to kill her.

Smith, Alexander Gordon. *Lockdown*. Farrar, Straus and Giroux, c2009. 273p. IL YA, Lexile: 1010
When fourteen-year-old Alex is framed for murder, he becomes an inmate in the Furnace Penitentiary, where brutal inmates and sadistic guards reign, boys who disappear in the middle of the night sometimes return weirdly altered, and escape might just be possible.
Sequel: *Solitary*

Stracher, Cameron. *The Water Wars*. Sourcebooks Fire, c2011. 240p. IL YA.
In a world where water has become a precious resource, Vera and her brother befriend a boy who seems to have unlimited access to water and who suspiciously disappears, prompting a dangerous search challenged by pirates, a paramilitary group, and corporations.

Wasserman, Robin. *Skinned*. Simon Pulse, c2008. 361p. IL YA, Lexile: 630
To save her from dying in a horrible accident, Lia's wealthy parents transplant her brain into a mechanical body.
Sequels: *Crashed; Wired*

Part 5

Subjects

Eighth-Grade Science

Anderson, Laurie Halse. *Fever, 1793.* Simon & Schuster Books for Young Readers, c2000. 251p. IL 5–8, Lexile: 580
Sixteen-year-old Matilda Cook, separated from her sick mother, learns about perseverance and self-reliance when she is forced to cope with the horrors of the yellow fever epidemic in Philadelphia in 1793.

Avi. *1937: Blue Heron.* Avon, 1993, c1992. 186p. IL 5–8, Lexile: 590
While spending the month of August on the Massachusetts shore with her father, stepmother, and their new baby, almost thirteen-year-old Maggie finds beauty in and draws strength from a great blue heron, even as the family around her unravels.

Cormier, Robert. *Fade.* Delacorte, 2004, c1988. 310p. IL YA, Lexile: 990
In the summer of 1938, Paul Moreaux, the thirteen-year-old son of French Canadian immigrants, inherits the ability to become invisible, but his power soon leads to death and destruction.

Funston, Sylvia. *It's All in Your Head: A Guide to Your Brilliant Brain.* Maple Tree Press, Distributed by Publishers Group West, c2005. 64p. IL 3–6, Lexile: 1080
This exploration of the mysteries and wonders of the brain describes its connections to the outside world, examines how the senses work in conjunction with the brain, and more.

Hiaasen, Carl. *Flush.* Alfred A. Knopf, 2005. 320p. IL 5–8, Lexile: 830,
When their father is jailed for sinking a riverboat, Noah Underwood and his younger sister, Abbey, must gather evidence proving that the owner of this floating casino is emptying his bilge tanks into the protected waters around their Florida Keys home.

Hiaasen, Carl. *Hoot.* Alfred A. Knopf, c2002. 292p. IL 5–8. Lexile: 760
Roy, who is new to his small Florida community, becomes involved in another boy's attempt to save a colony of burrowing owls from a proposed construction site.

Hiaasen, Carl. *Scat.* Knopf, c2009. 371p. IL 5–8, Lexile: 810
Nick and Marta are both suspicious when their biology teacher, the feared Mrs. Bunny Starch, disappears. They try to uncover the truth despite the police and headmaster's insistence that nothing is wrong.

Hickam, Homer H. *October Sky: A Memoir.* Dell, 2000, c1998. 428p, IL AD, Lexile: 900
Homer Hickam, the introspective son of a mine superintendent and a mother determined to get him out of Coalwood, West Virginia, forever, nurtures a dream to send rockets into outer space—an ambition that changes his life and the lives of everyone living in Coalwood in 1957.

Hobbs, Will. *Wild Man Island.* HarperCollins, c2002. 184p. IL 5–8, Lexile: 690
After fourteen-year-old Andy slips away from his kayaking group to visit the wilderness site of his archaeologist father's death, a storm strands him on Admiralty Island, Alaska. He manages to survive on the island, encounters unexpected animal and human inhabitants, and looks for traces of the earliest prehistoric immigrants to America.

Eighth-Grade Science

Mikaelsen, Ben. *Rescue Josh McGuire*. Hyperion Paperbacks for Children, 1993, c1991. 266p. IL 5–8, Lexile: 680

When thirteen-year-old Josh runs away to the mountains of Montana with an orphaned bear cub destined for laboratory testing, both must fight for their lives in a sudden snowstorm.

Mikaelsen, Ben. *Stranded*. Disney/Hyperion Books, c1995. 247p. IL 5–8, Lexile: 610

Twelve-year-old Koby, who has lost a foot in an accident, sees a chance to prove her self-reliance to her parents when she tries to rescue two stranded pilot whales near her home in the Florida Keys.

Taylor, Theodore. *Sniper*. Harcourt, c1989. 229p. IL YA, Lexile: 810

Fifteen-year-old Ben must cope alone when a mysterious sniper begins shooting the big cats in his family's private zoological preserve.

Zindel, Paul. *The Gadget*. Dell Laurel-Leaf, 2003, c2001. 184p. IL 5–8, Lexile: 590

In 1945, having joined his father in Los Alamos, New Mexico, where he and other scientists are working on a secret project to end World War II, thirteen-year-old Stephen becomes caught in a web of secrecy and intrigue.

Child Labor

Bartoletti, Susan Campbell. *Kids on Strike!* Houghton Mifflin, c1999. 208p, IL 5–8, Lexile: 920 (Non-fiction)

Describes the conditions and treatment that drove working American children to strike in the nineteenth and early twentieth centuries, discussing such events as the mill workers' strike in 1834; the coal strikes in 1897, 1900, and 1902; and Mother Jones's 125-mile "Children's Crusade" march in 1903.

Child Labor: A Global View. Greenwood Press, 2004. 221p. IL YA (Non-fiction)

Examines the various factors that contribute to child labor in fifteen countries, describing each country's child labor scene, the history of the problem, conditions faced by child workers, political policies, and social issues.

Child Labor and Sweatshops. Greenhaven Press, c2011. 125p. IL YA (Non-fiction)

Collects twelve essays that provide information about child labor and sweatshops, discussing their harm to children, legislation and laws related to working conditions, the influence of free trade agreements and globalization, government boycotts of sweatshop products, and other related topics.

D'Adamo, Francesco. *Iqbal: A Novel.* Atheneum Books for Young Readers, 2003. 120p. IL 3–6, Lexile: 730

A fictionalized account of the Pakistani child who escaped from bondage in a carpet factory and went on to help liberate other children like him, before being gunned down at the age of thirteen.

Freedman, Russell. *Kids at Work: Lewis Hine and the Crusade Against Child Labor.* Clarion Books, c1994. 104p. IL 5–8, Lexile: 1140 (Non-fiction)

Text and accompanying photographs show the use of children as industrial workers, interwoven with the story of Lewis W. Hine, who took these photographs and whose life's work made a significant difference in the lives of others.

Greenwood, Barbara. *Factory Girl.* Kids Can Press, c2007. 136p. IL 5–8, Lexile: 850

This work of historical fiction describes Emily, a young child who works eleven hours a day in a garment factory. The book also includes historical notes about child labor.

Hindman, Hugh D. *Child Labor: An American History.* M. E. Sharpe, c2002. 431p. IL AD (Non-fiction)

Examines the history of child labor in the United States, and attempts to identify lessons that could help eliminate the problem of child labor in countries on the path of economic development.

Jimenez, Francisco. *The Circuit: Stories from the Life of a Migrant Child.* Houghton Mifflin, 1999, c1997. 116p. IL 5–8, Lexile: 880

Explores a migrant family's experiences moving through labor camps, facing poverty and impermanence, and discusses how they endure through faith, hope, and back-breaking work.

Kielburger, Craig. *Free the Children: A Young Man Fights against Child Labor and Proves That Children Can Change the World.* HarperPerennial, 2000. 321p. IL YA (Non-fiction)

Chronicles the efforts of twelve-year-old Craig Kielburger and his human rights organization, Free the Children, to stop child labor in foreign countries.

Child Labor

Marrin, Albert. *Flesh & Blood So Cheap: The Triangle Fire and Its Legacy.* Alfred A. Knopf, c2011. 182p. IL 5–8 (Non-fiction)

>Provides a detailed account of the disastrous Triangle Shirtwaist Factory fire in New York City, which claimed the lives of 146 garment workers in 1911, and examines the impact of this event on the nation's working conditions and labor laws.

Paterson, Katherine. *Bread and Roses, Too.* Clarion Books, c2006. 275p. IL 5–8, Lexile: 810

>Twelve-year-old Rosa and thirteen-year-old Jake form an unlikely friendship as they try to survive and understand the 1912 Bread and Roses strike of mill workers in Lawrence, Massachusetts.

Paterson, Katherine. *Lyddie.* Lodestar Books, c1991. 182p. IL 5–8, Lexile: 860

>Impoverished Vermont farm girl Lyddie Worthen is determined to gain her independence by becoming a factory worker in Lowell, Massachusetts, in the 1840s.

Tsukiyama, Gail. *Women of the Silk.* St. Martin's Press, 1991. 278p. IL AD, Lexile: 890

>Two women struggle for economic independence while performing silk work in 1926 in a small village in China.

The Civil War

Bruchac, Joseph. *March Toward the Thunder.* Dial Books, c2008. 298p. IL YA, Lexile: 850
Louis Nollette, a fifteen-year-old Abenaki Indian, joins the Irish Brigade in 1864 to fight for the Union in the Civil War.

Durrant, Lynda. *Imperfections.* Clarion Books, c2008. 172p. IL 5-8, Lexile: 710
Fourteen-year-old Rosemary Elizabeth tries to fit into the world of the Shaker sisters in 1862 Pleasant Hill, Kentucky, but yearns to be reunited with her mother and siblings from whom she was separated when they sought refuge from her abusive father. Includes facts about Shakers and Morgan's Raiders.

Durrant, Lynda. *My Last Skirt: The Story of Jennie Hodgers, Union Soldier.* Clarion Books, c2006. 199p. IL 5-8, Lexile: 760
Enjoying the freedom afforded her while dressing as a boy in order to earn higher pay after emigrating from Ireland, Jennie Hodgers serves in the 95th Illinois Infantry as Private Albert Cashier, a Union soldier in the American Civil War.

Ernst, Kathleen. *Hearts of Stone.* Dutton Children's Books, c2006. 248p. IL 5-8
Orphaned when their father dies fighting for the Union and mother expires from exhaustion, and also estranged from their Confederate neighbors, fifteen-year-old Hannah and her siblings struggle to find a way to survive during the Civil War in Tennessee.

Klein, Lisa M. *Two Girls of Gettysburg.* Bloomsbury, 2008. 393p. IL YA, Lexile: 830
When the Civil War breaks out, two cousins, Lizzie and Rosanna, find themselves on opposite sides of the conflict until the war reunites them in the town of Gettysburg.

Kluger, Jeffrey. *Freedom Stone.* Philomel Books, c2011. 316p. IL 5-8, Lexile: 1030
With the help of a magical stone from Africa, a thirteen-year-old slave travels to the battle of Vicksburg to clear her father's name and free her family from bondage.

Lawlor, Laurie. *He Will Go Fearless.* Simon & Schuster Books for Young Readers, c2006. 210p. IL 5-8
With the Civil War ended and Reconstruction begun, fifteen-year-old Billy resolves to make the dangerous and challenging journey West in search of real fortune—his true father.

Lyons, Mary E. *Letters from a Slave Boy: The Story of Joseph Jacobs.* Atheneum Books for Young Readers, 2007., 197p. IL YA, Lexile: 710
A fictionalized look at the life of Joseph Jacobs, son of a slave, told in the form of letters that he might have written during his life in pre-Civil War North Carolina, on a whaling expedition, in New York, New England, and finally in California during the Gold Rush.

Myers, Walter Dean. *Riot.* Egmont USA, 2009. 164p. IL YA, Lexile: NP
In 1863, fifteen-year-old Claire, the daughter of an Irish mother and an African father, faces ugly truths and great danger when Irish immigrants, enraged by the Civil War and a federal draft, lash out against African-Americans and wealthy "swells" of New York City.

The Civil War

Rinaldi, Ann. *Juliet's Moon*. Harcourt, c2008. 249p. IL 5-8, Lexile: 630
In Missouri in 1863, twelve-year-old Juliet Bradshaw learns to rely on herself and her brother, a captain with Quantrill's Raiders, as she sees her family home burned, is imprisoned by Yankees, and then kidnapped by a blood-crazed Confederate soldier.

Rinaldi, Ann. *Leigh Ann's Civil War: A Novel*. Harcourt, 2009. 308p. IL 5-8, Lexile: 620
Spunky Leigh Ann Conners, eleven years old when the Civil War erupts, faces the biggest challenge of her life when she is arrested and charged as a traitor after placing a French flag on top of the family mill in Roswell, Georgia, in hopes of convincing the invading Yankees to spare the business.

Wells, Rosemary. *Red Moon at Sharpsburg: A Novel*. Viking, 2007. 236p. IL YA, Lexile: 760
Even though the odds are against her and the Civil War has ruined her home and given her a view of the darker side of humanity, thirteen-year-old India Moody continues to aspire to become a scientist and attend Oberlin College.

Cryptids

Coleman, Loren. *Cryptozoology A to Z: The Encyclopedia of Loch Monsters, Sasquatch, Chupacabras, and Other Authentic Mysteries of Nature.* Fireside, c1999. 270p. IL YA (Non-fiction)
Contains two hundred entries that profile unusual beasts, new animal finds, and the explorers and scientists who search for them.

Cox, Judy. *Weird Stories from the Lonesome Café.* Harcourt, Inc., c2000. 72p. IL 3–6, Lexile: 350
Sam moves to Nevada with his uncle to run a cafe in the middle of nowhere. Although Uncle Clem insists that nothing ever happens there, his clientele consists of a number of strange characters, including Dorothy and Toto, Elvis, and Bigfoot.

Duey, Kathleen. *Castle Avamir.* Aladdin Paperbacks, 2003. 73p. IL 3–6, Lexile: 460
Heart must solve the riddle of Castle Avamir, which is, among other things, "deep in a valley" and "over the moon," to find a safe haven for the unicorns as the Gypsies leave Lord Levin's mountains for Lord Kaybale's plains.

Duey, Kathleen. *True Heart.* Aladdin Paperbacks, 2003. 75p. IL 3–6, Lexile: 420
With Moonsilver the unicorn disguised in armor, young Heart Avamir, searching for her Gypsy friends, attempts to travel unnoticed through the crowds gathered for the crowning of a new lord.

Emmer, Rick. *Giant Anaconda and Other Cryptids: Fact or Fiction?* Chelsea House, c2010. 109p. IL 5–8 (Non-fiction)
Examines the evidence for the existence of giant animals that remain hidden from humans, such as the Tasmanian thylacine and a mermaid-like creature in the waters around a Pacific Ocean island.

Greenburg, Dan. *The Boy Who Cried Bigfoot.* Grosset & Dunlap, c2000. 58p. IL 3–6, Lexile: 440
After hearing stories that a Bigfoot-like monster is haunting Camp Weno-wanna-getta-wedgee, ten-year-old Zack begins to find evidence that the legend may be true.

Halls, Kelly Milner. *In Search of Sasquatch.* Houghton Mifflin, c2011. IL 3–6 (Non-fiction)
Draws on interviews with cryptozoologists, linguistics experts, anthropologists, biologists, and others to examine evidence for and against the existence of Sasquatch.

Halls, Kelly Milner. *Tales of the Cryptids: Mysterious Creatures That May or May Not Exist.* Darby Creek Publishing, c2006. 72p. IL 3–6, Lexile: 1160 (Non-fiction)
Introduces young readers to cryptozoology, the study of animals that may or may not be real.

Johnston, Tony. *Bigfoot Cinderrrrella.* Puffin Books, 2000, c1998. 32p. IL K–3, Lexile: 570
This version of the familiar story in which a mistreated stepchild finds happiness with the "man" of her dreams is set in the old-growth forest and features Bigfoot characters.

Kent, Jack. *There's No Such Thing as a Dragon.* Dragonfly Books, 2009, c1975. 32p. IL K–3
Billy Bixbee's mother will not admit that dragons exist until it is nearly too late.

Myers, Bill. *My Life as a Bigfoot Breath Mint.* Tommy Nelson, c1997. 113p. IL 3–6, Lexile: 690
Wally's visit to the Fantasmo World amusement park, where his Uncle Max works as a stuntman, turns into a disaster involving computer errors, runaway rides, and other outrageous mistakes.

Cryptids

Osborne, Mary Pope. *Blizzard of the Blue Moon.* Random House, c2006. 110p. IL 3–6, Lexile: 570
A magic tree house carries Jack and Annie to New York City in 1938 on a mission to rescue the last unicorn.

Pilkey, Dav. *Ricky Ricotta's Mighty Robot: An Adventure Novel.* Scholastic, c2000. 111p. IL K–3, Lexile: 340
Ricky Ricotta, a small mouse, saves a giant robot from his evil creator, Dr. Stinky. In turn, the robot protects Ricky from the bullies at school and saves the city from Dr. Stinky's plan to destroy it.

Roberts, Rachel. *Song of the Unicorns.* Seven Seas, c2008. 223p. IL 3–6
Emily, Adriane, and Kara—three friends who have learned they are destined to be magic masters—travel to New Mexico to visit Emily's father and become involved in a quest to save a herd of baby unicorns from an evil hunter.

Robertson, M. P. *Hieronymus Betts and His Unusual Pets.* Frances Lincoln Children's Books, 2005. 26p. IL K–3
This book for early readers describes the strange pets of Hieronymus Betts.

Rodda, Emily. *The Unicorn.* HarperCollins, c2004. 106p. IL 3–6, Lexile: 530
When wicked Queen Valda of the Outlands threatens both the Fairy Realm and the human world, Jessie seeks the help of the unicorns.

Smith, Roland. *Cryptid Hunters.* Hyperion Paperbacks for Children, 2006, c2005. 348p. IL 5–8, Lexile: 750
Grace and Marty, along with their mysterious uncle, are dropped into the middle of the Congolese jungle, where they search for the twins' missing photojournalist parents.

Smith, Roland. *Sasquatch.* Hyperion Paperbacks for Children, 1999, c1998. 188p. IL 5–8, Lexile: 680
Thirteen-year-old Dylan follows his father into the woods on the slopes of Mount St. Helens, which is on the brink of another eruption, in an attempt to protect the resident Sasquatch from ruthless hunters.

Yomtov, Nelson. *Tracking Sea Monsters, Bigfoot, and Other Legendary Beasts.* Capstone Press, c2011. 48p. IL 5–8
This account describes the search for animals that may or may not exist, including evidence for and against the existence of cryptids.

Yorke, Malcolm. *Beastly Tales: Yeti, Bigfoot, and the Loch Ness Monster.* DK Publishing, 1998. 48p. IL K–3, Lexile: 850 (Non-fiction)
Using simple text with illustrations, this book presents information on mysterious monsters, such as Bigfoot, Yeti, and the Loch Ness monster, and includes real-life stories of people who claim to have seen these beasts.

DNA and Genetics

Brown, Jeremy. *Body of Evidence.* Scholastic, c2006. 197p. IL 5–8, Lexile: 850
Readers are challenged to solve fifty-one short mysteries from the crime files of CSI West Burton. Answers are provided for each case.

Cadbury, Deborah. *The Lost King of France: How DNA Solved the Mystery of the Murdered Son of Louis XVI and Marie-Antoinette.* St. Martin's Griffin, 2003, c2002. 299p. IL AD (Non-fiction)
Explains how twenty-first-century researchers, with the help of DNA testing, finally solved the two-hundred-year-old mystery about the true fate of Marie Antoinette's son.

Collins, Max Allan. *CSI: Crime Scene Investigation Omnibus. Volume 1.* IDW Publishing, c2009. 361p. IL AD (Non-fiction)
A collection of graphic stories based on the popular television show *CSI*, in which a group of forensic investigators use their skills to solve crimes in the Las Vegas area.

Cornwell, Patricia Daniels. *At Risk.* Berkley Books, 2007, c2006, 289p. IL AD
A Massachusetts district attorney running for governor decides to use a radical new DNA technology to solve a long-ago murder, but his efforts spur another outbreak of violence.

Ferguson, Alane. *The Angel of Death: A Forensic Mystery.* Sleuth/Viking, 2006. 258p. IL YA, Lexile: 770
While investigating the murder of her English teacher, seventeen-year-old Cameryn Mahoney, who works as an assistant coroner for her father, begins a romance with the most popular guy in school, awaits the arrival of her long-missing mother, and puts her life in danger.

Ferguson, Alane. *The Christopher Killer: A Forensic Mystery.* Sleuth/Viking, 2006. 274p. IL YA, Lexile: 800
On the payroll as an assistant to her coroner father, seventeen-year-old Cameryn Mahoney uses her knowledge of forensic medicine to catch the killer of a friend while putting herself in terrible danger.

Halam, Ann. *Dr. Franklin's Island.* Dell Laurel-Leaf, 2003, c2002. 245p. IL YA, Lexile: 690
When their plane crashes over the Pacific Ocean, three science students are left stranded on a tropical island and then imprisoned by a doctor who is performing horrifying experiments on humans involving the transfer of animal genes.

Junkin, Tim. *Bloodsworth.* Algonquin Books of Chapel Hill, 2005, c2004. 294p. IL AD (Non-fiction)
This account examines the case of Kirk Bloodsworth, who was sentenced to death for the rape and murder of a nine-year-old girl in 1984, discussing how his continuous claims of innocence led to the evidence from the crime scene being subjected to the new technology of DNA testing. Bloodsworth was eventually pardoned by the governor of Maryland.

Picoult, Jodi. *My Sister's Keeper: A Novel.* Atria Books, c2004. 423p. IL AD, Lexile: 840
Thirteen-year-old Anna was conceived specifically to provide blood and bone marrow for her sister Kate, who was diagnosed with a rare form of leukemia at the age of two. Anna decides to sue her parents for control of her body when her mother wants her to donate a kidney to Kate.

DNA and Genetics

Picoult, Jodi. *Second Glance: A Novel.* Atria Books, c2003. 425p. IL AD, Lexile: 840
When an old man puts a piece of land up for sale in Vermont, the local Abenaki Indian tribe protests, claiming the site is a burial ground. When odd, supernatural events start plaguing the town, a ghost hunter is hired by the developer to help convince residents that there is nothing spiritual about the property.

Preston, Richard. *The Cobra Event.* Ballantine Books, 1998. 432p. IL AD, Lexile: 840
Dr. Alice Austen, an officer with the Epidemic Intelligence Service branch of the Centers for Disease Control and Prevention, goes to New York to investigate the hideous and mysterious death of a seventeen-year-old girl. In the course of her investigation, she uncovers a terrorist plot involving the use of biological weapons.

Reichs, Kathleen J. *Fatal Voyage.* Scribner, c2001. 527p. IL AD
Forensic anthropologist Temperance Brennan finds her involvement in the aftermath of an airplane crash becoming increasingly dangerous as she attempts to discover why the plane went down and who is responsible.

Reichs, Kathy. *Virals.* Razorbill, c2010. 454p. IL YA, Lexile: 480
Tory Brennan and her friends are exposed to a canine parvovirus when they rescue a dog from a medical testing facility. They soon realize they have heightened senses, which they use to solve a cold-case murder.

Reilly, Philip. *Abraham Lincoln's DNA and Other Adventures in Genetics.* Cold Spring Harbor Laboratory Press, c2000. 339p. IL AD (Non-fiction)
In these twenty-four stories, the author summarizes what is being learned from the study of human genes and considers the effects of those discoveries on society.

Roach, Mary. *Stiff: The Curious Lives of Human Cadavers.* W. W. Norton, c2003. 303p. IL AD, Lexile: 1230 (Non-fiction)
This account explores how human cadavers have been used throughout history, including how the use of dead bodies has benefited every aspect of human existence.

Rose, Malcolm. *Lost Bullet.* Kingfisher, 2005. 204p. IL 5–8, Lexile: 770
Recently qualified as a forensic investigator, sixteen-year-old Luke Harding is assigned to the slums of London, where he and his robotic sidekick Malc investigate a doctor's murder.

Werlin, Nancy. *Double Helix.* Sleuth/Puffin, 2005, c2003. 250p. IL YA, Lexile: 690
Eighteen-year-old Eli discovers a shocking secret about his life and his family while working for a Nobel Prize–winning scientist whose specialty is genetic engineering.

Weyn, Suzanne. *The Bar Code Tattoo.* Scholastic, c2004. 252p. IL YA, Lexile: 720
Kayla is ostracized at school because she refused to get the required tattooed bar code; now she and her family must go on the run to avoid the threats made against them.

Investing

Bailey, Gerry. *Get Rich Quick?: Earning Money.* Compass Point Books, 2006. 47p. IL 3–6 (Non-fiction), Lexile: 1000

This introduction to earning money, presented in simple text with illustrations, explains banks, inflation, investing, and more.

Bochner, Arthur Berg. *The New Totally Awesome Money Book for Kids (and Their Parents).* Newmarket Press, c2007. 189p. IL 5–8 (Non-fiction)

The author discusses topics such as budgeting, credit cards, saving, investing, and paying for college, and provides games, riddles, and quizzes related to financial issues.

Clements, Andrew. *Lunch Money.* Simon & Schuster Books for Young Readers, c2005. 222p. IL 3–6, Lexile: 840

Twelve-year-old Greg, who has always been good at money-making projects, is surprised to find himself teaming up with his lifelong rival, Maura, to create a series of comic books to sell at school.

Croke, Liam. *I'm Broke!: The Money Handbook.* Crabtree Publishing, 2009. 48p. IL 5–8, Lexile: 1030 (Non-fiction)

This introduction to personal finances provides advice, facts, and quizzes on budgeting, saving, banking, the economy, loans, investments, credit cards, and more.

Fradin, Dennis B. *Investing.* Marshall Cavendish Benchmark, c2011. 64p. IL 3–6 (Non-fiction)

The author answers basic questions that students ask when learning about the financial skills needed for adulthood, including investing money in the stock market, bonds and mutual funds, gold, and collectibles.

Holyoke, Nancy. *A Smart Girl's Guide to Money: How to Make It, Save It, and Spend It.* Pleasant Company, c2006. 95p. IL 3–6 (Non-fiction)

This practical guide to money smarts for girls offers advice on how to identify spending style, tips on running a business, and information on saving and investing. It also includes 101 money-making ideas.

Karlitz, Gail. *Growing Money: A Complete Investing Guide for Kids.* Price Stern Sloan, c2010. 143p. IL 3–6 (Non-fiction)

The author explains different types of investing—savings accounts, bonds, stocks, and mutual funds—and provides information to help children make decisions on each kind of investment.

McGillian, Jamie Kyle. *The Kids' Money Book: Earning, Saving, Spending, Investing, Donating.* Sterling, 2004, c2003. 96p. IL 3–6 (Non-fiction)

This introduction to personal finance explains how to manage money, from earning an allowance to budgeting to saving for college.

Minden, Cecilia. *Investing: Making Your Money Work for You.* Cherry Lake Pub., c2008. 32p. IL 3–6 (Non-fiction)

This introduction to financial literacy looks at ways in which people can put their money to work for them through investing. It includes notes designed to help readers identify the skills needed

Investing

for success in the twenty-first century in the areas of learning and innovation, business and money, and life and career.

Paulsen, Gary. *Lawn Boy.* Wendy Lamb Books, c2007. 88p. IL 5–8, Lexile: 780
Things get out of hand for a twelve-year-old boy when a neighbor convinces him to expand his summer lawn mowing business.

Justice

Alphin, Elaine Marie. *The Perfect Shot.* Carolrhoda Books, c2005. 360p. IL YA, Lexile: 990
Brian uses basketball to block out memories of his girlfriend and her family, who were murdered; however, the upcoming trial and a high school history assignment force him to face the past.

Crutcher, Chris. *Whale Talk.* Greenwillow Books, c2001. 220p. IL YA, Lexile: 1000
Intellectually and athletically gifted, TJ, a multiracial, adopted teenager, shuns organized sports and the gung-ho athletes at his high school—until he agrees to form a swimming team and recruits some of the school's less popular students to join it.

Farmer, Nancy. *The House of the Scorpion.* Atheneum Books for Young Readers, c2002. 380p. IL 5–8, Lexile: 660
In a future where humans despise clones, Matt enjoys special status as the young clone of El Patron, the 142-year-old leader of a corrupt drug empire nestled between Mexico and the United States.

Flinn, Alex. *Fade to Black.* HarperTempest, 2006, c2005. 184p. IL YA, Lexile: 590
An HIV-positive high school student hospitalized after being attacked, the bigot accused of the crime, and the only witness, a classmate with Down syndrome, reveal how the assault has changed their lives as they tell of its aftermath.

Frank, E. R. *America: A Novel.* Simon Pulse, 2003, c2002. 242p. IL YA, Lexile: 610
America, a runaway boy who is being treated at Ridgeway, a New York hospital, finds himself opening up to one of the doctors on staff and revealing things about himself that he had always vowed to keep secret.

Klass, David. *Dark Angel.* Farrar, Straus and Giroux, 2005. 311p. IL YA, Lexile: 820
When his older brother is released from prison, seventeen-year-old Jeff's family secret is revealed, causing upheaval in his home, school, and love life.

McCarthy, Susan Carol. *Lay That Trumpet in Our Hands.* Bantam, 2002. 281p. IL AD
After Florida Klansmen abduct and kill a nineteen-year-old African American citrus picker in the spring of 1951, Reesa McMahon finds the world she knows and the people she loves have been forever changed by the tragedy.

Morpurgo, Michael. *Private Peaceful.* Scholastic Press, 2004, c2003. 202p. IL YA, Lexile: 860
When Thomas Peaceful's older brother is forced to join the British Army, Thomas decides to sign up as well, even though he is only fourteen years old, to prove himself to his country, his family, his childhood love Molly, and himself.

Myers, Walter Dean. *Monster.* HarperCollins, c1999. 281p. IL YA, Lexile: 670
While on trial as an accomplice to a murder, sixteen-year-old Steve Harmon records his experiences in prison and in the courtroom in the form of a film script as he tries to come to terms with the course his life has taken.

Rose, Reginald. *Twelve Angry Men.* Penguin Books, 2006. 73p. IL AD
In this play, a juror in a murder trial holds out on a guilty verdict and tries to get the other jurors to look at the situation without being swayed by their personal prejudices or biases.

From *101 Great, Ready-to-Use Book Lists for Teens* by Nancy J. Keane. Santa Barbara, CA: Libraries Unlimited. Copyright © 2012.

Justice

Strasser, Todd. *Give a Boy a Gun.* Simon Pulse, 2002, c2000. 208p. IL YA, Lexile: 760
Events leading up to a night of terror at a high school dance are told from the point of view of various people involved.

Volponi, Paul. *Black and White.* Viking, 2005. 185p. IL YA, Lexile: 710
Two star high school basketball players—one black and one white—experience the justice system differently after committing a crime together and getting caught.

Zusak, Markus. *The Book Thief.* Knopf, c2006. 552p. IL YA, Lexile: 730
Trying to make sense of the horrors of World War II, Death relates the story of Liesel—a young German girl whose book-stealing and story-telling talents help sustain her family and the Jewish man they are hiding, as well as their neighbors.

Narrative Non-fiction about the Civil War

Abnett, Dan. *The Battle of Gettysburg: Spilled Blood on Sacred Ground.* Rosen Central, 2007. 48p. IL 5–8 (Non-fiction)
> Presents a brief depiction of the Civil War battle at Gettysburg, Pennsylvania, in July 1863. The book describes major Union and Confederate generals as well as details of the fight.

Abnett, Dan. *The Battle of the Wilderness: Deadly Inferno.* Rosen, 2007. 48p. IL 5–8 (Non-fiction)
> Tells the story of the Battle of the Wilderness in graphic novel format, also providing introductory information on the important commanders, the Civil War itself, and the course of the two days of fighting.

Abnett, Dan. *The* Monitor *versus the* Merrimac*: Ironclads at War.* Rosen Central, 2007. 48p. IL 5–8 (Non-fiction)
> Presents a brief depiction of the Civil War clash between the Confederate ironclad *Merrimac*— renamed the *Virginia*—and the Union ironclad *Monitor* at Hampton Roads, Virginia, in March 1862.

Allen, Thomas B. *Mr. Lincoln's High-Tech War: How the North Used the Telegraph, Railroads, Surveillance Balloons, Iron-Clads, High-Powered Weapons, and More to Win the Civil War.* National Geographic, c2009. 144p. IL 5–8, Lexile: 1180 (Non-fiction)
> Examines how Abraham Lincoln's interest in technology played a role in the outcome of the Civil War. The book explains how the telegraph, railroads, surveillance balloons, and other inventions helped the North win the war and rebuild the economy in the war's aftermath.

Burgan, Michael. *Battle of the Ironclads.* Compass Point Books, c2006. 48p. IL 5–8, Lexile: 860 (Non-fiction)
> Presents an account of the first naval battle between metal ships, which took place during the U.S. Civil War at Hampton Roads, Virginia, in 1862, between the *Monitor* and the *Virginia*.

Burgan, Michael. *Fort Sumter.* Compass Point Books, c2006. 48p. IL 5–8, Lexile: 920 (Non-fiction)
> Provides an account of the Confederacy's attack on Fort Sumter in Charleston Harbor in April 1861, which marked the beginning of the American Civil War.

Burgan, Michael. *The Gettysburg Address.* Compass Point Books, c2006. 48p. IL 5–8 (Non-fiction)
> Examines the events surrounding Lincoln's famous "Gettysburg Address" given in November 1863, and describes Lincoln's views on slavery, the aftermath of the Battle of Gettysburg, and other important dates and people.

Burgan, Michael. *The Lincoln–Douglas Debates.* Compass Point Books, c2006. 48p. IL 5–8, Lexile: 890 (Non-fiction)
> This account of the Lincoln–Douglas debates of 1858 over slavery in the United States explains how these debates helped Lincoln win the presidential election.

Burgan, Michael. *The Missouri Compromise.* Compass Point Books, c2006. 48p. IL 5–8, Lexile: 910 (Non-fiction)
> An account of the Missouri Compromise of 1820, which banned slavery above the latitude of Missouri's southern border, except in the state of Missouri itself.

Narrative Non-fiction about the Civil War

Burgan, Michael. *The Reconstruction Amendments.* Compass Point Books, c2006. 48p. IL 5–8, Lexile: 980 (Non-fiction)

A history of the role of the Thirteenth, Fourteenth, and Fifteenth Amendments to the U.S. Constitution in the reconstruction of the southern states after the Civil War.

Butzer, C. M. *Gettysburg: The Graphic Novel.* Bowen Press/Collins, c2009. 80p. IL 5–8 (Non-fiction)

A comic book–style depiction of the Battle of Gettysburg; the national movement to create a memorial at the battle site; and the day of Lincoln's Gettysburg Address in 1863, drawn from first-person letters, speeches, and other primary sources.

Doeden, Matt. *The Civil War: An Interactive History Adventure.* Capstone Press, c2010. 112p. IL 5–8, Lexile: 650 (Non-fiction)

Reveals historical details from the perspective of a Union soldier at Gettysburg, a civilian during the siege of Vicksburg, and a Confederate soldier at Chancellorsville.

Dougherty, Terri. *America's Deadliest Day: The Battle of Antietam.* Capstone Press, c2009. 32p. IL 5–8, Lexile: 740 (Non-fiction)

Offers a brief overview of the Battle of Antietam, describing the events surrounding the bloodiest battle of the Civil War and its impact on American history.

Figley, Marty Rhodes. *President Lincoln, Willie Kettles, and the Telegraph Machine.* Millbrook Press, c2011. 48p. IL 3–6, Lexile: 590 (Non-fiction)

Fifteen-year-old Willie Kettles awaits good news from Richmond, Virginia, while working during the Civil War as a telegraph operator in the War Department building in Washington, D.C.

Gillis, Jennifer Blizin. *The Confederate Soldier.* Compass Point Books, c2007. 48p. IL 5–8, Lexile: 1060 (Non-fiction)

Describes the lives of Confederate soldiers in the Civil War, covering recruitment, camp life, and battle, as well as soldiers' experiences after General Robert E. Lee surrendered to the Union army.

Hama, Larry. *The Battle of Antietam: "The Bloodiest Day of Battle."* Rosen Central, 2007. 48p. IL 5–8 (Non-fiction)

Presents a brief depiction of the Civil War battle near Antietam Creek in Sharpsburg, Maryland, in September 1862. The book describes major Union and Confederate generals and provides details of the fight.

Hama, Larry. *The Battle of First Bull Run: The Civil War Begins.* Rosen, 2007. 48p. IL 5–8 (Non-fiction)

Tells the story of the Battle of First Bull Run in graphic novel format, while also providing introductory information on the important commanders and each side of the conflict's preparation for war.

Heinrichs, Ann. *The Underground Railroad.* Compass Point Books, c2001. 48p. IL 5–8, Lexile: 820 (Non-fiction)

Examines the lives of some of the people involved with the Underground Railroad, a network by which slaves were able to escape to the North. The book includes photographs and engravings, a glossary, listings of important dates and people, and an index.

Narrative Non-fiction about the Civil War

Jarrow, Gail. *Lincoln's Flying Spies: Thaddeus Lowe and the Civil War Balloon Corps.* Calkins Creek, c2010. 109p. IL 5-8, Lexile: 1060 (Non-fiction)
   Provides an account of Thaddeus Lowe's efforts to provide intelligence to Union forces during the American Civil War, detailing how he managed to telegraph messages to the War Department in Washington, D.C., from a silk hydrogen balloon that floated over the battlefields.

Johnson, Jennifer. *Gettysburg: The Bloodiest Battle of the Civil War.* Franklin Watts, c2010. 64p. IL 5–8, Lexile: 890 (Non-fiction)
   A collection of brief stories about the Battle of Gettysburg, which took place in early July 1863.

Lassieur, Allison. *The Battle of Bull Run: An Interactive History Adventure.* Capstone Press, c2009. 112p. IL 5–8, Lexile: 630 (Non-fiction)
   A brief description of the events surrounding the Battle of Bull Run during the Civil War, including historical details from the perspective of a Union soldier, a Confederate soldier, and a civilian.

McNeese, Tim. *The Civil War Era, 1851–1865.* Chelsea House, c2010. 144p. IL 5–8 (Non-fiction)
   Chronicles the history of the Civil War, discussing the reasons why the North and South turned against each other, and highlighting key battles and events from 1861 to 1865. The book includes a chronology and a timeline.

Nemeth, Jason D. *Voices of the Civil War: Stories from the Battlefields.* Capstone Press, c2011. 32p. IL 3–6 (Non-fiction)
   Describes the experiences of some of the people who lived through the Civil War.

O'Shei, Tim. *Civil War Spies.* Capstone Press, c2008. 32p. IL 5–8, Lexile: 760 (Non-fiction)
   An exploration of the history of spying during the Civil War, which provides information on significant individuals and intelligence gathering techniques. The book includes fact boxes, photographs, a glossary, and suggestions for further reading.

Raatma, Lucia. *African-American Soldiers in the Revolutionary War.* Compass Point Books, c2009. 48p. IL 5–8, Lexile: 1020 (Non-fiction)
   Describes the experiences of African Americans who were recruited by the Union to fight in the Civil War.

Raatma, Lucia. *The Carpetbaggers.* Compass Point Books, c2005. 48p IL 5–8, Lexile: 970 (Non-fiction)
   Presents a study of the Reconstruction period following the Civil War and discusses both the positive and negative effects of Northern carpetbaggers and the reasons why reconstruction failed.

Ratliff, Thomas M. *You Wouldn't Want to Be a Civil War Soldier!: A War You'd Rather Not Fight.* Franklin Watts, 2004. 32p. IL 3–6, Lexile: 960 (Non-fiction)
   Brief text, sidebars, labeled illustrations, and humorous cartoons depict life and events during the four years of the Civil War.

Rebman, Renee C. *The Union Soldier.* Compass Point Books, c2007. 48p. IL 5–8, Lexile: 940 (Non-fiction)
   Describes the life of the average Union soldier in the Civil War, the leadership of generals Ulysses S. Grant and William Tecumseh Sherman, the enlistment of women posing as men, and the experiences and contributions of African American troops.

Narrative Non-fiction about the Civil War

Santella, Andrew. *Surrender at Appomattox.* Compass Point Books, c2006. 48p. IL 5–8, Lexile: 880 (Non-fiction)

Provides an account of Confederate General Robert E. Lee's surrender to Union General Ulysses S. Grant at Appomattox Court House in April 1865, which ended the U.S. Civil War.

Senior, Kathryn. *You Wouldn't Want to Be a Nurse During the American Civil War!: A Job That's Not for the Squeamish.* Franklin Watts, 2010. 32p. IL 3–6, Lexile: 930 (Non-fiction)

A reporter is sent to the battlefields of the South to learn what it takes to be a nurse during the Civil War.

Sheinkin, Steve. *Two Miserable Presidents: Everything Your Schoolbooks Didn't Tell You about the Civil War.* Roaring Brook Press, 2009, c2008. 244p. IL 5–8, Lexile: 920 (Non-fiction)

Describes all the issues and events—large, small, and even personal—that led up to the Civil War, covering the stories of the soldiers and statesmen involved.

Silvey, Anita. *I'll Pass for Your Comrade: Women Soldiers in the Civil War.* Clarion Books, c2008. 115p. IL 5–8, Lexile: 1130 (Non-fiction)

Profiles the lives and service of a number of women who disguised themselves as men and fought during the Civil War.

Skog, Jason. *The Weeping Time.* Compass Point Books, c2008. 48p. IL 5–8, Lexile: 1020 (Non-fiction)

Historical photographs and text describe the Weeping Time, an event in which 436 slaves were sold on a racetrack in Savannah, Georgia, in 1859.

Warren, Andrea. *Under Siege!: Three Children at the Civil War Battle for Vicksburg.* Melanie Kroupa Books, 2009. 166p. IL 5–8, Lexile: 1110 (Non-fiction)

Tells the story of Lucy McRae and Willie Lord, survivors of the battle for Vicksburg in 1863. The book describes how they lived in caves and underground bunkers as Union artillery bombarded the town for six weeks; it also tells of young Frederick Grant, son of General Ulysses S. Grant, who witnessed the carnage of that battle.

Westwell, Ian. *The Civil War, 1861–1865.* Brown Bear Books, c2008. 48p. IL 5–8 (Non-fiction)

Presents a brief description of how and why the Civil War was fought, with biographies of major players on both sides of the conflict and eyewitness accounts.

Worth, Richard. *African Americans during Reconstruction.* Chelsea House Publishers, c2006. 112p. IL 5–8 (Non-fiction)

Examines the challenges faced by African Americans during the Reconstruction era following the Civil War, discussing the expanded social and political rights granted to former slaves by the Reconstruction Act of 1867, as well as the continuing discrimination, segregation, and violence against African Americans.

Physical Science for Ninth Grade

Avi. *Blue Heron.* Avon, 1993, c1992. 186p. IL 5–8, Lexile: 590
    While spending the month of August on the Massachusetts shore with her father, stepmother, and their new baby, almost thirteen-year-old Maggie finds beauty in and draws strength from a great blue heron, even as the family around her unravels.

Burnford, Sheila Every. *The Incredible Journey.* Delacorte Press, 1996, c1961. 148p. IL 5–8, Lexile: 1320
    A Siamese cat, an old bull terrier, and a young Labrador retriever travel together 250 miles through the Canadian wilderness to find their family.

Dickinson, Peter. *A Bone from a Dry Sea.* Bantam Doubleday Dell Books for Young Readers, 1995, c1992. 199p. IL YA, Lexile: 1040
    In two parallel stories, an intelligent female member of a prehistoric tribe becomes instrumental in advancing the lot of her people, and the daughter of a paleontologist is visiting him on a dig in Africa when important fossil remains are discovered.

Hesse, Karen. *The Music of Dolphins.* Scholastic, 2005, c1996. 181p. IL 3–6, Lexile: 560
    Using sophisticated computer technology, a fifteen-year-old girl who has been raised by dolphins records her thoughts about her reintroduction to the human world.

Hiaasen, Carl. *Hoot.* Alfred A. Knopf, c2002. 292p. IL 5–8, Lexile: 760
    Roy, who is new to his small Florida community, becomes involved in another boy's attempt to save a colony of burrowing owls from a proposed construction site.

Hickam, Homer H. *October Sky: A Memoir.* Dell, 2000, c1998. 428p, IL AD, Lexile: 900
    Homer Hickam, the introspective son of a mine superintendent and a mother determined to get him out of Coalwood, West Virginia, forever, nurtures a dream to send rockets into outer space—an ambition that changes his life and the lives of everyone living in Coalwood in 1957.

Hobbs, Will. *Wild Man Island.* HarperCollins, c2002. 184p. IL 5–8, Lexile: 690
    After fourteen-year-old Andy slips away from his kayaking group to visit the wilderness site of his archaeologist father's death, a storm strands him on Admiralty Island, Alaska. He manages to survive on the island, encounters unexpected animal and human inhabitants, and looks for traces of the earliest prehistoric immigrants to America.

Mikaelsen, Ben. *Rescue Josh McGuire.* Hyperion Paperbacks for Children, 1993, c1991. 266p. IL 5–8, Lexile: 680
    When thirteen-year-old Josh runs away to the mountains of Montana with an orphaned bear cub destined for laboratory testing, both must fight for their lives in a sudden snowstorm.

Mikaelsen, Ben. *Stranded.* Disney/Hyperion Books, c1995. 247p. IL 5–8, Lexile: 610
    Twelve-year-old Koby, who has lost a foot in an accident, sees a chance to prove her self-reliance to her parents when she tries to rescue two stranded pilot whales near her home in the Florida Keys.

Mowat, Farley. *Never Cry Wolf.* Holt, Rinehart and Winston, 1999, c1963. 215p. IL YA (Non-fiction)
    The author reports his observations of the Keewatin Lands northwest of the Hudson Bay, and the caribou and wolf populations living in the region. The book includes an afterword section with assorted writings about wolves.

Physical Science for Ninth Grade

North, Sterling. *Rascal.* Dutton, 1984, c1963. 189p. IL 5–8, Lexile: 1140
   The author recalls his carefree life in a small Midwestern town at the close of World War I, and his adventures with his pet raccoon, Rascal.

Smith, Dominic. *The Beautiful Miscellaneous: A Novel.* Washington Square Press, 2008, c2007. 329p. IL AD
   Seventeen-year-old Nathan Nelson awakens from a two-week coma and finds he has an extraordinary memory. Even with his new ability and a change of schools, however, he cannot live up to his genius father's high expectations.

Taylor, Theodore. *Sniper.* Harcourt, 2007, c1989. 229p. IL YA
   Fifteen-year-old Ben must cope alone when a mysterious sniper begins shooting the big cats in his family's private zoological preserve.

Taylor, Theodore. *The Weirdo.* Harcourt, 2006, c1991. 292p. IL YA, Lexile: 770
   Seventeen-year-old Chip Clewt fights to save the black bears in the Powhatan Swamp, a National Wildlife Refuge in North Carolina.

Poems for Two Voices

Ciardi, John. *You Read to Me, I'll Read to You.* HarperTrophy, 1987, c1962. 64p. IL 3–6, Lexile: NP
Contains poetry for parents to read to their children and simpler poems for children to read to their parents.

Fleischman, Paul. *I Am Phoenix: Poems for Two Voices.* HarperTrophy, 1989, c1985. 51p. IL 5–8, Lexile: NP
A collection of poems about birds to be read aloud by two voices.

Fleischman, Paul. *Joyful Noise: Poems for Two Voices.* HarperCollins, c1988. 44p. IL 5–8, Lexile: NP
A collection of poems describing the characteristics and activities of a variety of insects.

Franco, Betsy. *Messing around on the Monkey Bars: And Other School Poems for Two Voices.* Candlewick Press, 2009. 45p. IL K–3
A collection of nineteen poems for children about what happens on a normal school day.

Hall, Donald. *I Am the Dog, I Am the Cat.* Dial Books, c1994. 32p. IL K–3, Lexile: NP
A dog and a cat take turns explaining what is wonderful about being who they are.

Harrison, David L. *Farmer's Dog Goes to the Forest: Rhymes for Two Voices.* Wordsong/Boyds Mills Press, 2005. 32p. IL K–3
A collection of illustrated rhymes to be read aloud in two voices, in which a curious dog interviews all the animals on a farm.

Harrison, David L. *Farmer's Garden: Rhymes for Two Voices.* Wordsong, 2003, c2000. 32p. IL K–3
A curious dog asks various animals what they are doing in the garden in this picture book featuring verse with questions and answers.

Hoberman, Mary Ann. *You Read to Me, I'll Read to You: Very Short Mother Goose Tales to Read Together.* Little, Brown, c2005. 32p. IL K–3, Lexile: NP
A collection of short retellings of familiar Mother Goose fairy tales, each told in two voices and designed especially for young children and adults to read together.

Shakespeare Alternatives

Asher, Sandy. *Romeo and Juliet—Together (and Alive!) At Last: A Middle-School Romantic Farce in Two Acts.* Dramatic Publishing, c2004. 93p. IL YA
> Eighth-graders Pete Saltz and Anabell Stackpoole, who are in love but too shy to speak to each other, are voted to play the lead roles in their class performance of *Romeo and Juliet*. Even though the production does not run smoothly, their classmates succeed in bringing the couple together.

Blackwood, Gary L. *The Shakespeare Stealer.* Puffin Books, 2000, 1998. 216p. IL 3–6, Lexile: 840
> A young orphan boy is ordered by his master to infiltrate Shakespeare's acting troupe and steal the script of *Hamlet*, but instead he discovers the meaning of friendship and loyalty.

Cooper, Susan. *King of Shadows.* Margaret K. McElderry Books, c1999. 186p. IL 5–8, Lexile: 1010
> While in London as part of an all-boy acting company preparing to perform in a replica of the famous Globe Theatre, Nat Field suddenly finds himself transported back to 1599 and performing in the original theater under the tutelage of Shakespeare himself.

Cover, Arthur Byron. *Macbeth: The Graphic Novel.* Puffin Books, 2005. 176p. IL 5–8
> A science-fiction graphic novel adaptation of William Shakespeare's tragedy of brutal ambition, in which Macbeth, a dragon-riding nobleman in a future world, kills his king with the help of his power-hungry wife and finds himself battling rivals and vengeance seekers for his life and the throne.

Coville, Bruce. *The Skull of Truth.* Harcourt, 2002, c1997. 194p. IL 3–6, Lexile: 700
> Charlie, a sixth grader with a compulsion to tell lies, acquires a mysterious skull that forces its owner to tell only the truth, causing some awkward moments before he understands its power.

Davies, Katharine. *The Madness of Love: A Novel.* Random House Trade Paperbacks, 2005, c2004. 253p. IL AD
> After learning her twin brother has broken their childhood promise and left her behind in London, Valentina masquerades as a gardener to Leo, who dreams of restoring his estates gardens to their former splendor. Valentina soon finds herself falling for Leo, despite his attraction to another woman.

Dean, Pamela. *Tam Lin.* Firebird, 2006, c1991. 468p. IL YA
> Janet, a coed at a small Midwestern college in Vietnam-era America, becomes involved with a group of theater and classics students and uncovers a world of strange rumors and traditions.

Draper, Sharon M. *Romiette and Julio.* Atheneum Books for Young Readers, c1999. 236p. IL YA, Lexile: 610
> Romiette, an African American girl, and Julio, a Hispanic American boy, discover that they attend the same high school after falling in love on the Internet, but are harassed by a gang whose members object to their interracial dating.

Fiedler, Lisa. *Dating Hamlet: Ophelia's Story.* Holt, 2002. 183p. IL YA
> In a story based on the Shakespeare play, Ophelia describes her relationship with Hamlet, learns the truth about her own father, and recounts the complicated events following the murder of Hamlet's father.

Shakespeare Alternatives

Fiedler, Lisa. *Romeo's Ex: Rosaline's Story.* Holt, 2006. 246p. IL YA, Lexile: 910
  In a story based on the Shakespeare play, sixteen-year-old Rosaline, who is studying to be a healer, becomes romantically entangled with the Montague family, even as her beloved young cousin, Juliet Capulet, defies the family feud and secretly marries Romeo.

Gehrman, Jody Elizabeth. *Confessions of a Triple Shot Betty.* Speak, 2009, c2008. 255p. IL YA, Lexile: 750
  Sixteen-year-olds Geena, Hero, and Amber spend the summer working at a Sonoma, California, coffee shop, where they experience romance, identity crises, and newfound friendships.

Gratz, Alan. *Something Rotten: A Horatio Wilkes Mystery.* Dial Books, c2007. 207p. IL YA, Lexile: 790
  In this contemporary story based on Shakespeare's play *Hamlet*, Horatio Wilkes seeks to solve the murder of his friend Hamilton Prince's father in Denmark, Tennessee.

Gratz, Alan. *Something Wicked: A Horatio Wilkes Mystery.* Speak, 2009. 265p. IL YA, Lexile: 740
  In this adaptation of Shakespeare's *Macbeth*, Horatio Wilkes seeks to solve the murder of Duncan MacKae at the Scottish Highland Games in Pigeon Forge, Tennessee, after his friend Malcolm, the son of Duncan MacKae, is identified as the lead suspect.

Klein, Lisa M. *Lady Macbeth's Daughter.* Bloomsbury, 2009. 291p. IL YA, Lexile: 730
  This tale based on Shakespeare's *Macbeth* is told by two voices speaking in alternating chapters. Ambitious Lady Macbeth tries to bear a son and win the throne of Scotland for her husband. Albia, their daughter who was banished at birth and raised by three weird sisters, falls in love, learns of her parentage, and seeks to free Scotland from tyranny.

Klein, Lisa M. *Ophelia: A Novel.* Bloomsbury, 2006. 328p. IL YA, Lexile: 860
  In this story based on Shakespeare's *Hamlet*, Ophelia tells of her life in the court at Elsinore, her love for Prince Hamlet, and her escape from the violence in Denmark.

Korman, Gordon. *Son of the Mob.* Hyperion Paperbacks, 2004, c2002. 262p. IL YA, Lexile: 690
  Seventeen-year-old Vince's life is constantly complicated by the fact that he is the son of a powerful Mafia boss—a relationship that threatens to destroy his romance with the daughter of an FBI agent.

Lawlor, Laurie. *The Two Loves of Will Shakespeare: A Novel.* Holiday House, c2006. 278p. IL YA, Lexile: 720
  After falling in love, eighteen-year-old Will Shakespeare, a bored apprentice in his father's glove business and often in trouble for various misdeeds, vows to live an upstanding life and pursue his passion for writing.

Marsden, John. *Hamlet: A Novel.* Candlewick Press, 2009, c2008. 229p. IL YA, Lexile: 760
  Grieving for the recent death of his beloved father and appalled by his mother's quick remarriage to his uncle, Hamlet, heir to the Danish throne, struggles with conflicting emotions, particularly after his father's ghost appeals to him to avenge his death.

Shakespeare Alternatives

Meyer, Carolyn. *Loving Will Shakespeare.* Harcourt, c2006. 265p. IL YA, Lexile: 950
Anne Hathaway has always dreamed of leaving the small cottage where she and her siblings live with their critical stepmother. When Will Shakespeare returns home and begins showing a serious interest in her, Anne must decide whether to follow her heart or play by the rules.

Myers, Walter Dean. *Street Love.* Amistad/HarperTeen, 2007, c2006. 134p. IL YA, Lexile: NP
In this story told in free verse, Damien, a seventeen-year-old from Harlem, takes a bold step to ensure that he and his new love, Junice, will not be separated.

Peet, Mal. *Exposure.* Candlewick Press, 2009. 430p. IL YA, Lexile: 760
Paul Faustino, South America's best soccer journalist, reports on the series of events that hurl Otello from the heights of being a beloved and successful soccer star, happily married to the pop singer Desdemona, into a downward spiral, in this novel loosely based on Shakespeare's play *Othello.*

Rees, Celia. *The Fool's Girl.* Bloomsbury, 2010. 297p. IL YA, Lexile: 780
Violetta travels to London with her comic companion, Feste, to recover the holy relic that was stolen from their kingdom by evil Malvolio, only to encounter the playwright William Shakespeare.

Scott, Michael. *The Alchemist.* Delacorte Press, c2007. 375p. IL YA, Lexile: 890
Fifteen-year-old twins, Sophie and Josh, find themselves caught up in the deadly struggle between rival alchemists, Nicholas Flamel and John Dee, over the possession of an ancient book that holds the secret formulas for alchemy and everlasting life.

Shulman, Irving. *West Side Story: A Novelization.* Pocket, 1967, c1961. 160p. IL YA
Maria, a young Puerto Rican girl living in New York, who is sister to Sharks gang leader Bernardo, falls in love with Tony, former leader of the rival gang, the Jets, setting the stage for tragedy.

Smiley, Jane. *A Thousand Acres: A Novel.* Anchor Books, 2003, c1991. 371p. IL AD
Dark truths and long-suppressed emotions come to the surface in 1979 when a successful Iowa farmer decides to cut one of his daughters out of his will.

Stoppard, Tom. *Rosencrantz & Guildenstern Are Dead.* Grove Press, 1967. 126p. IL YA, Lexile: NP
This play-within-a-play presents the story of Hamlet as seen through the eyes of Rosencrantz and Guildenstern.

Zindel, Lizabeth. *A Girl, a Ghost, and the Hollywood Hills.* Viking, 2010. 306p. IL YA, Lexile: 700
When the ghost of Holly's mother claims she was murdered by Holly's aunt, Claudia, Holly must decide how far she will go to get revenge.

Part 6

Teaching Literary Elements

Alliteration

Atwood, Margaret Eleanor. *Bashful Bob and Doleful Dorinda.* Bloomsbury Children's Books, Distributed by Holtzbrinck Publishers, 2006. 31p. IL K–3, Lexile: 960
> A story told mainly with words that begin with the letters "b" and "d," in which bashful Bob, who has been abandoned and raised by dogs, meets doleful Dorinda, who deals with dirty dishes, and the two become friends and eventually heroes.

Atwood, Margaret Eleanor. *Princess Prunella and the Purple Peanut.* Workman Publishing, c1995. 32p. IL K–3, Lexile: 530
> Prunella, a proud, prissy princess, plans to marry a pinheaded prince who will pamper her—until a wise old woman's spell puts a purple peanut on the princess's pretty nose.

Base, Graeme. *Animalia.* H. N. Abrams, 1987, c1986. 32p. IL K–3, Lexile: 860
> This alphabet book contains fantastic and detailed pictures, bearing such labels as "Lazy lions lounging in the local library."

Bayer, Jane. *A My Name Is Alice.* Dial Books for Young Readers, 1984. 30p IL K–3, Lexile: 370
> The well-known jump rope ditty, which is built on letters of the alphabet, is illustrated with animals from all over the world.

Buzzeo, Toni. *Dawdle Duckling.* Puffin Books, 2005, c2003. 32p. IL K–3, Lexile: 460
> Mama Duck tries to keep Dawdle Duckling together with his siblings, but he wants to dawdle and dream, preen and play, splash and spin.

Crimi, Carolyn. *Henry & the Buccaneer Bunnies.* Candlewick Press, 2005. 34p. IL K–3, Lexile: 910
> Captain Barnacle Black Ear, baddest of the Buccaneer Bunnies, is ashamed of his book-loving son, Henry, until the day a great storm approaches.

Edwards, Pamela Duncan. *Clara Caterpillar.* HarperCollins, c2001. 33p. IL K–3, Lexile: 660
> By camouflaging herself, Clara Caterpillar, who becomes a cream-colored butterfly, courageously saves Catisha the crimson-colored butterfly from a hungry crow.

Edwards, Pamela Duncan. *Dinorella: A Prehistoric Fairy Tale.* Hyperion Books for Children, c1997. 32p. IL K–3, Lexile: 530
> In this story, loosely based on the Cinderella tale but featuring dinosaurs, the Duke falls in love with Dinorella when she rescues him from the dreaded deinonychus at the Dinosaur Dance.

Edwards, Pamela Duncan. *Four Famished Foxes and Fosdyke.* HarperCollins, c1995. 32p. IL K–3, Lexile: 570
> This alliterative tale describes four fox kits who go hunting for meat in the barnyard while their gourmet brother fixes a vegetarian feast.

Edwards, Pamela Duncan. *Some Smug Slug.* HarperCollins, c1996. 32p. IL K–3, Lexile: 620
> A smug slug that will not listen to the animals around it comes to an unexpected end.

Fox, Mem. *Feathers and Fools.* Harcourt, c1989. 34p. IL K–3, Lexile: 960
> This modern fable focuses on some peacocks and swans who allow the fear of their differences to become so great that they end up destroying each other.

Alliteration

Gerstein, Mordicai. *The Absolutely Awful Alphabet.* Harcourt, c1999. 32p. IL K–3, Lexile: 690
This illustrated alphabet book for young readers features outrageous characters in the shape of each letter.

Palatini, Margie. *The Web Files.* Hyperion Books for Children, c2001. 32p. IL K–3, Lexile: 220
Ducktective Web and his partner try to quack the case of the pilfered peck of perfectly picked pickled peppers.

Seeger, Laura Vaccaro. *Walter Was Worried.* Roaring Brook Press, c2005. 34p. IL K–3, Lexile: 210
Children's faces, depicted with letters of the alphabet, react to the onset of a storm and its aftermath in this picture book, with the illustrations accompanied by simple alliterative text.

Sendak, Maurice. *Alligators All Around: An Alphabet.* Harper & Row, c1962. 32p. IL K–3, Lexile: NP
The letters of the alphabet are introduced by alligators engaged in a variety of activities.

Shaw, Nancy. *Sheep on a Ship.* Houghton Mifflin, 1989. 32p. IL K–3, Lexile: 160
Sheep on a deep-sea voyage run into trouble when a storm arises; they are glad to come paddling into port.

Steig, William. *Wizzil.* Farrar Straus Giroux, 2000. 32p, IL K–3, Lexile: 690
A bored witch causes trouble when she decides to take revenge on an old man, but her mischief leads to a happy ending.

Stevens, Janet. *The Great Fuzz Frenzy.* Harcourt, c2005. 48p. IL K–3, Lexile: 420
When a tennis ball lands in a prairie dog town, the residents find that their newfound frenzy for fuzz creates a fiasco.

Van Allsburg, Chris. *The Alphabet Theatre Proudly Presents "The Z Was Zapped": A Play in Twenty-Six Acts.* Houghton Mifflin, c1987. 56p. IL K–3, Lexile: BR
This illustrated book depicts how A was in an avalanche, B was badly bitten, C was cut to ribbons, and the other letters of the alphabet suffered similar mishaps.

From *101 Great, Ready-to-Use Book Lists for Teens* by Nancy J. Keane. Santa Barbara, CA: Libraries Unlimited. Copyright © 2012.

Analogies

Brisson, Pat. *Beach Is to Fun: A Book of Relationships*. Holt, 2004. 34p. IL K–3, Lexile: 120
A day at the beach is the occasion for this rhyming look at the relationships between things.

Jonas, Ann. *The Trek*. Mulberry Books, 1989, c1985. 32p. IL K–3, Lexile: 250
The city streets become a jungle, and then a desert, as a child forges her way to school, observing and avoiding all the wild animals posing as trees, chimneys, fences, and even fruit.

Lionni, Leo. *Matthew's Dream*. Knopf, 1995, c1991. 32p. IL K–3, Lexile: 560
A visit to an art museum inspires a young mouse to become a painter.

Lionni, Leo. *Swimmy.* Knopf, c1991. 32p. IL K–3, Lexile: 640
Swimmy, a small black fish, finds a way to protect a school of small red fish from their natural enemies.

Steig, William. *Rotten Island*. D. R. Godine, 1984, c1969. 32p. IL K–3, Lexile: 790
Rotten Island has always been a paradise for nasty creatures, until one awful day a beautiful flower begins to grow, threatening to spoil the island forever.

Wisniewski, David. *Golem*. Clarion Books, c1996. 32p. IL K–3, Lexile: 690
A saintly rabbi miraculously brings to life a clay giant who helps him watch over the Jews of sixteenth-century Prague.

Wisniewski, David. *Tough Cookie*. Lothrop, Lee & Shepard Books, c1999. 28p. IL 3–6, Lexile: 90
When his friend Chips is snatched and chewed, Tough Cookie sets out to stop Fingers.

Yolen, Jane. *Welcome to the Green House*. Putnam & Grosset, 1997, c1993. 32p IL K–3, Lexile: 770
Describes the tropical rainforest and the life found there.

Cause and Effect

Aardema, Verna. *Bringing the Rain to Kapiti Plain: A Nandi Tale.* Dial Books for Young Readers, c1981. 32p. IL K–3, Lexile: NP
A cumulative rhyme relating how Ki-pat brought rain to the drought-stricken Kapiti Plain.

Aardema, Verna. *Why Mosquitoes Buzz in People's Ears: A West African Tale.* Dial Books for Young Readers, c1975. 32p. IL K–3, Lexile: 770
Reveals the meaning of the mosquito's buzz.

Brown, Margaret Wise. *The Runaway Bunny.* HarperCollins, 2005, c1942. 38p. IL K–3, Lexile: 600
A little rabbit who wants to run away tells his mother how he will escape, but she is always right behind him.

Carle, Eric. *The Grouchy Ladybug.* HarperCollins, 1996, c1977. 42p. IL K–3. Lexile: 560
A grouchy ladybug who is looking for a fight challenges everyone she meets regardless of their size or strength.

Carle, Eric. *The Very Hungry Caterpillar.* Philomel Books, c1987. 18p. IL K–3, Lexile: 460
Follows the progress of a hungry little caterpillar as he eats his way through a varied and very large quantity of food until, full at last, he forms a cocoon around himself and goes to sleep. Die-cut pages illustrate what the caterpillar ate on successive days.

Christelow, Eileen. *Five Little Monkeys Jumping on the Bed.* Clarion, c1989. 32p. IL K–3, Lexile: 310
A counting book in which, one by one, the little monkeys jump on the bed, only to fall off and bump their heads.

Cleary, Beverly. *Muggie Maggie.* Morrow Junior Books, c1990. 70p. IL 3–6, Lexile: 730
Maggie resists learning cursive writing in the third grade, until she discovers that knowing how to read and write cursive promises to open up an entirely new world of knowledge for her.

DePaola, Tomie. *The Legend of the Bluebonnet: An Old Tale of Texas.* Putnam, 1993, c1983. 30p. IL 3–6, Lexile: 740
A retelling of the Comanche Indian legend of how a little girl's sacrifice brought the flower called bluebonnet to Texas.

Giff, Patricia Reilly. *Today Was a Terrible Day.* Puffin Books, 1984, c1980. 25p. IL K–3, Lexile: 460
Follows the humorous mishaps of a second grader who is learning to read.

Hogrogian, Nonny. *One Fine Day.* Simon & Schuster Books for Young Readers, c1971. 32p. IL K–3, Lexile: 1080
After the old woman cuts off his tail when he steals her milk, the fox must go through a long series of transactions before she will sew it back on again.

Hutchins, Pat. *Rosie's Walk.* Simon & Schuster, c1968. 32p. IL K–3, Lexile: NP
Although unaware that a fox is after her as she takes a walk around the farmyard, Rosie the hen still manages to lead her pursuer into one accident after another.

Keats, Ezra Jack. *The Snowy Day.* Viking Press, 1962. 32p. IL K–3, Lexile: 500
The adventures of a little boy in the city on a very snowy day.

From *101 Great, Ready-to-Use Book Lists for Teens* by Nancy J. Keane. Santa Barbara, CA: Libraries Unlimited. Copyright © 2012.

Cause and Effect

Kellogg, Steven. *Chicken Little.* HarperCollins, c1985. 32p. IL K–3, Lexile: 690
Chicken Little and his feathered friends, alarmed that the sky seems to be falling, are easy prey for hungry Foxy Loxy when he poses as a police officer in hopes of tricking them into his truck.

Noble, Trinka Hakes. *The Day Jimmy's Boa Ate the Wash.* Dial Press, c1980. 32p. IL K–3, Lexile: 540
Jimmy's boa constrictor wreaks havoc on the class trip to a farm.

Numeroff, Laura Joffe. *If You Give a Moose a Muffin.* Laura Geringer Book, c1991. 32p. IL K–3, Lexile: 590
Shows the chaos that can ensue if one gives a moose a muffin and starts him on a cycle of urgent requests.

Numeroff, Laura Joffe. *If You Give a Mouse a Cookie.* Laura Geringer Books, c1985. 32p. IL K–3, Lexile: 660
Relates the cycle of requests a mouse is likely to make after you give him a cookie, taking the reader through a young child's day.

Numeroff, Laura Joffe. *If You Give a Pig a Pancake.* Laura Geringer Book, c1998. 32p. IL K–3, Lexile: 570
Presents a children's story of the chaos that can happen in the house when you give a pig a pancake.

Peet, Bill. *Big Bad Bruce.* Houghton Mifflin, c1977. 38p. IL K–3, Lexile: 890
Bruce, a bear bully, never picks on anyone his own size—until he is diminished in more ways than one by a small but very independent witch.

Peet, Bill. *Pamela Camel.* Houghton Mifflin, c1984. 30p. IL K–3, Lexile: 1070
A tired and dejected circus camel finds long-sought-after recognition along a railroad track.

Smith, Robert Kimmel. *Chocolate Fever.* Puffin Books, 2006, c1972. 93p. IL 3–6, Lexile: 680
After eating too much chocolate, Henry breaks out in brown bumps that help him foil some hijackers and teach him a valuable lesson about self-indulgence.

Steig, William. *Sylvester and the Magic Pebble.* Simon and Schuster Books for Young Readers, 2005, c1969. 36p. IL K–3, Lexile: 700
Sylvester the donkey finds a magic pebble that grants his every wish, but in a moment of fright he wishes he were a rock, and then cannot hold the pebble to wish himself back to normal again.

Viorst, Judith. *Alexander and the Terrible, Horrible, No Good, Very Bad Day.* Atheneum, c1972. 32p. IL K–3, Lexile: 970
On a day when everything goes wrong for him, Alexander is consoled by the thought that other people have bad days, too.

Wood, Audrey. *The Napping House.* Harcourt, c1984. 32p. IL K–3, Lexile: NP
In this cumulative tale, a wakeful flea atop a number of sleeping creatures causes a commotion, with just one bite.

Persuasive Writing

Child, Lauren. *I Will Never Not Ever Eat a Tomato.* Candlewick Press, 2000. 32p. IL K–3, Lexile: 370
A fussy eater decides to sample the carrots after her brother convinces her that they are really orange twiglets from Jupiter.

Cronin, Doreen. *Duck for President.* Simon & Schuster Books for Young Readers, c2004. 40p. IL K–3, Lexile: 680
When Duck gets tired of working for Farmer Brown, his political ambition eventually leads to his being elected president.

Hoose, Phillip M. *Hey, Little Ant.* Tricycle Press, c1998. 26p. IL K–3, Lexile: NP
A song in which an ant pleads with the kid who is tempted to squish it.

Kasza, Keiko. *My Lucky Day.* G. P. Putnam's Sons, c2003. 32p. IL K–3, Lexile: 270
When a young pig knocks on a fox's door, the fox thinks dinner has arrived, but the pig has other plans.

Kellogg, Steven. *Can I Keep Him?* Puffin, 1976, c1971. 32p. IL K–3, Lexile: 510
Mother objects to every pet Arnold asks to keep, except one—a person.

Khalsa, Dayal Kaur. *I Want a Dog.* Tundra, 2002, c1987. 24p. IL K–3, Lexile: 610
When her parents refuse to get her a dog, May creates an imaginary dog out of a roller skate.

LaRochelle, David. *The Best Pet of All.* Dutton Children's Books, c2004. 32p. IL K–3
A young boy enlists the help of a dragon to persuade his mother to let him have a dog as a pet.

Orloff, Karen Kaufman. *I Wanna Iguana.* Putnam, c2004. 32p. IL K–3, Lexile: 460
Alex and his mother write notes back and forth in which Alex tries to persuade her to let him have a baby iguana for a pet.

Pomerantz, Charlotte. *The Piggy in the Puddle.* Aladdin Paperbacks, 1989, c1974. 32p. IL K–3, Lexile: NP
Unable to persuade a young pig not to frolic in the mud, her family finally joins her for a mud party.

Scieszka, Jon. *The True Story of the 3 Little Pigs.* Viking, 1989. 32p. IL K–3, Lexile: 570
The wolf gives his own outlandish version of what really happened when he tangled with the three little pigs.

Teague, Mark. *Dear Mrs. Larue: Letters from Obedience School.* Scholastic Press, 2002. 32p. IL K–3, Lexile: 500
Gertrude LaRue receives typewritten and paw-written letters from her dog Ike, entreating her to let him leave the Igor Brotweiler Canine Academy and come back home.

Viorst, Judith. *Earrings!* Atheneum Books for Young Readers, c1990. 32p. IL K–3, Lexile: 470
A young girl uses a variety of arguments to try to convince her parents to let her get her ears pierced.

Persuasive Writing

Willems, Mo. *Don't Let the Pigeon Drive the Bus!* Hyperion Books for Children, c2003. 34p. IL K–3, Lexile: 120

A pigeon that longs to drive a bus sees a chance to make its dream come true when the bus driver takes a short break.

Wilson, Karma. *Bear's New Friend.* Margaret K. McElderry Books, c2006. 32p. IL K–3, Lexile: NP

Bear and his friends persuade a bashful owl to play with them.

Prediction

Brett, Jan. *The Mitten: A Ukrainian Folktale.* G. P. Putnam's Sons, 2009, c1989. 32p. IL K–3, Lexile: 800
   Several animals sleep snugly in Nicki's lost mitten—until the bear sneezes.

Halpern, Monica. *How Many Seeds?* Steck-Vaughn, c1999. 8p. IL K–3 (Non-fiction)
   Simple text and pictures help students learn about the amount of seeds in different types of fruit.

Krauss, Ruth. *The Carrot Seed.* HarperCollins, c1973. 25p. IL K–3
   Despite everyone's dire predictions, a little boy has faith in the carrot seed he plants.

Numeroff, Laura Joffe. *If You Give a Mouse a Cookie.* Laura Geringer Books, 2000, c1985. 32p. IL K–3, Lexile: 660
   Relates the cycle of requests a mouse is likely to make after you give him a cookie, taking the reader through a young child's day.

Park, Barbara. *Junie B., First Grader: Shipwrecked.* Random House, c2004. 88p. IL K–3
   Junie B.'s journal entries start with Room One's stomach virus excitement, the first-grade Columbus Day play, and getting the part of the *Pinta*, the fastest ship in Columbus's fleet.

Portis, Antoinette. *Not a Box.* HarperCollins, c2006. 32p. IL K–3
   To an imaginative little bunny, a box is not always just a box.

Portis, Antoinette. *Not a Stick.* HarperCollins, c2008. 32p. IL K–3
   An imaginative young pig shows some of the many things that a stick can be.

Sequencing

Andersen, H. C. *The Emperor's New Clothes*. Houghton Mifflin, c1977. 44p. IL K–3
A vain emperor is duped into parading through town without clothes by a pair of swindlers posing as tailors.

Andersen, H. C. *The Princess and the Pea*. North-South Books, 1985. 24p. IL K–3, Lexile: 580
A young girl feels a pea through twenty mattresses and twenty featherbeds, proving she is a real princess.

Asbjornsen, Peter Christen. *The Three Billy Goats Gruff*. Clarion, c1973. 31p. IL K–3, Lexile: 500
Three clever billy goats outwit a big ugly troll who lives under the bridge they must cross on their way up the mountain.

Aston, Dianna Hutts. *A Seed Is Sleepy*. Chronicle Books, c2007. 34p. IL K–3, Lexile: 750 (Non-fiction)
This introduction to seeds explains their varying shapes and sizes, the locations where they are found, and their life cycles.

Barry, Robert E. *Mr. Willowby's Christmas Tree*. Random House Children's Books, 2000, c1991. 32p. IL K–3
Mr. Willowby's Christmas tree is too tall, so he trims off the top and gives the top to the upstairs maid for her tree, and she finds it too tall, so she cuts off the top, which the gardener uses for his tree, but it is too tall . . .

Brett, Jan. *Berlioz the Bear*. Putnam, c1991. 32p. IL K–3, Lexile: 540
Berlioz the bear and his fellow musicians are due to play for the town ball when the mule pulling their bandwagon refuses to move. A strange buzzing in Berlioz's double bass turns into a surprise that saves the day.

Brett, Jan. *Gingerbread Baby*. G. P. Putnam's, c1999. 32p. IL K–3, Lexile: 430
A young boy and his mother bake a gingerbread baby that escapes from their oven and leads a crowd on a chase similar to the one in the familiar tale about a not-so-clever gingerbread man.

Bunting, Eve. *Sunflower House*. Harcourt Brace, c1996. 32p. IL K–3, Lexile: 530
A young boy creates a summer playhouse by planting sunflowers and saves the seeds to make another house the next year.

Burton, Virginia Lee. *Mike Mulligan and His Steam Shovel*. Houghton Mifflin, 1999, c1967. 44p. IL K–3, Lexile: 820
Although Mike Mulligan's steam shovel, named Mary Anne, is too old-fashioned to compete with newer models, the people of Popperville find a way to keep Mike and Mary Anne working.

Buzzeo, Toni. *Little Loon and Papa*. Dial Books for Young Readers, c2004. 32p. IL K–3
Motivated by a challenging situation and his supportive father, Little Loon finally learns to dive.

Carle, Eric. *The Very Hungry Caterpillar*. Philomel Books, c1987. 18p. IL K–3
Follows the progress of a hungry little caterpillar as he eats his way through a varied and very large quantity of food until, full at last, he forms a cocoon around himself and goes to sleep. Die-cut pages illustrate what the caterpillar ate on successive days.

Sequencing

Cronin, Doreen. *Click, Clack, Moo: Cows That Type*. Simon & Schuster Books for Young Readers, c2006. 32p. IL K–3, Lexile: 160
> When Farmer Brown's cows find a typewriter in the barn, they start making demands, and go on strike when the farmer refuses to give them what they want.

Cronin, Doreen. *Duck for President*. Simon & Schuster Books for Young Readers, c2004. 40p. IL K–3, Lexile: 680
> When Duck gets tired of working for Farmer Brown, his political ambition eventually leads to his being elected president.

Cronin, Doreen. *Giggle, Giggle, Quack*. Simon & Schuster Books for Young Readers, c2006. 32p. IL K–3, Lexile: 330
> When Farmer Brown goes on vacation, leaving his brother Bob in charge, Duck makes trouble by changing all his instructions to notes the animals like much better.

DePaola, Tomie. *Charlie Needs a Cloak*. Aladdin Paperbacks, c1973. 32p. IL K–3, Lexile: 500 (Non-fiction)
> A shepherd shears his sheep, cards and spins the wool, weaves and dyes the cloth, and sews a beautiful new red cloak.

Donaldson, Julia. *The Gruffalo*. Dial Books for Young Readers, c1999. 28p. IL K–3, Lexile: 200
A clever mouse uses the threat of a terrifying creature to keep from being eaten by a fox, an owl, and a snake—only to have to outwit that creature as well.

Ernst, Lisa Campbell. *Stella Louella's Runaway Book*. Simon & Schuster Books for Young Readers, c1998. 34p. IL K–3, Lexile: 640
> As she tries to find the book that she must return to the library that day, Stella gathers a growing group of people who have all enjoyed reading the book.

Frost, Helen. *Monarch and Milkweed*. Atheneum Books for Young Readers, c2008. 34p. IL K–3, Lexile: 970 (Non-fiction)
> Illustrations and text describe the life cycle of the monarch butterfly and its link with the milkweed plant.

Kimmel, Eric A. *I Took My Frog to the Library*. Puffin Books, 1992. 28p. IL K–3, Lexile: 430
> A young girl brings her pets to the library—with predictably disastrous results.

Levenson, George. *Pumpkin Circle: The Story of a Garden*. Tricycle Press, c1999. 38p. IL K–3, Lexile: NP (Non-fiction)
> Rhyming text and photographs follow a pumpkin patch as it grows and changes, from seeds to plants to pumpkins ready to harvest, to jack-o-lanterns, and then to seeds again.

Lobel, Arnold. *Frog and Toad All Year.* HarperCollins, c1976. 64p. IL K–3, Lexile: 300
> Two friends share experiences in each season of the year.

London, Jonathan. *Froggy Gets Dressed.* Viking, 1992. IL K–3, Lexile: 300
> Rambunctious Froggy hops out into the snow for a winter frolic, but is called back by his mother to put on some necessary articles of clothing.

Sequencing

Lowry, Lois. *Gooney Bird Greene.* Yearling, 2004, c2002. 88p. IL 3–6, Lexile: 590
A most unusual new student who loves to be the center of attention entertains her teacher and fellow second graders by telling absolutely true stories about herself, including how she got her name.

Martin, Bill. *The Ghost-Eye Tree.* Holt, 1988, c1985. 32p. IL K–3, Lexile: NP
Walking down a dark lonely road on an errand one night, a brother and sister argue over who is afraid of the dreaded Ghost-Eye tree.

McClintock, Marshall. *A Fly Went by.* Beginner Books, c1986. 62p. IL K–3, Lexile: 270
A sheep with its foot caught in a tin can sets off a chase with a fly in the lead.

McKissack, Pat. *Flossie & the Fox.* Dial Books for Young Readers, c1986. 32p. IL K–3, Lexile: 610
A wily fox, notorious for stealing eggs, meets his match when he encounters a bold little girl in the woods who insists upon proof that he is a fox before she will become frightened.

McPhail, David. *Mole Music.* H. Holt, 1999. 32p. IL K–3, Lexile: 380
Feeling that something is missing in his simple life, Mole acquires a violin and learns to make beautiful, joyful music.

Meddaugh, Susan. *Cinderella's Rat.* Houghton Mifflin, c1997. 32p. IL K–3, Lexile: 420
One of the rats that was turned into a coachman by Cinderella's fairy godmother tells his story.

Meddaugh, Susan. *Martha Speaks.* Houghton Mifflin, c1992. 32p. IL K–3, Lexile: 420
Problems arise when Martha, the family dog, learns to speak after eating alphabet soup.

Noble, Trinka Hakes. *The Day Jimmy's Boa Ate the Wash.* Dial Press, c1980. 32p. IL K–3, Lexile: 540
Jimmy's boa constrictor wreaks havoc on the class trip to a farm.

Numeroff, Laura Joffe. *Beatrice Doesn't Want to.* Candlewick Press, 2004. 32p. IL K–3, Lexile: 140
On the third afternoon of going to the library with her brother Henry, Beatrice finally finds something she enjoys doing.

Numeroff, Laura Joffe. *If You Give a Pig a Pancake.* Laura Geringer Book, c1998. 32p. IL K–3, Lexile: 570
Presents a children's story of the chaos that can happen in the house when you give a pig a pancake.

Parish, Peggy. *Amelia Bedelia.* HarperCollins, 1992. 63p. IL K–3, Lexile: 140
A literal-minded housekeeper causes a ruckus in the household when she attempts to make sense of some instructions.

Pearson, Emily. *Ordinary Mary's Extraordinary Deed.* Gibbs Smith, c2002. 32p. IL K–3
A young girl's good deed is multiplied as it is passed on by those who have been touched by the kindness of others.

Rathmann, Peggy. *10 Minutes till Bedtime.* G. P. Putnam's, c1998. 48p. IL K–3, Lexile: NP
A boy's hamster leads an increasingly large group of hamsters on a tour of the boy's house, while his father counts down the minutes to bedtime.

Sequencing

Robart, Rose. *The Cake That Mack Ate.* Little, Brown, c1986. 24p. IL K–3
A cumulative tale about the chain of events surrounding the making of a cake by a farmer's wife, eventually leading to its consumption in surprising circumstances.

Sendak, Maurice. *Where the Wild Things Are.* HarperCollins, 1991, c1963. 40p. IL K–3, Lexile: 740
After he is sent to bed without supper for behaving like a wild thing, Max dreams of a voyage to the island where the wild things are.

Seuss, Dr. *The 500 Hats of Bartholomew Cubbins.* Random House, c1965. 47p. IL K–3, Lexile: 520
Each time Bartholomew Cubbins attempts to obey the king's order to take off his hat, he finds there is another one on his head.

Shannon, David. *A Bad Case of Stripes.* Blue Sky Press, c1998. 32p. IL K–3, Lexile: 540
To ensure her popularity, Camilla Cream always does what is expected, until the day arrives when she no longer recognizes herself.

Shannon, David. *No, David!* Blue Sky Press, c1998. 32p. IL K–3, Lexile: BR
A young boy is depicted doing a variety of naughty things for which he is repeatedly admonished, but finally he gets a hug.

Sierra, Judy. *Wild about Books.* Knopf, c2004. 34p. IL K–3, Lexile: NP
A librarian named Mavis McGrew introduces the animals in the zoo to the joy of reading when she drives her bookmobile to the zoo by mistake.

Steig, William. *Brave Irene.* Farrar, Straus, Giroux, 1986. 32p. IL K–3, Lexile: 630
Plucky Irene, a dressmaker's daughter, braves a fierce snowstorm to deliver a new gown to the duchess in time for the ball.

Taback, Simms. *There Was an Old Lady Who Swallowed a Fly.* Viking, 1997. 32p. IL K–3, Lexile: NP
Ever-expanding die-cut holes show exactly what is happening in the old lady's stomach as she swallows an assortment of creatures, beginning with a small fly, and ending with a fatal horse.

Van Allsburg, Chris. *Two Bad Ants.* Houghton Mifflin, c1988. 31p. IL K–3, Lexile: 780
When two bad ants desert from their colony, they experience a dangerous adventure that convinces them to return to their former place of safety.

Wood, Audrey. *The Napping House.* Harcourt, c1984. 32p. IL K–3, Lexile: NP
In this cumulative tale, a wakeful flea atop a number of sleeping creatures causes a commotion, with just one bite.

Part 7

Readalikes

If You Liked *Thirteen Reasons Why* by Jay Asher, You May Like . . .

Adoff, Jaime. *Names Will Never Hurt Me.* Speak, 2005, c2004. 186p. IL YA, Lexile: 510
Several high school students relate their feelings about school, themselves, and the events that unfold on the fateful one-year anniversary of the killing of a fellow student.

Anderson, Laurie Halse. *Speak.* Farrar Straus Giroux, 1999. 197p. IL YA, Lexile: 690
A traumatic event near the end of the summer has a devastating effect on Melinda's freshman year in high school.

Anderson, Laurie Halse. *Wintergirls.* Viking, 2009. 278p. IL YA, Lexile: 730
Eighteen-year-old Lia comes to terms with her best friend's death from anorexia as she struggles with the same disorder.

Brown, Jennifer. *Hate List.* Little, Brown, 2009. 408p. IL YA, Lexile: 760
Sixteen-year-old Valerie, whose boyfriend Nick committed a school shooting at the end of their junior year, struggles to cope with integrating herself back into high school life, unsure herself whether she was a hero or a villain.

Cohn, Rachel. *You Know Where to Find Me.* Simon & Schuster Books for Young Readers, c2008. 204p. IL YA, Lexile: 900
In the wake of her cousin's suicide, overweight and introverted seventeen-year-old Miles experiences significant changes in her relationships with her mother and father, her best friend Jamal and his family, and her cousin's father, while gaining insights about herself, both positive and negative.

Crutcher, Chris. *Deadline.* Greenwillow Books, c2007. 316p. IL YA, Lexile: 880
Given the medical diagnosis of one year to live, high school senior Ben Wolf decides to fulfill his greatest fantasies, ponders his life's purpose and legacy, and converses through dreams with a spiritual guide known as "Hey-Soos."

Downham, Jenny. *Before I Die.* David Fickling Books, 2009, c2007. 326p. IL YA, Lexile: 580
A terminally ill teenage girl makes and carries out a list of things to do before she dies.

Forman, Gayle. *If I Stay: A Novel.* Dutton Books, c2009. 201p. IL YA, Lexile: 830
While in a coma following an automobile accident that killed her parents and younger brother, seventeen-year-old Mia, a gifted cellist, weighs whether to live with her grief or join her family in death.

Giles, Gail. *What Happened to Cass McBride?: A Novel.* Little, Brown, 2006. 211p. IL YA, Lexile: 520
After his younger brother commits suicide, Kyle Kirby decides to exact revenge on the person he holds responsible for his death.

Green, John. *Looking for Alaska: A Novel.* Dutton, c2005. 221p. IL YA. Lexile: 930
For sixteen-year-old Miles, his first year at Culver Creek Preparatory School in Alabama includes good friends and great pranks, but is defined by his search for answers about life and death after a fatal car crash.

If You Liked *Thirteen Reasons Why* by Jay Asher, You May Like . . .

Green, John. *Paper Towns.* Dutton Books, c2008. 305p. IL YA, Lexile: 850
One month before graduating from his Central Florida high school, Quentin "Q" Jacobsen basks in the predictable boredom of his life—until the beautiful and exciting Margo Roth Spiegelman, Q's neighbor and classmate, takes him on a midnight adventure and then mysteriously disappears.

Hopkins, Ellen. *Identical.* Margaret K. McElderry Books, c2008. 565p. IL YA, Lexile: 590
Sixteen-year-old identical twin daughters of a district court judge and a candidate for the U.S. House of Representatives, Kaeleigh and Raeanne Gardella desperately struggle with secrets that have already torn them and their family apart.

Huntley, Amy. *The Everafter.* Balzer + Bray, c2009. 244p. IL YA, Lexile: 680
After her death, seventeen-year-old Maddy finds a way to revisit moments in her life by using objects that she lost while she was alive. She uses this method to try to figure out the complicated emotions, events, and meaning of her existence.

Knowles, Johanna. *Lessons from a Dead Girl.* Candlewick Press, 2007. 215p. IL YA, Lexile: 620
Laine struggles to come to terms with her friendship with troubled Leah Greene, whose secrets were too much for Laine to bear and whose actions sent Laine on a painful journey of self-discovery.

Peters, Julie Anne. *By the Time You Read This, I'll Be Dead.* Hyperion DBG, c2010. 200p. IL YA
High school student Daelyn Rice, who has been bullied throughout her school career and has attempted suicide multiple times, again makes plans to kill herself, despite the persistent attempts of an unusual boy to draw her out.

Picoult, Jodi. *The Pact: A Love Story.* Avon Books, 1998. 496p. IL AD, Lexile: 820
The Hartes and the Golds, long-time neighbors and friends, are not surprised when their children Chris and Emily fall in love. The bond between the families is placed under an enormous strain when Emily is killed, leaving behind the question of whether her death was a suicide or murder.

Smith, Alexander Gordon. *Lockdown: Escape from Furnace.* Farrar Straus and Giroux, 2009. 273p. IL YA, Lexile: 1010
When fourteen-year-old Alex is framed for murder, he becomes an inmate in the Furnace Penitentiary, where brutal inmates and sadistic guards reign, boys who disappear in the middle of the night sometimes return weirdly altered, and escape might just be possible.

Summers, Courtney. *Some Girls Are.* St. Martin's Griffin, 2010, c2009. 245p. IL YA, Lexile: 600
Regina, a high school senior in the popular—and feared—crowd, suddenly falls out of favor and becomes the object of the same sort of vicious bullying that she used to inflict on others, until she finds solace with one of her former victims.

Williams-Garcia, Rita. *Jumped.* HarperTeen, c2009. 169p. IL YA, Lexile: 600
The lives of Leticia, Dominique, and Trina become irrevocably intertwined through the course of one day in an urban high school after Leticia overhears Dominique's plans to beat up Trina and must decide whether to get involved.

If You Liked *Thirteen Reasons Why* by Jay Asher, You May Like...

Zevin, Gabrielle. *Elsewhere*. Farrar, Straus and Giroux, 2005. 275p. IL YA, Lexile: 720
  After fifteen-year-old Liz Hall is hit by a taxi and killed, she finds herself in a place that is both like and unlike Earth, where she must adjust to her new status and figure out how to "live."

If You Liked *Timeless* by Alexandra Monir, You May Like . . .

Babbitt, Natalie. *Tuck Everlasting.* Farrar, Straus, Giroux, 1975. 139p. IL 5–8, Lexile: 770
The Tuck family is confronted with an agonizing situation when they discover that a ten-year-old girl and a malicious stranger now share their secret about a spring whose water prevents those who drink it from ever growing any older.

Condie, Allyson Braithwaite. *Matched.* Dutton Books, c2010. 369p. IL YA, Lexile: 680
Cassia has always had complete trust in the Society to make decisions for her. When she is being paired with her ideal mate, however, a second face flashes on the screen—and Cassia begins to doubt the Society's infallibility as she tries to decide which man she truly loves.

Cooney, Caroline B. *Both Sides of Time.* Bantam Doubleday Dell Books for Young Readers, 1995. 210p. IL YA, Lexile: 750
The summer after her senior year, Annie, wishing she could have lived a hundred years ago in a more romantic time, finds herself in the 1890s. The experience is, indeed, romantic—and very painful.

Davis, Heather. *The Clearing.* Graphia, 2010. 215p. IL YA
Amy, a sixteen-year-old girl recovering from an abusive relationship, moves to the country in Washington to live with her great-aunt. In a mysterious clearing in the woods there, she meets Henry, a boy stuck in the summer of 1944.

Donnelly, Jennifer. *Revolution.* Delacorte Press, c2010. 471p. IL YA, Lexile: 560
An angry, grieving seventeen-year-old musician facing expulsion from her prestigious private school in Brooklyn travels to Paris to complete a school assignment. There, she discovers a diary written during the French revolution by a young actress attempting to help a tortured, imprisoned little boy—Louis Charles, the lost king of France.

Dunlap, Susanne Emily. *Anastasia's Secret.* Bloomsbury, 2010. 333p. IL YA
As world war and the looming Russian Revolution threaten all they hold dear, Anastasia, the youngest daughter of Czar Nicholas II, and her family are held in captivity. During their confinement, Anastasia falls in love with one of their guards, a young man who has espoused the ideals of Lenin.

Fantaskey, Beth. *Jessica's Guide to Dating on the Dark Side.* Harcourt, 2009. 354p. IL YA, Lexile: 700
Seventeen-year-old Jessica, adopted and raised in Pennsylvania, learns that she is descended from a royal line of Romanian vampires and that she is betrothed to a vampire prince, who poses as a foreign exchange student while courting her.

Finney, Jack. *Time and Again.* Buccaneer Books, c1970. 399p. IL YA, Lexile: 1020
Illustrator Si Morley steps out of his twentieth-century New York apartment one night—and right into the winter of 1882.

Fitzpatrick, Becca. *Hush, Hush.* Simon & Schuster Books for Young Readers, c2009. 391p. IL YA, Lexile: 640
High school sophomore Nora has always been very cautious in her relationships, but when Patch, who has a dark side she can sense, enrolls at her school, she is mysteriously and strongly drawn to him, despite warnings from her best friend, the school counselor, and her own instincts.

If You Liked *Timeless* by Alexandra Monir, You May Like . . .

Gabaldon, Diana. *Outlander.* Delacorte Press, 1991. 627p. IL AD
While on vacation in Scotland, Clare touches an ancient stone circle and is hurled two hundred years back in time, to 1743.

Garcia, Kami. *Beautiful Creatures.* Little, Brown, 2009. 563p. IL YA, Lexile: 670
In a small South Carolina town, where it seems little has changed since the Civil War, sixteen-year-old Ethan is powerfully drawn to Lena, a new classmate with whom he shares a psychic connection and whose family hides a dark secret that may be revealed on her sixteenth birthday.

Guibord, Maurissa. *Warped.* Delacorte Press, c2011. 339p. IL YA
When seventeen-year-old Tessa Brody comes into possession of an ancient unicorn tapestry, she is plummeted back in time to sixteenth-century England. There, her life becomes intertwined with that of a handsome nobleman who is desperately trying to escape a terrible fate.

Kate, Lauren. *Fallen.* Delacorte Press, c2009. 452p. IL YA, Lexile: 830
Suspected in the death of her boyfriend, seventeen-year-old Luce is sent to a Savannah, Georgia, reform school, where she meets two intriguing boys and learns the truth about the strange shadows that have always haunted her.

Klein, Lisa M. *Cate of the Lost Colony.* Bloomsbury, 2010. 329p. IL YA, Lexile: 820
When Lady Catherine has an affair with Sir Walter Raleigh, she is banished to Raleigh's colony of Roanoke by Queen Elizabeth. Surviving alongside other colonists with help from Native Americans, she gradually falls in love with Manteo, a native of the area, just as Raleigh sets sail for the New World.

MacCullough, Carolyn. *Once a Witch.* Clarion Books, 2009. 292p. IL YA, Lexile: 790
Born into a family of witches, seventeen-year-old Tamsin is raised believing that she alone lacks a magical "Talent." When her beautiful and powerful sister is taken by an age-old rival of the family in an attempt to change the balance of power, however, Tamsin discovers her true destiny.

Miller, Kirsten. *The Eternal Ones: What if Love Refused to Die?* Razorbill, c2010. 411p. IL YA, Lexile: 760
Haven Moore, a high school girl living with her widowed mother and grandmother in Snopes, Tennessee, is plagued by visions of a past life in New York with a boy named Ethan. When a series of circumstances force her to flee her home, she heads to the city in search of answers.

Mitchell, Saundra. *The Vespertine.* Harcourt, 2011. 296p. IL YA
In the summer of 1889, Amelia van den Broek's time with her stylish cousin Zora in Baltimore is interrupted by a series of disturbing visions that offer glimpses of the future and threaten her future with Nathaniel, a young man who is keeping secrets of his own and seems to be linked to Amelia's darkest visions.

If You Liked *Alchemyst* by Michael Scott, You May Like . . .

Series

Brennan, Herbie. *Faerie Wars Chronicles.* Bloomsbury, 2003– . IL YA

Henry finds his life taking a new dimension when he becomes involved with Prince Pyrgus Malvae, who has been sent away from the faerie world to escape the treacherous Faeries of the Night.

Colfer, Eoin. *Artemis Fowl Series.* Hyperion Books for Children, c2001– . IL 5–8

When a twelve-year-old evil genius tries to capture a fairy demanding a ransom in gold, the fairies fight back with magic, technology, and a particularly nasty troll.

Riordan, Rick. *Percy Jackson & the Olympians: The Complete Series.* Disney/Hyperion Books, c2005–c2009. IL 5–8

After learning that he is the son of a mortal woman and Poseidon, god of the sea, young Percy is sent to Camp Half-Blood, a camp for training demigods like himself. There, he gets into adventures, battles evil, and moves toward the prophecy that awaits him on his sixteenth birthday.

Walden, Mark. *H.I.V.E.* Simon & Schuster Books for Young Readers, 2004– . IL 5–8

Thirteen-year-old orphan Otto Malpense, identified as a boy with a special talent for villainy, is kidnapped and taken to the remote Higher Institute of Villainous Education (H.I.V.E.), where he is enrolled in a six-year training program and immediately begins formulating a plan to escape.

If You Liked *Gallagher Girls* by Ally Carter, You May Like . . .

Abrahams, Peter. *Down the Rabbit Hole: An Echo Falls Mystery.* Laura Geringer Books, 2006, c2005. 407p. IL 5–8, Lexile: 680
> Like her idol Sherlock Holmes, eighth grader Ingrid Levin-Hill uses her intellect to solve a murder case in her home town of Echo Falls.

Barnes, Jennifer. *The Squad. Perfect Cover.* Laurel-Leaf, c2008. 275p. IL YA
> High school sophomore Toby Klein enjoys computer hacking and wearing combat boots, so she thinks it is a joke when she is invited to join the cheerleading squad. Soon, however, she learns cheering is just a cover for an elite group of government operatives.

Black, Holly. *White Cat.* Margaret K. McElderry Books, c2010. 310p. IL YA, Lexile: 700
> When Cassel Sharpe discovers that his older brothers have used him to carry out their criminal schemes and then stolen his memories, he figures out a way to turn their evil machinations against them.

Cabot, Meg. *The Mediator.* HarperTeen, 2011. 515p. IL YA
> These two stories follow the adventures of Suze Simon, a sixteen-year-old girl who can talk to the dead, as she deals with a sexy, nineteenth-century ghost named Jesse and the troubled spirit of a murdered woman.

Cassidy, Kay. *The Cinderella Society.* Egmont USA, 2010. 322p. IL YA, Lexile: 800
> Sixteen-year-old Jess Parker fears she will never fit in at her new school, until she is invited to join the Cinderella Society, a secret sisterhood of the most popular girls in school. The group needs Jess in their battle of good versus evil, as they face off against the Wickeds, who are targeting innocent girls in their war against the Cinderellas.

Clement-Moore, Rosemary. *Prom Dates from Hell: A Novel.* Delacorte Press, c2007. 308p. IL YA
> High school senior and yearbook photographer Maggie thought she would rather die than go to the prom, but when a classmate summons a revenge-seeking demon, she has no choice except to buy herself a dress and prepare to face jocks, cheerleaders, and Evil Incarnate.

Gerber, Linda C. *Death by Bikini.* Sleuth, c2008. 223p. IL YA, Lexile: 640
> Sixteen-year-old Aphra Behn Connolly investigates why her father let an unknown family stay at their exclusive tropical island resort, who strangled a famous rock star's girlfriend with the woman's own bikini top, and what secret a smoldering teenaged guest is hiding.

Lockhart, E. *The Boy Book: (A Study of Habits and Behaviors, Plus Techniques for Taming Them): A Ruby Oliver Novel.* Delacorte Press, 2008, c2006. 193p. IL YA, Lexile: 820
> A high school junior continues her quest for relevant data on the male species, while enjoying her freedom as a newly licensed driver and examining her friendship with a clean-living vegetarian classmate.

Lockhart, E. *The Disreputable History of Frankie Landau-Banks: A Novel.* Disney/Hyperion Books, 2009, c2008. 345p. IL YA, Lexile: 890
> When Frankie Landau-Banks attempts to take over a secret, all-male society at her exclusive prep school, her antics with the group soon draw some unlikely attention and have unexpected consequences that could change her life forever.

If You Liked *Gallagher Girls* by Ally Carter, You May Like...

Meyer, L. A. *My Bonny Light Horseman: Being an Account of the Further Adventures of Jacky Faber, in Love and War.* Harcourt, c2008. 436p. IL YA, Lexile: 950
> Jacky Faber, forced to go behind enemy lines in Paris as an American dancer, seduces a French general to obtain military secrets and save her friends, then dresses in male clothing and penetrates the French army to fight with Napoleon.

Scott, Elizabeth. *Stealing Heaven.* HarperTeen, c2008. 307p. IL YA, Lexile: 690
> Eighteen-year-old Danielle grew up learning how to steal under her mother's tutelage, and the two have spent their lives traveling around and targeting wealthy homes. In the beach town of Heaven, when Dani realizes her new friend's home is actually her next target and her potential boyfriend is a police officer, she must try to hide her true identity.

White, Kiersten. *Paranormalcy.* HarperTeen, c2010. 335p. IL YA, Lexile: 580
> When a dark prophecy begins to come true, sixteen-year-old Evie of the International Paranormal Containment Agency must not only try to stop it, but also uncover its connection to herself and the alluring shapeshifter, Lend.

If You Liked *Because of Winn Dixie* by Kate DiCamillo, You May Like . . .

Bunting, Eve. *The Summer of Riley*. HarperTrophy, 2002, c2001. 170p. IL 3–6, Lexile: 540
Shortly after he gets Riley, the perfect dog, eleven-year-old William must fight for his dog's life after Riley is taken away when he chases and injures an elderly neighbor's old horse.

Byars, Betsy Cromer. *Wanted—Mud Blossom*. Holiday House, 2008, c1991. 180p. IL 3–6
Convinced that Mud is responsible for the disappearance of the school hamster, which was his responsibility for the weekend, Junior Blossom is determined that the dog should be tried for his "crime."

Giff, Patricia Reilly. *Pictures of Hollis Woods*. Wendy Lamb Books, c2002. 166p. IL 5–8, Lexile: 650
A troublesome twelve-year-old orphan, staying with an elderly artist who needs her, remembers the only other time she was happy in a foster home, with a family that truly seemed to care about her.

Hannigan, Katherine. *Ida B—: and Her Plans to Maximize Fun, Avoid Disaster, and (Possibly) Save the World*. Greenwillow Books, c2004. 246p. IL 3–6, Lexile: 970
In Wisconsin, fourth grader Ida B spends happy hours being home-schooled and playing in her family's apple orchard, until her mother begins treatment for breast cancer and her parents must sell part of the orchard and send her to public school.

Hesse, Karen. *Just Juice*. Scholastic Signature, 1998. 138p. IL 3–6, Lexile: 690
Realizing that her father's lack of work has endangered her family, nine-year-old Juice decides that she must return to school and learn to read to help the family's chances of surviving and keeping their house.

Hill, Kirkpatrick. *The Year of Miss Agnes*. Aladdin Paperbacks, 2002, c2000. 115p. IL 3–6
Ten-year-old Fred (short for Frederika) narrates the story of school and village life among the Athapascans in Alaska during 1948, when Miss Agnes arrived as the new teacher.

Korman, Gordon. *No More Dead Dogs*. Hyperion Paperbacks for Children, 2002, c2000. 180p. IL 3–6, Lexile: 610
Eighth-grade football hero Wallace Wallace is sentenced to detention attending rehearsals of the school play. In spite of himself, he becomes wrapped up in the production and begins to suggest changes that improve not only the play but also his life.

Lisle, Janet Taylor. *Afternoon of the Elves*. Puffin Books, c1989. 122p. IL 3–6, Lexile: 820
As Hillary works in the miniature village, allegedly built by elves, in Sara-Kate's backyard, she becomes more and more curious about Sara-Kate's real life inside her big, gloomy house with her mysterious, silent mother.

Madden, Kerry. *Gentle's Holler: A Novel*. Viking, 2005. 237p. IL 5–8, Lexile: 950
In the early 1960s, twelve-year-old songwriter Livy Two Weems dreams of seeing the world beyond the Maggie Valley, North Carolina, holler where she lives in poverty with her parents and eight brothers and sisters, but understands that she must put family first.

If You Liked *Because of Winn Dixie* by Kate DiCamillo, You May Like . . .

Morris, Willie. *My Dog Skip.* Vintage Books, 1996. 118p. IL YA, Lexile: 1380
> The story of a dog and his closest companion, the author, during their growing years in a small town in Mississippi.

O'Connor, Barbara. *Fame and Glory in Freedom, Georgia.* Farrar Straus Giroux, 2003. 104p. IL 3–6, Lexile: 740
> Unpopular sixth grader Burdette "Bird" Weaver persuades the new boy at school, whom everyone thinks is mean and dumb, to be her partner for a spelling bee that might win her everything she's ever wanted.

Paterson, Katherine. *The Same Stuff as Stars.* Clarion Books, c2002. 242p. IL 5–8, Lexile: 670
> When Angel's self-absorbed mother leaves her and her younger brother with their poor great-grandmother, the eleven-year-old girl worries not only about her mother and brother, her imprisoned father, and the frail old woman, but also about a mysterious man who begins sharing with her the wonder of the stars.

Peck, Richard. *A Year Down Yonder.* Dial Books for Young Readers, c2000. 130p. IL 5–8, Lexile: 610
> During the recession of 1937, fifteen-year-old Mary Alice is sent to live with her feisty, larger-than-life grandmother in rural Illinois and comes to a better understanding of this fearsome woman.

Wallace, Bill. *A Dog Called Kitty.* Holiday House, c1980. 153p. IL 3–6, Lexile: 710
> Afraid of dogs since he was attacked by a mad one, Ricky resists taking in a homeless pup that shows up at the farm.

Wallace, Bill. *Snot Stew.* Aladdin Paperbacks, 2008, c1989. 81p. IL 3–6, Lexile: 500
> Brother and sister cats are taken in by a family and learn the pleasures and dangers of living alongside humans.

Welch, Sheila Kelly. *The Shadowed Unicorn.* Front Street/Cricket Books, 2000. 185p. IL 5–8, Lexile: 630
> When their father dies suddenly, twelve-year-old twins Brendan and Nick, along with their mother and older sister Ami, move to an isolated old farm in the country. There, the twins find themselves pulled into Ami's obsession with capturing a unicorn.

Wiles, Deborah. *Each Little Bird That Sings.* Harcourt, c2005. 247p. IL 3–6, Lexile: 760
> Comfort Snowberger is well acquainted with death—her family runs the funeral parlor in their small southern town. Even so, the ten-year-old is unprepared for the series of heart-wrenching events that begins on the first day of Easter vacation with the sudden death of her beloved great-uncle Edisto.

Wiles, Deborah. *Love, Ruby Lavender.* Harcourt, c2001. 188p. IL 3–6, Lexile: 570
> When her quirky grandmother goes to Hawaii for the summer, nine-year-old Ruby learns to survive on her own in Mississippi by writing letters, befriending chickens as well as the new girl in town, and finally coping with her grandfather's death.

If You Liked *Bud, Not Buddy* by Christopher Paul Curtis, You May Like...

De Young, C. Coco. *A Letter to Mrs. Roosevelt.* Dell Yearling, 2000, c1999. 105p. IL 3–6, Lexile: 690
Eleven-year-old Margo fulfills a class assignment by writing a letter to Eleanor Roosevelt, asking for help to save her family's home during the Great Depression.

Hesse, Karen. *Out of the Dust.* Scholastic Press, 1997. 227p. IL 3–6, Lexile: NP
In a series of poems, fifteen-year-old Billie Jo relates the hardships of living on her family's wheat farm in Oklahoma during the Dust Bowl years of the Depression.

Levine, Gail Carson. *Dave at Night.* HarperTrophy, 2001, c1999. 281p. IL 3–6, Lexile: 490
When orphaned Dave is sent to the Hebrew Home for Boys, where he is treated cruelly, he sneaks out at night and is welcomed into the music- and culture-filled world of the Harlem Renaissance.

Mackall, Dandi Daley. *Rudy Rides the Rails: A Depression Era Story.* Sleeping Bear Press, Thomson/ Gale, c2007. 36p. IL 3–6
In 1932, during the Depression in Ohio, thirteen-year-old Rudy, who is determined to help his family weather the hard times, hops a train going west to California and experiences the hobo life.

Porter, Tracey. *Billy Creekmore.* Joanna Cotler Books, c2007. 305p. IL 5–8, Lexile: 930
One day a stranger comes to claim Billy Creekmore from the Guardian Angels Home for Boys; he embarks on a cross-country journey in search of his past, his future, and his own true self.

Schwartz, Ellen. *Stealing Home.* Tundra Books, Tundra Books of Northern New York, c2006. 217p. IL 3–6, Lexile: 630
Nine-year-old Yankees fan and Bronx native Joey Sexton is sent to Brooklyn after his mother's death and finds himself battling prejudice in his own family, as he tries to win the acceptance of his white, Jewish grandfather, who looks down on him because he is half African American.

If You Liked Clique Novels, You May Like...

Cabot, Meg. *The Princess Diaries*. HarperCollins, c2000. 238p. IL YA, Lexile: 920
Fourteen-year-old Mia, who is trying to lead a normal life as a teenage girl in New York City, is shocked to learn that her father is the Prince of Genovia, a small European principality, and that she is a princess and the heir to the throne.

Harper, Charise Mericle. *Flashcards of My Life: A Novel*. Little, Brown, 2007. 235p. IL 3–6.
Emily uses the journaling flashcards her aunt gave her as a birthday gift to help her sort out her friendships, attitudes, and family oddities.

Jaffe, Michele. *Bad Kitty*. HarperTeen, 2007, c2006. 268p. IL YA, Lexile: 830
While vacationing with her family in Las Vegas, seventeen-year-old Jasmine stumbles upon a murder mystery that she attempts to solve with the help of her friends, recently arrived from California.

Koss, Amy Goldman. *The Girls*. Dial Books for Young Readers, c2000. 121p. IL 5–8, Lexile: 710
Each of the girls in a middle school clique reveals the strong, manipulative hold that one of the group exerts on the others, causing hurt and self-doubt among the girls.

Mackler, Carolyn. *The Earth, My Butt, and Other Big Round Things*. Candlewick Press, 2003. 246p. IL YA, Lexile: 790
Feeling as if she does not fit in with the other members of her family, who are all thin, brilliant, and good-looking, fifteen-year-old Virginia tries to deal with her self-image, her first physical relationship, and her disillusionment with some of the people closest to her.

Myracle, Lauren. *The Fashion Disaster That Changed My Life*. Dutton Children's Books, c2005. 135p. IL 5–8, Lexile: 680
Seventh grader Alli describes in her journal the ups and downs of being in junior high, her doubts about where she fits in, and her belief about what it means to be a real friend.

Scott, Kieran. *I Was a Non-blonde Cheerleader*. Speak, 2007, c2005. 246p. IL YA, Lexile: 750
As a brunette on the all-blonde cheerleading squad at her new Florida high school, New Jersey–born sophomore Annisa Gobrowski tries to fit in with her popular teammates without losing the friendship of Bethany, the only other non-blonde at the school, and hopes something might develop with her new, guitar-playing neighbor, who has an evil girlfriend.

Shulman, Polly. *Enthusiasm*. Speak, 2007, c2006. 198p. IL YA, Lexile: 820
Julie and her best friend Ashleigh find themselves at odds when they both fall for the same boy, forcing them to choose between their loyalty to each other and the love of the perfect guy.

Spinelli, Jerry. *Stargirl*. A. Knopf, c2000. 186p. IL 5–8, Lexile: 590
Stargirl, a teen who animates quiet Mica High with her colorful personality, suddenly finds herself shunned for her refusal to conform.

Vega, Denise. *Click Here: (To Find out How I Survived Seventh Grade): A Novel*. Little, Brown, 2006, c2005. 211p. IL 3–6, Lexile: 690
Seventh-grader Erin Swift writes about her friends and classmates in her private blog, but when it accidentally gets posted on the school intranet site, she learns some important lessons about friendship.

If You Liked Clique Novels, You May Like . . .

Wood, Maryrose. *Sex Kittens and Horn Dawgs Fall in Love.* Delacorte Press, c2006. 243p. IL YA
A group of girls calling themselves the Sex Kittens and their male counterparts, the Horn Dogs, face love, karate, and science experiments in an unstructured private school setting in New York City.

Series

Brashares, Ann. *Sisterhood Series.* Delacorte, 2001– . IL YA
Carmen decides to discard an old pair of jeans, but Tibby, Lena, and Bridget think they are great and decide that whoever the pants fit best will get them. When the jeans fit everyone perfectly, a sisterhood begins.

Dean, Zoey. *The A-List Series.* Little, Brown, c2003– . IL YA
Seventeen-year-old blueblood Anna Percy leaves Manhattan to spend the second half of her senior year with her father in Los Angeles and quickly becomes involved in the lives of the rich and famous at Beverly Hills High School

Hopkins, Cathy. *Mates, Dates, and . . . Series.* Simon Pulse, 2001– . IL YA
Mates! Dates! Can these girls ever have enough of either?

Rennison, Louise. *Confessions of Georgia Nicolson Series.* HarperTempest, 1999– . IL YA
In her outrageously funny and angst-filled diaries, a British teen, Georgia Nicolson, deals with the Elderly Mad (also known as "parents"), tries to prevent her Scottish wildcat Angus from eating Mr. Next Door's poodles, organizes emergency meetings with her friends the Ace Gang, and does everything within her power to get off the rack of romance and into the cakeshop of love once and for all.

Von Ziegesar, Cecily. *Gossip Girl Series.* Little, Brown, 2002– . IL YA
Gossip Girl, the unnamed narrator, shares the inside scoop on her friends and foes in a privileged private school in New York City.

If You Liked *The Crucible* by Arthur Miller, You May Like . . .

Asher, Jay. *Thirteen Reasons Why: A Novel.* Razorbill, c2007. 288p. IL YA, Lexile: 550
High school student Clay Jenkins receives a box in the mail containing seven cassette tapes recorded by his crush, Hannah Baker, who committed suicide. He spends a bewildering and heartbreaking night crisscrossing their town, listening to Hannah's voice recounting the events leading up to her death.

Avi. *Nothing But the Truth: A Documentary Novel.* Scholastic, 2010, c1991. 177p. IL 5–8, Lexile: NP
A ninth grader's suspension for humming *The Star-Spangled Banner* during homeroom becomes a national news story, and leads to him and his teacher both leaving the school.

Bradbury, Ray. *Fahrenheit 451.* Ballantine Books, 1991, c1953. 179p. IL YA, Lexile: 890
A book-burning official in a future fascist state finds out that books are a vital part of a culture he never knew. He clandestinely pursues reading, until he is betrayed.

Butler, Dori Hillestad. *The Truth about Truman School.* Whitman, 2008. 170p. IL 3–6, Lexile: 640
Tired of being told what to write by the school newspaper's advisor, Zibby and her friend Amr start an underground newspaper online where everyone is free to post anything. Unfortunately, things spiral out of control when a cyberbully starts using the site to harass one popular girl.

Chbosky, Stephen. *The Perks of Being a Wallflower.* MTV Books/Pocket Books, c1999. 213p. IL YA, Lexile: 720
Charlie, a freshman in high school, explores the dilemma of growing up through a collection of letters he sends to an unknown receiver.

Cormier, Robert. *The Chocolate War.* Knopf, 2004, c1974. 253p. IL YA, Lexile: 820
A high school freshman discovers the devastating consequences of refusing to join in the school's annual fundraising drive and arousing the wrath of the school bullies.

DeVita, James. *The Silenced.* Eos, c2007. 504p. IL YA, Lexile: 700
Consigned to a prison-like Youth Training Facility because of her parents' political activities, Marena organizes a resistance movement to combat the restrictive policies of the ruling Zero Tolerance party.

Emerson, Kevin. *Carlos Is Gonna Get It.* Arthur A. Levine Books, 2008. 291p. IL 3–6, Lexile: 870
At the end of seventh grade, a group of friends plan to trick Carlos, an annoying "problem" student who says he is visited by aliens, while they are on a field trip in the mountains of New Hampshire.

Faulkner, William. *The Sound and the Fury.* Modern Library, 1992. 348p. IL YA, Lexile: 870
The members of a genteel Southern family are portrayed as petty failures, drunkards, suicides, pathological perverts, and idiots.

Golding, William. *Lord of the Flies.* Berkley, 2003, c1954. 315p. IL YA
After a plane crash strands them on a tropical island while the rest of the world is ravaged by war, a group of British schoolboys attempts to form a civilized society but descends into brutal anarchy.

If You Liked *The Crucible* by Arthur Miller, You May Like . . .

Hawthorne, Nathaniel. *The Scarlet Letter.* Signet Classics, 2009. 274p. IL AD, Lexile: 1420
This classic tale about Hester Prynne, her lover, their child, and Hester's husband deals with the effect of sin on the mind and spirit of these characters.

Hemphill, Stephanie. *Wicked Girls: A Novel of the Salem Witch Trials.* Balzer + Bray, c2010. 408p. IL YA, Lexile: 700
This fictionalized account of the Salem witch trials is told in verse form from the perspectives of three young women living in Salem in 1692—Mercy Lewis, Margaret Walcott, and Ann Putnam, Jr.

Hinton, S. E. *The Outsiders.* Viking Press, 1967. 188p. IL YA, Lexile: 750
Three brothers struggle to stay together after their parent's death and question their identity among the conflicting values of their adolescent society.

Lee, Harper. *To Kill a Mockingbird.* Harper, 2010, c1988. 323p. IL YA
Scout Finch, the young daughter of a local attorney in the Deep South during the 1930s, tells of her father's defense of an African American man charged with the rape of a white girl.

Lowry, Lois. *The Giver.* Houghton Mifflin, 1993. 180p. IL 5–8, Lexile: 760
Given his lifetime assignment at the Ceremony of Twelve, Jonas becomes the receiver of memories shared by only one other member of his community and discovers the terrible truth about the society in which he lives.

Ness, Patrick. *The Ask and the Answer.* Candlewick Press, 2009. 519p. IL YA, Lexile: 770
Alternate chapters follow teenagers Todd and Viola, who become separated as the Mayor's oppressive new regime takes power in New Prentisstown, a space colony where residents can hear one another's thoughts.

Ness, Patrick. *The Knife of Never Letting Go.* Candlewick Press, 2008. 479p. IL YA, Lexile: 860
Todd, one month away from an important birthday, learns the tough lessons of adulthood when he is forced to flee after discovering a secret near the town where he lives.

Orwell, George. *Animal Farm.* Harcourt, 1990. 124p. IL YA
In this political satire, the animals take over running the farm, but find their utopian state turning into a dictatorship.

Preller, James. *Bystander.* Feiwel and Friends, 2009. 226p. IL 5–8, Lexile: 600
Thirteen-year-old Eric discovers there are consequences to not standing by and watching as the bully at his new school hurts people. Although school officials are aware of the problem, Eric may be the one with a solution.

Sleator, William. *House of Stairs.* Puffin Books, 1991, c1974. 166p. IL 5–8, Lexile: 810
Five sixteen-year-old orphans with widely varying personalities are involuntarily placed in a house of endless stairs as subjects for a psychological experiment on conditioned human response.

If You Liked *The Crucible* by Arthur Miller, You May Like . . .

Spinelli, Jerry. *Stargirl.* A. Knopf, c2000. 186p. IL 5–8, Lexile: 590

Stargirl, a teen who animates quiet Mica High with her colorful personality, suddenly finds herself shunned for her refusal to conform.

Strasser, Todd. *The Wave.* Dell Laurel-Leaf, c1981. 138p. IL YA, Lexile: 770

In this account of an actual classroom experiment in establishing a fascist society, Laurie tries to persuade Mr. Ross to call off the experiment.

Williams-Garcia, Rita. *Jumped.* HarperTeen, c2009. 169p. IL YA, Lexile: 600

The lives of Leticia, Dominique, and Trina become irrevocably intertwined during the course of one day in an urban high school after Leticia overhears Dominique's plans to beat up Trina and must decide whether to get involved.

Zusak, Markus. *The Book Thief.* Knopf, Distributed by Random House, c2006. 552p. IL YA, Lexile: 730

Trying to make sense of the horrors of World War II, Death relates the story of Liesel—a young German girl whose book-stealing and story-telling talents help sustain her family and the Jewish man they are hiding, as well as their neighbors.

If You Liked *Diary of a Wimpy Kid* by Jeff Kinney, You May Like . . .

Angleberger, Tom. *The Strange Case of Origami Yoda.* Amulet Books, 2010. 141p. IL 3–6, Lexile: 760

Sixth grader Tommy and his friends describe their interactions with a paper finger puppet of Yoda, worn by their weird classmate Dwight, as they try to figure out whether the puppet can really predict the future. The book includes instructions for making an origami Yoda.

Colfer, Eoin. *Eoin Colfer's Legend of—Spud Murphy.* Miramax Books/Hyperion Paperbacks for Children, 2005, c2004. 95p. IL 3–6, Lexile: 580

When their mother starts dropping them off at the library several afternoons a week, nine-year-old William and his brother dread boredom and the overbearing librarian, but they are surprised at how things turn out.

Kowitt, Holly. *The Loser List.* Scholastic Press, c2011. 213p. IL 3–6, Lexile: 480

Danny Shine tries to get his name off the "Loser List" posted in the girls' bathroom and winds up in detention, where the school bullies discover Danny's artistic talents and encourage him to draw tattoos and graffiti. When the bullies steal a comic book from his favorite store, Danny needs to find a way to steal it back, return it, and end his association with the bullies before he gets new reputation.

O'Dell, Kathleen. *Agnes Parker—Girl in Progress.* Puffin Books, 2004, c2003. 156p. IL 5–8, Lexile: 660

As she starts sixth grade, Agnes faces challenges with her old best friend, a longtime bully, a wonderful new classmate and neighbor, and herself.

Weeks, Sarah. *Oggie Cooder.* Scholastic Press, 2008. 172p. IL 3–6, Lexile: 880

Quirky fourth grader Oggie Cooder goes from being shunned to being everyone's best friend when his uncanny ability to chew slices of cheese into the shapes of states wins him a slot on a popular television talent show. He soon learns the perils of being a celebrity—and having a neighbor girl as his manager.

Series

Benton, Jim. *Dear Dumb Diary.* Scholastic, c2004– . IL 3–6

The hilarious, candid, and sometimes not-so-nice diaries of Jamie Kelly, who promises that everything she writes is true, or at least as true as it needs to be.

Gantos, Jack. *Joey Pigza Series.* Farrar, Straus and Giroux, 1998– . IL 5–8

Hilarious and emotionally honest—some of the problems this hyperactive hero has had to deal with include controlling his mood swings when his prescription wears off, dealing with his dysfunctional family, and developing a friendship with Olivia Lapp.

Peirce, Lincoln. *Big Nate Series.* Harper, c2010– . IL 3–6

Meet Nate Wright—sixth grader, class clown, self-described genius, and the all-time record holder for school detentions! With black-and-white illustrations, comics, and doodles throughout, Big Nate blazes an unforgettable trail through middle school.

If You Liked *Diary of a Wimpy Kid* by Jeff Kinney, You May Like...

Pilkey, Dav. *The Adventures of Captain Underpants Series.* Blue Sky Press, c1997–2003. IL 3–6
   The outrageous adventures of the world's greatest superhero!

Russell, Rachel Renee. *Dork Diaries Series.* Aladdin, c2009– . IL 3–6
   Hilarious and heartwarming stories from the personal diary of Nikki Maxwell. Included are drawings, doodles, and comic strips that chronicle the daily drama of her life in middle school.

Vernon, Ursula. *Dragonbreath Series.* Dial Books, c2009– . IL 3–6
   This series is written in the author's trademark hybrid style of comic-book panels and text. Danny Dragonbreath and his friend Wendell get an up-close underwater tour of the Sargasso Sea from Danny's sea-serpent cousin, encountering giant squid and mako sharks.

If You Liked *Fallen Angels* by Walter Dean Myers, You May Like . . .

Bradley, Kimberly Brubaker. *For Freedom: The Story of a French Spy.* Dell Laurel-Leaf, 2005, c2003. 181p. IL 5–8, Lexile: 520

> This novel is based on the experiences of Suzanne David Hall, who, as a teenager in Nazi-occupied France, worked as a spy for the French Resistance while training to be an opera singer.

Hughes, Dean. *Search and Destroy.* Atheneum Books for Young Readers, c2005. 216p. IL YA, Lexile: 740

> Recent high school graduate Rick Ward, undecided about his future and eager to escape from his unhappy home life, joins the army and experiences the horrors of the war in Vietnam.

Paulsen, Gary. *Soldier's Heart: Being the Story of the Enlistment and Due Service of the Boy Charley Goddard in the First Minnesota Volunteers: A Novel of the Civil War.* Delacorte Press, c1998. 106p. IL YA, Lexile: 1000

> Eager to enlist, fifteen-year-old Charley has a change of heart after experiencing both the physical horrors and mental anguish of Civil War combat.

Remarque, Erich Maria. *All Quiet on the Western Front.* Little Brown, c1958. 291p. IL YA, Lexile: 830

> This classic novel depicts the experiences of a group of young German soldiers fighting and suffering during the last days of World War I.

Rylant, Cynthia. *I Had Seen Castles.* Harcourt, 1995, c1993. 97p. IL YA, Lexile: 950

> Now an old man, John is haunted by his memories of enlisting to fight in World War II, a decision that forced him to face the horrors of war and changed his life forever.

Trumbo, Dalton. *Johnny Got His Gun.* Bantam, 1982. 243p. IL AD, Lexile: 970

> A young man who was severely wounded in World War I thinks about his life and about the horror and futility of war and its toll on him.

Dear America: Letters Home from Vietnam. W. W. Norton, 2002, c1985. 344p. IL AD, Lexile: 1010 (Non-fiction)

> In these letters and poems written to families and friends by American soldiers fighting in Vietnam, the correspondents express their homesickness and the horrors of war.

If You Liked *Ghost Soldier* by Elaine Marie Alpin, You May Like . . .

Alphin, Elaine Marie. *Ghost Cadet.* Hither Page Press, c2010. 174p. IL 5–8
  Twelve-year-old Benjy, in Virginia visiting the grandmother whom he has never met, meets the ghost of a Virginia Military Institute cadet who was killed in the Battle of New Market in 1864 and helps him recover his family's treasured gold watch.

Asfar, Dan. *Ghost Stories of the Civil War.* Ghost House Books, c2003. 215p. IL 5–8 (Non-fiction)
  A collection of ghost stories set in the Civil War era. Stories about the ghosts of such famous men as Abraham Lincoln, Jefferson Davis, and even Edgar Allen Poe are told. The disembodied head of a fallen soldier terrifies visitors in Georgia, and Confederate soldiers rise from the dead.

Avi. *Iron Thunder: The Battle Between the* **Monitor** *&* **the** **Merrimac:** *A Civil War Novel.* Hyperion Books for Children, c2007. 203p. IL 3–6, Lexile: 620
  Thirteen-year-old Tom Carroll takes his place as head of the family after his father dies fighting for the Union. His job at the local ironworks, where he helps build an iron ship for the Union army, and his loyalty come into question when he is approached by Confederate spies to sell secrets about the ship to the South.

Avi, *Something Upstairs.* Scholastic, 2010, c1988. 140p. IL 5–8
  When Kenny moves from Los Angeles to Providence, Rhode Island, he discovers that his new house is haunted by the spirit of a slave boy, who asks Kenny to return with him to the early nineteenth century and prevent his murder.

Belanger, Jeff. *Ghosts of War: Restless Spirits of Soldiers, Spies, and Saboteurs.* Rosen Publishing, 2009. 235p. IL YA (Non-fiction)
  Contains accounts of reportedly true ghost sighting on more than twenty battlefields and describes the battles that took place at each site.

Civil War Ghosts. August House Publishers, c1991. 205p. IL YA
  A compilation of nine stories about ghosts of the Civil War, including pieces by Ambrose Bierce and John Jakes.

If You Liked *Gone* by Michael Grant, You May Like . . .

Armstrong, Jennifer. *Fire-Us Trilogy.* HarperCollins, c2002–2003. IL YA
In 2007, a small band of children join together in a Florida town, trying to survive in a world where it seems that all the adults have been killed off by a catastrophic virus.

Dashner, James. *The Maze Runner.* Delacorte Press, c2009. 375p. IL YA, Lexile: 770
Sixteen-year-old Thomas wakes up with no memory in the middle of a maze and realizes he must work with the community in which he finds himself if he is to escape.

Dobkin, Bonnie. *Neptune's Children.* Walker, 2008. 262p. IL YA, Lexile: 740
A group of children, stranded at an amusement park following a biological terrorist attack that has killed all the adults on Earth, work together to survive with the help of Milo, a boy whose father was an engineer at the park. When new threats arise and suspicions grow, however, rebellion erupts.

Higson, Charles. *The Enemy.* Hyperion, 2010, c2009. 440p. IL YA, Lexile: 590
A group of young survivors are offered safety from the roaming packs of zombie-like adults in Buckingham Palace. Even after they survive their perilous journey through London to the palace, the teens discover that their fight is far from over.

Nelson, O. T. *The Girl Who Owned a City.* First Avenue Editions, c1995. 200p. IL 5–8, Lexile: 660
When a plague sweeps over the earth, killing everyone except children younger than age twelve, ten-year-old Lisa organizes a group to build a new way of life.

Nix, Garth. *Shade's Children.* EOS, 2003, c1997. 344p. IL YA, Lexile: 980
In a savage future world, four young fugitives attempt to overthrow the bloodthirsty rule of the Overlords with the help of Shade, their mysterious mentor.

Pullman, Philip. *The Subtle Knife.* Knopf, c1997. 326p. IL 5–8, Lexile: 890
As the boundaries between worlds begin to dissolve, Lyra and her daemon help Will Parry in his search for his father and for a powerful, magical knife.

Shusterman, Neal. *Everlost.* Simon & Schuster Books for Young Readers, c2006. 313p. IL YA, Lexile: 860
When Nick and Allie are killed in a car crash, they end up in Everlost, or limbo for lost souls. Although Nick is satisfied there, Allie will stop at nothing—even skinjacking—to break free.

Shusterman, Neal. *Everwild.* Simon & Schuster Books for Young Readers, c2009. 424p. IL YA, Lexile: 870
Nick, enamored with Mary Hightower, leader of a group of Afterlights living in the ruins of the World Trade Center, joins with her and the Chocolate Ogre in a battle to save the land of Everlost.

Series

Testa, Dom. *Galahad Series.* Tor, 2009– . IL YA
Desperate to save the human race after a comet's deadly particles devastate the adult population, scientists create a ship that will carry a crew of 251 teenagers to a home in a distant solar system

From *101 Great, Ready-to-Use Book Lists for Teens* by Nancy J. Keane. Santa Barbara, CA: Libraries Unlimited. Copyright © 2012.

If You Liked *Graceling* by Kristin Cashore, You May Like . . .

Durrant, Lynda. *My Last Skirt: The Story of Jennie Hodgers, Union Soldier.* Clarion Books, c2006. 199p. IL 5–8, Lexile: 760
Enjoying the freedom afforded her while dressing as a boy so as to earn higher pay after emigrating from Ireland, Jennie Hodgers serves in the 95th Illinois Infantry as Private Albert Cashier, a Union soldier in the American Civil War.

Friesner, Esther M. *Nobody's Princess.* Random House, 2008, c2007. 305p. IL YA, Lexile: 910
Determined to fend for herself in a world where only men have real freedom, headstrong Helen—who will be called queen of Sparta and Helen of Troy one day—learns to fight, hunt, and ride horses while disguised as a boy, and goes on an adventure throughout the Mediterranean world.

Hale, Shannon. *Enna Burning.* Bloomsbury, 2004. 317p. IL YA, Lexile: 800
Enna hopes that her new knowledge of how to wield fire will help protect her good friend Isi—the Princess Anidori—and all of Bayern against their enemies. The need to burn proves uncontrollable, however, and puts Enna and her loved ones in grave danger.

Jones, Frewin. *Warrior Princess.* Eos, c2009. 346p. IL YA, Lexile: 780
After a deadly attack on her home, fifteen-year-old Princess Branwen meets a mystical woman in white who prophesies that Branwen will save her homeland from falling to the Saxons.

Landman, Tanya. *I Am Apache.* Candlewick Press, 2008. 305p. IL YA, Lexile: 860
Fourteen-year-old Siki vows revenge on the Mexican raiders who brutally murdered her little brother, and turns away from the tradition roles that women in her tribe fill to become an Apache warrior.

McKinley, Robin. *The Blue Sword.* Greenwillow Books, c1982. 272p. IL 5–8, Lexile: 1030
Harry, bored with her sheltered life in the remote orange-growing colony of Daria, discovers magic in herself when she is kidnapped by a native king with mysterious powers.

McKinley, Robin. *The Hero and the Crown.* Greenwillow, c1985. 246p. IL 5–8, Lexile: 1120
Aerin, with the guidance of the wizard Luthe and the help of the blue sword, wins the birthright due her as the daughter of the Damarian king and a witchwoman of the mysterious, demon-haunted North.

Nix, Garth. *Sabriel.* HarperTrophy, 1996. 491p. IL YA, Lexile: 1060
Sabriel, daughter of the necromancer Abhorsen, must journey into the mysterious and magical Old Kingdom to rescue her father from the Land of the Dead.

Pierce, Tamora. *Alanna: The First Adventure.* Atheneum Books for Young Readers, 2010, c1983. 249p. IL 5–8, Lexile: 690
Eleven-year-old Alanna, who aspires to be a knight even though she is a girl, disguises herself as a boy to become a royal page, learning many hard lessons along her path to high adventure.

If You Liked *Graceling* by Kristin Cashore, You May Like . . .

Rees, Celia. *Pirates!: The True and Remarkable Adventures of Minerva Sharpe and Nancy Kington, Female Pirates.* Bloomsbury, 2003. 379p. IL YA, Lexile: 800

At the dawn of the eighteenth century, Nancy Kington and Minerva Sharpe set sail from Jamaica on a pirate vessel, hoping to escape from an arranged marriage and slavery.

Rinaldi, Ann. *Girl in Blue.* Scholastic, 2001. 310p. IL 5–8, Lexile: 680

To escape an abusive father and an arranged marriage, fourteen-year-old Sarah, dressed as a boy, leaves her Michigan home to enlist in the Union Army. She becomes a soldier on the battlefields of Virginia as well as a Union spy working in the house of Confederate sympathizer Rose O'Neal Greenhow in Washington, D.C.

Tingle, Rebecca. *The Edge on the Sword.* Speak, 2003, c2001. 277p. IL YA, Lexile: 930

In ninth-century Britain, fifteen-year-old Aethelflaed, daughter of King Alfred of West Saxony, finds she must assume new responsibilities much sooner than expected when she is betrothed to Ethelred of Mercia as part of a plan to strengthen a strategic alliance against the Danes.

Wilson, Diane L. *I Rode a Horse of Milk White Jade.* Sourcebooks Jabberwocky, c2010. 257p. IL YA, Lexile: 1010

In early fourteenth-century China, Oyuna tells her granddaughter of her girlhood in Mongolia and how love for her horse enabled her to win an important race and bring good luck to her family.

Series

Collins, Suzanne. *The Hunger Games Trilogy.* Scholastic Press, 2008–2010. IL YA

Contains *The Hunger Games*, in which sixteen-year-old Katniss Everdeen becomes a contender in a gravely serious competition hosted by the Capitol, in which young boys and girls are pitted against each other in a televised fight to the death; *Catching Fire*, in which Katniss and Peeta win the competition and become the faces of an impending rebellion; and *Mockingjay*, in which Katniss and her family and friends are in danger because the Capitol holds her responsible for the unrest.

Meyer, L. A. *Bloody Jack Adventures.* Harcourt, c2002– . IL YA

Reduced to begging and thievery in the streets of London, thirteen-year-old orphan Jacky Faber disguises herself as a boy and connives her way onto a British warship set for high seas adventure in search of pirates.

If You Liked *Anthony Horwitz*, You May Like . . .

Butcher, A. J. *The Paranoia Plot.* Little, Brown, 2004, c2003. 236p. IL YA
Due to her unusual behavior, the Bond Team suspects Rebecca Dee is a double agent.

Butcher, A. J. *The Serpent Scenario.* Little, Brown, 2004, c2003. 218p. IL YA
The Bond Team sets out to avenge the death of Jennifer and stop drug lords from taking over Undertown; however, the Wallachian government is also looking to eliminate Talon and take over the drug market.

Butcher, A. J. *Spy High: Mission One.* Little, Brown, 2004, c2003. 214p. IL YA
As students at a special high school that trains them to be secret agents, six teenagers struggle to complete the training exercises as a team before being sent out into the field to sink or swim.

Clancy, Tom. *Tom Clancy's Net Force.* Berkley Books, 1999, c1998. 372p. IL AD
In the year 2010, Congress creates Net Force, an FBI agency designed to regulate and maintain the computers that are the new superpowers. When someone sabotages the computer mainframes and kills Net Force's director, Alex Michaels is forced to take on the director's position and find the killers before they take over the world.

Rose, Malcolm. *Framed!* Kingfisher, 2007, c2005. 223p. IL 5–8, Lexile: 760
Forensic scientist Luke Harding and his robot assistant must solve a series of on-campus murders, especially since Luke is being framed for the murders.

Rose, Malcolm. *Lost Bullet.* Kingfisher, 2005. 204p. IL 5–8, Lexile: 770
Recently qualified as a forensic investigator, sixteen-year-old Luke Harding is assigned to the slums of London, where he and his robotic sidekick Malc investigate a doctor's murder.

Yancey, Richard. *The Extraordinary Adventures of Alfred Kropp.* Bloomsbury Publishing, 2005. 339p. IL YA, Lexile: 810
Through a series of dangerous and violent misadventures, teenage loser Alfred Kropp rescues King Arthur's legendary sword Excalibur from the forces of evil.

Series

Flanagan, John. *Ranger's Apprentice Series.* Philomel Books, 2005– . IL 5–8
When Will is rejected by battleschool, he becomes a reluctant apprentice to the mysterious Ranger Halt, and winds up protecting the kingdom from danger.

Korman, Gordon. *On the Run Series.* Scholastic, c2005– . IL 3–6
Two nationally known fugitives, Aiden and Meg, are finding it harder and harder to find the evidence to clear their parents.

If You Liked *I Am Number Four* by Pittacus Lore, You May Like . . .

Curley, Marianne. *Old Magic.* Simon Pulse, 2002. 316p. IL YA, Lexile: 810
Witch-in-training Kate is mesmerized by her new classmate Jarrod Thornton; she realizes that he is the victim of a centuries-old family curse but he has difficulty believing her.

Dashner, James. *The Maze Runner.* Delacorte Press, c2009. 375p. IL YA, Lexile: 770
Sixteen-year-old Thomas wakes up with no memory in the middle of a maze and realizes he must work with the community in which he finds himself if he is to escape.

Gill, David Macinnis. *Black Hole Sun.* Greenwillow Books, c2010. 340p. IL YA, Lexile: 610
Sixteen-year-old Durango and his crew of mercenaries are hired by the settlers of a mining community on Mars to protect their most valuable resource from a feral band of marauders.

Gould, Steven. *Jumper: Griffin's Story.* Tor, 2008, c2007. 286p. IL YA , Lexile: 800
Griffin O'Connor, a boy who can teleport, seeks revenge against a group of men who are interested in his ability and are responsible for the deaths of his parents.

Herbert, Frank. *Dune.* Ace Books, 1999, c1984. 517p. IL YA, Lexile: 800
This story follows a young prince, Paul Artreides, scion of a star-crossed dynasty, on his journey from boy to warrior to ruler of a dying planet destined to become a paradise regained.

Patterson, James. *The Dangerous Days of Daniel X.* Little, Brown, 2010, c2008. 234p. IL 3–6
Fifteen-year-old Daniel has followed in his parents' footsteps as the Alien Hunter, exterminating beings on the List of Alien Outlaws on Terra Firma. When he faces his first of the top ten outlaws, the very existence of Earth and another planet are at stake.

Smith, Tara Bray. *Betwixt.* Little, Brown, 2009, c2007. 487p. IL YA, Lexile: 710
Three alienated teenagers are drawn to a strange outdoor concert in the woods outside Seattle, where they discover that they possess magical powers and that their destinies are intertwined.

Teague, Mark. *The Doom Machine: A Novel.* Blue Sky Press, c2009. 376p. IL 5–8, Lexile: 610
When a spaceship lands in the small town of Vern Hollow in 1956, juvenile delinquent Jack Creedle and prim, studious Isadora Shumway form an unexpected alliance as they try to keep a group of extraterrestrials from stealing eccentric Uncle Bud's space travel machine.

Weyn, Suzanne. *Reincarnation.* Scholastic Press, 2008. 293p. IL YA, Lexile: 770
When a young couple dies in prehistoric times, their love—and link to various green stones—endures through the ages as they are reborn into new bodies and somehow find a way to connect.

Yansky, Brian. *Alien Invasion and Other Inconveniences.* Candlewick Press, 2010. 227p. IL YA
When a race of aliens quickly takes over the earth, leaving most people dead, high schooler Jesse finds himself a slave to an inept alien leader—a situation that brightens as Jesse develops telepathic powers and attracts the attention of two beautiful girls.

If You Liked *Into Thin Air* by Jon Krakauer, You May Like . . .

Armstrong, Jennifer. *Shipwreck at the Bottom of the World: The Extraordinary True Story of Shackleton and the* **Endurance.** Crown, 2000, c1998. 134p. IL 5–8, Lexile: 1090 (Non-fiction)
Describes the events of the 1914 Antarctic expedition led by Ernest Shackleton. After being trapped in a frozen sea for nine months, the group's ship, *Endurance*, was finally crushed, forcing Shackleton and his men to make a very long and perilous journey to reach inhabited land.

Capuzzo, Mike. *Close to Shore: The Terrifying Shark Attacks of 1916.* Broadway Books, 2002, c2001. 317p. IL AD, Lexile: 1200 (Non-fiction)
Recreates the events of the summer of 1916, when a rogue great white shark attacked swimmers along the New Jersey shore.

George, Jean Craighead. *My Side of the Mountain.* Dutton, c1988. 177p. IL 5–8, Lexile: 810
A young boy relates his adventures during the year he spends living alone in the Catskill Mountains, including his struggle for survival, his dependence on nature, his animal friends, and his ultimate realization that he needs human companionship.

McKernan, Victoria. *Shackleton's Stowaway.* Laurel-Leaf, 2006, c2005. 317p. IL 5–8, Lexile: 740
A fictionalized account of the adventures of eighteen-year-old Perce Blackborow, who stowed away for the 1914 Antarctic expedition led by Ernest Shackleton. After the group's ship, *Endurance*, was crushed by ice, Blackborow endured many hardships, including the loss of his toes to frostbite, during the nearly two-year return journey across sea and ice.

Mikaelsen, Ben. *Touching Spirit Bear.* HarperCollins, c2001. 241p. IL 5–8, Lexile: 670
After his anger erupts into violence, fifteen year-old Cole, to avoid going to prison, agrees to participate in a sentencing alternative based on the Native American circle justice. He is sent to a remote Alaskan island, where an encounter with a huge Spirit Bear changes his life.

Paulsen, Gary. *Hatchet.* Atheneum Books for Young Readers, c1987. 195p. IL 5–8, Lexile: 1020
After a plane crash, thirteen-year-old Brian spends fifty-four days in the wilderness, learning to survive with only the aid of a hatchet given him by his mother, and learning to survive his parents' divorce.

Paulsen, Gary. *The Transall Saga.* Delacorte Press, c1998. 248p. IL YA, Lexile: 630
While backpacking in the desert, thirteen-year-old Mark falls into a tube of blue light and is transported into a more primitive world, where he must use his knowledge and skills to survive.

Pfetzer, Mark. *Within Reach: My Everest Story.* Puffin Books, 2000, c1998. 224p. IL 5–8, Lexile: 970 (Non-fiction)
The author describes how he spent his teenage years climbing mountains in the United States, South America, Africa, and Asia, with an emphasis on his two expeditions up Mount Everest.

Smith, Roland. *Peak.* Harcourt, c2007. 246p. IL YA, Lexile: 760
A fourteen-year-old boy attempts to be the youngest person to reach the top of Mount Everest.

If You Liked *Into Thin Air* by Jon Krakauer, You May Like...

Stark, Peter. *Last Breath: The Limits of Adventure.* Ballantine Books, 2002, c2001. 300p. IL AD
In this collection of short stories, adventurers find themselves on the brink of death from hypothermia, drowning, mountain sickness, avalanche, scurvy, heatstroke, falling, predators, the bends, cerebral malaria, and dehydration.

White, Robb. *Deathwatch.* Bantam Doubleday Dell Books for Young Readers, 1973, c1972. 220p. IL YA, Lexile: 990
Needing money for school, a college student accepts a job as a guide on a desert hunting trip and nearly loses his life.

Series

Korman, Gordon. *Everest Series.* Scholastic, c2002. IL 3–6
Four climbers—winners of an American Junior Alpine Association contest—vie to become the youngest person ever to reach the peak of Mount Everest.

If You Liked *Lemonade Mouth* by Mark Peter Hughes, You May Like...

Avi. *Never Mind!: A Twin Novel.* HarperTrophy, 2005, c2004. 200p. IL 5–8, Lexile: 620
Twelve-year-old New York City twins Meg and Edward have nothing in common, so they are just as shocked as everyone else when Meg's hopes for popularity and Edward's mischievous schemes collide in a hilarious showdown.

Benway, Robin. *Audrey, Wait!* Razorbill, c2008. 313p. IL YA, Lexile: 760
Audrey Cuttler's life is turned upside down when her ex-boyfriend's song about their breakup hits the top of the charts. Audrey becomes a prime target for the paparazzi, who are documenting her every move, hoping to catch her messing up, and causing her nothing but misery.

Choyce, Lesley. *Thunderbowl.* Orca Book, 2004. 102p. IL YA, Lexile: 520
Sixteen-year-old Jeremy, caught up in the excitement of playing guitar for the hot band Thunderbowl, begins to lose control of the rest of his life.

Craft, Liz. *Bass Ackwards and Belly Up: A Novel.* Little, Brown, 2006. 386p. IL YA, Lexile: 790
Three best friends decide to forego college and pursue their individual dreams, while the fourth chooses to stay in school.

Crutcher, Chris. *Whale Talk.* Greenwillow Books, c2001. 220p. IL YA, Lexile: 1000
Intellectually and athletically gifted, TJ, a multiracial, adopted teenager, shuns organized sports and the gung-ho athletes at his high school—until he agrees to form a swimming team and recruits some of the school's less popular students to join it.

Going, Kelly. *Fat Kid Rules the World.* G. P. Putnam's Sons, c2003. 187p. IL YA, Lexile: 700
Seventeen-year-old Troy—depressed, suicidal, and weighing nearly three hundred pounds—gets a new perspective on life when Curt, a semi-homeless teen who is a genius on guitar, asks Troy to be the drummer in a rock band.

Graham, Rosemary. *Thou Shalt Not Dump the Skater Dude: And Other Commandments I Have Broken.* Speak, 2008, c2005. 281p. IL YA
Having endured the vicious rumors spread by her professional-skateboarder ex-boyfriend, high school sophomore Kelsey Wilcox tries to salvage her reputation while attempting to earn a place on her high school newspaper.

High, Linda Oatman. *Sister Slam and the Poetic Motormouth Roadtrip.* Bloomsbury, Distributed by Holtzbrinck Publishers, c2004. 256p. IL YA
In this novel told in slam verse, best friends and aspiring poets Laura and Twig embark on a road trip after graduating from high school, traveling from Pennsylvania to New York City while participating in slam poetry events.

Katcher, Brian. *Almost Perfect.* Delacorte Press, c2009. 360p IL YA, Lexile: 620
With his mother working long hours and in pain from a romantic breakup, eighteen-year-old Logan feels alone and unloved until a zany new student—who is hiding a big secret—arrives at his small-town Missouri high school.

If You Liked *Lemonade Mouth* by Mark Peter Hughes, You May Like . . .

Kluger, Steve. *My Most Excellent Year: A Novel of Love, Mary Poppins, & Fenway Park.* Dial Books, c2008. 403p. IL YA, Lexile: 1030

Three teenagers in Boston narrate their experiences of a year of new friendships, first loves, and coming into their own.

Manning, Sarra. *Guitar Girl.* Speak, 2005, c2003. 217p. IL YA

As her band, The Hormones, becomes an international sensation, seventeen-year-old Molly begins to question the high cost of fame.

Nelson, Blake. *Rock Star, Superstar.* Speak, 2005, c2004. 229p. IL YA, Lexile: 530

When Pete, a talented bass player, moves from playing in the high school jazz band to playing in a popular rock group, he finds the experience exhilarating, even as his new fame jeopardizes his relationship with girlfriend Margaret.

Oates, Joyce Carol. *Big Mouth & Ugly Girl.* HarperTempest, 2003, c2002. 266p. IL YA, Lexile: 720

When sixteen-year-old Matt is falsely accused of threatening to blow up his high school and his friends turn against him, an unlikely classmate comes to his aid.

Tashjian, Janet. *The Gospel According to Larry.* Dell Laurel-Leaf, 2003, c2001. 227p. IL YA, Lexile: 800

Seventeen-year-old Josh, a loner-philosopher who wants to make a difference in the world, tries to maintain his secret identity as the author of a website that is receiving national attention.

If You Liked *Leviathan* by Scott Westerfeld, You May Like . . .

Blackwood, Gary L. *The Year of the Hangman*. Speak, 2004, c2002. 261p. IL YA, Lexile: 820
In 1777, having been kidnapped and taken forcibly from England to the American colonies, fifteen-year-old Creighton becomes part of developments in the political unrest there that may spell defeat for the patriots and change the course of history.

Harland, Richard. *Worldshaker*. Simon & Schuster Books for Young Readers, 2010, c2009. 388p. IL YA, Lexile: 640
Sixteen-year-old Col Porpentine is being groomed as the next Commander of Worldshaker, a juggernaut where elite families live on the upper decks while the Filthies toil below. When he meets Riff, a Filthy girl on the run, he discovers how ignorant he is of his home and its residents.

Heiligman, Deborah. *Charles and Emma: The Darwins' Leap of Faith*. Holt, 2009. 268p. IL YA, Lexile: 1020 (Non-fiction)
This biography of English naturalist Charles Darwin provides an account of the personality behind evolutionary theory and the effect of his work on his personal life, including his relationship with his religious wife.

Oppel, Kenneth. *Airborn*. Eos, c2004. 355p. IL YA, Lexile: 760
Matt, a young cabin boy aboard an airship, and Kate, a wealthy young girl traveling with her chaperone, team up to search for the existence of mysterious winged creatures reportedly living hundreds of feet above the Earth's surface.

Oppel, Kenneth. *Skybreaker*. Eos, 2007, c2006. 544p. IL YA, Lexile: 750
Matt Cruse, a student at the Airship Academy, and Kate de Vries, a young heiress, team up with a gypsy and a daring captain to find a long-lost airship, rumored to carry a treasure beyond imagination.

Oppel, Kenneth. *Starclimber*. Eos, c2009. 390p. IL YA, Lexile: 700
As members of the first crew of astralnauts, Matt Cruse and Kate De Vries journey into outer space on the *Starclimber* and face a series of catastrophes that threaten the survival of all on board.

Reeve, Philip. *Fever Crumb*. Scholastic Press, 2010, c2009. 325p IL YA, Lexile: 1000
Foundling Fever Crumb has been raised as an engineer even though females in the future London, England, are not believed capable of rational thought. At age fourteen, she leaves her sheltered world and begins to learn startling truths about her past while facing danger in the present.

Reeve, Philip. *Larklight, or, The Revenge of the White Spiders!, Or, To Saturn's Rings and Back!: A Rousing Tale of Dauntless Pluck in the Farthest Reaches of Space*. Bloomsbury Children's, 2006. 399p. IL 5–8, Lexile: 1170
In an alternate-universe Victorian England, young Arthur and his sister Myrtle, who are residents of Larklight, a floating house in one of Her Majesty's outer space territories, uncover a spidery plot to destroy the solar system.

If You Liked *Leviathan* by Scott Westerfeld, You May Like . . .

Reeve, Philip. *Mortal Engines Quartet.* Scholastic Press, c2004– . IL YA

Tom is a third-class apprentice in a distant future in which technology has been lost and tiered cities move about the Earth on caterpillar tracks, often absorbing smaller locales. He has many dangerous adventures after being pushed off London by Thaddeus Valentine, a historian who is trying to resurrect an ancient atomic weapon.

Reeve, Philip. *Starcross, or, The Coming of the Moobs, Or, Our Adventures in the Fourth Dimension!: A Stirring Adventure of Spies, Time Travel and Curious Hats.* Bloomsbury Children's Books, 2007. 368p. IL 5–8, Lexile: 1150

Young Arthur Mumby, his sister Myrtle, and their mother accept an invitation to take a holiday at an up-and-coming resort in the asteroid belt. There, they become involved in a dastardly plot involving spies, time travel, and mind-altering clothing.

If You Liked *Little Brother* by Corey Doctorow, You May Like . . .

Anderson, M. T. *Feed.* Candlewick Press, 2002. 299p. IL YA, Lexile: 770
In a future where most people have computer implants in their heads to control their environment, a boy meets an unusual girl who is in serious trouble.

Bachorz, Pam. *Candor.* Egmont USA, 2009. 249p. IL YA, Lexile: 350
For a fee, "model teen" Oscar Banks has been secretly—and selectively—sabotaging the subliminal messages that program the behavior of the residents of Candor, Florida—until his attraction to a rebellious new girl threatens to expose his subterfuge.

Bodeen, S. A. *The Compound.* Feiwel and Friends, 2008. 248p. IL YA, Lexile: 570
Fifteen-year-old Eli and his family have been locked inside a radiation-proof compound built by his father to keep them safe following a nuclear attack. As the family's situation steadily disintegrates over the course of six years, Eli begins to question his future, as well as his father's grip on sanity.

Bray, Libba. *Going Bovine.* Delacorte Press, c2009. 480p. IL YA, Lexile: 680
Cameron Smith, a disaffected sixteen-year-old diagnosed with mad cow disease, sets off on a road trip with a death-obsessed, video-gaming dwarf whom he meets in the hospital in an attempt to find a cure.

Child, Lincoln. *Utopia.* Fawcett Books, 2003, c2002. 434p. IL AD
When the computerized infrastructure of Utopia, the world's most popular and technologically advanced theme park, is overtaken by mercenaries, Andrew Warne, the computer engineer who designed the park's robotics, becomes the best chance for its thousands of visitors—including Warne's daughter—to survive.

Dashner, James. *The Maze Runner.* Delacorte Press, c2009. 375p. IL YA, Lexile: 770
Sixteen-year-old Thomas wakes up with no memory in the middle of a maze and realizes he must work with the community in which he finds himself if he is to escape.

Deuker, Carl. *Runner.* Houghton Mifflin, 2005. 216p. IL YA, Lexile: 670
Living with his alcoholic father on a broken-down sailboat on Puget Sound has been hard on seventeen-year-old Chance Taylor. When his love of running leads to a high-paying job, however, he quickly learns that the money is not worth the risk.

Doctorow, Cory. *For the Win.* Tor, 2010. 475p. IL YA, Lexile: 1070
A group of teens from around the world find themselves drawn into an online revolution arranged by a mysterious young woman known as Big Sister Nor, who hopes to challenge the status quo and change the world using her virtual connections.

Fisher, Catherine. *Incarceron.* Dial Books, 2010, c2007. 442p. IL YA, Lexile: 600
To free herself from an upcoming arranged marriage, Claudia, the daughter of the Warden of Incarceron, a futuristic prison with a mind of its own, decides to help a young prisoner escape.

If You Liked *Little Brother* by Corey Doctorow, You May Like . . .

Fukui, Isamu. *Truancy.* Tor, 2008. 429p. IL YA, Lexile: 1000
In the City, where the iron-fisted Mayor's goal is perfect control through education, fifteen-year-old Tack is torn between a growing sympathy for the Truancy, an underground movement determined to bring down the system at any cost, and the desire to avenge a death caused by a Truant.

Henderson, Jan-Andrew. *Bunker 10.* Harcourt, 2007. 253p. IL YA, Lexile: 680
Something is going terribly wrong at the top-secret Pinewood Military Installation, and the teenage geniuses who study and work there are about to discover a horrible truth as they lead a small military force trying to retrieve data and escape before the compound self-destructs.

Huxley, Aldous. *Brave New World.* Harper Perennial, 2006, c1932. 259p. IL YA, Lexile: 870
This satirical novel is set in the utopia of the future, a world in which babies are decanted from bottles and the great Ford is worshipped.

Kass, Pnina. *Real Time: A Novel.* Clarion, c2004. 186p. IL YA, Lexile: 640
Sixteen-year-old Tomas Wanninger persuades his mother to let him leave Germany to volunteer at a kibbutz in Israel, where he experiences a violent political attack and finds answers about his own past.

Lloyd, Saci. *The Carbon Diaries 2015.* Holiday House, 2009, c2008. 330p. IL YA, Lexile: 690
In 2015, England becomes the first nation to introduce carbon dioxide rationing in a drastic bid to combat climate change. Sixteen-year-old Laura documents the first year of rationing as her family spirals out of control.

Lowry, Lois. *The Giver.* Houghton Mifflin, 1993. 180p. IL 5–8, Lexile: 760
Given his lifetime assignment at the Ceremony of Twelve, Jonas becomes the receiver of memories shared by only one other member of his community—and discovers the terrible truth about the society in which he lives.

Nelson, Blake. *Paranoid Park.* Speak, 2008, c2006. 180p. IL YA
A sixteen-year-old Portland, Oregon, skateboarder, whose parents are going through a difficult divorce, is engulfed by guilt and confusion when he accidentally kills a security guard at a train yard.

Orwell, George. *1984: A Novel.* Signet Classic, 1977, c1949. 328p. IL YA, Lexile: 1090
This classic novel depicts life in a totalitarian regime of the future.

Pearson, Mary. *The Adoration of Jenna Fox.* Henry Holt, 2008. 266p. IL YA, Lexile: 570
In the not-too-distant future, when biotechnological advances have made synthetic bodies and brains possible but illegal, a seventeen-year-old girl, recovering from a serious accident and suffering from memory lapses, learns a startling secret about her existence.

Plum-Ucci, Carol. *Streams of Babel.* Harcourt, c2008. 424p. IL YA, Lexile: 840
When six teens face a bioterrorist attack on American soil, four of them are infected with the mysterious disease affecting their small New Jersey neighborhood and the other two, both brilliant computer hackers, assist the United States Intelligence Coalition in tracking the perpetrators.

If You Liked *Little Brother* by Corey Doctorow, You May Like . . .

Richards, Justin. *The Chaos Code*. Bloomsbury, 2007. 388p. IL YA
Fifteen-year-old Matt and his new friend Robin travel the globe on a quest to retrieve an ancient code—rumored to have brought down the ancient civilization of Atlantis—from the hands of a madman who is bent on destroying the modern world.

Sandford, John. *The Hanged Man's Song*. Berkley Books, 2004, c2003. 340p. IL AD
Kidd—an artist, computer whiz, and professional crook—teams up with his sometime partner and lover LuEllen in an effort to retrieve an incriminating laptop that was stolen when its owner Bobby, a superhacker, was murdered.

Shusterman, Neal. *Unwind*. Simon & Schuster Books for Young Readers, c2007. 335p. IL YA, Lexile: 740
Three teens embark upon a cross-country journey to escape from a society that salvages body parts from children ages thirteen to eighteen.

Smith, Alexander Gordon. *Lockdown: Escape from Furnace*. Farrar Straus and Giroux, 2009. 273p. IL YA, Lexile: 1010
When fourteen-year-old Alex is framed for murder, he becomes an inmate in the Furnace Penitentiary, where brutal inmates and sadistic guards reign, boys who disappear in the middle of the night sometimes return weirdly altered, and escape might just be possible.

Sorrells, Walter. *First Shot: What Would You Do If Your Dad Was a Murderer?* Speak, 2009, c2007. 279p. IL YA, Lexile: 580
During his sophomore year, high school senior David Crandall's mother was murdered. Now, after learning about a family embezzlement secret and witnessing his father burying a shotgun, he begin to suspect that his dad was the murderer.

Updike, John. *Terrorist*. Knopf, 2006. 310p. IL AD
Eighteen-year-old Ahmad Ashmawy Mulloy, son of a pale, freckled Irish American mother and dark-skinned Egyptian father, feels alienated from his New Jersey classmates because of his dun-colored skin and his Muslim faith. His lack of self-confidence makes him an easy target for the unscrupulous iman of the local mosque, who steers Ahmad in the direction of a terrorist cell planning an attack on the Holland Tunnel.

Volponi, Paul. *Rikers High*. Viking, 2010. 246p. IL YA, Lexile: 790
Arrested on a minor offense, a New York City teenager attends high school in the jail facility on Rikers Island while waiting for his case to go to court.

Wasserman, Robin. *Hacking Harvard: A Novel*. Simon Pulse, 2007. 320p. IL YA, Lexile: 840
Four pranksters decide that they will use their intelligence to get an unqualified student into Harvard University.

Westerfeld, Scott. *Leviathan*. Simon Pulse, 2009. 440p. IL YA, Lexile: 790
In an alternate 1914 Europe, fifteen-year-old Austrian Prince Alek is on the run from the Clanker Powers, who are attempting to take over the globe using mechanical machinery. He forms an uneasy alliance with Deryn, who, disguised as a boy to join the British Air Service, is learning to fly genetically engineered beasts.

If You Liked *Little Brother* by Corey Doctorow, You May Like . . .

Westerfeld, Scott. *So Yesterday: A Novel.* Razorbill, c2004. 225p. IL YA, Lexile: 770
Hunter Braque, a New York City teenager who is paid by corporations to spot what is "cool," combines his analytical skills with his girlfriend Jen's creative talents to find a missing person and thwart a conspiracy directed at the heart of consumer culture.

Whyman, Matt. *Icecore: A Thriller.* Atheneum Books for Young Readers, 2007. 307p. IL YA, Lexile: 890
Seventeen-year-old Englishman Carl Hobbes meant no harm when he hacked into Fort Knox's security system. Nevertheless, at Camp Twilight in the Arctic Circle, known as "the Guantanamo Bay of the north," he is tortured to reveal information about a conspiracy of which he was never a part.

Series

Collins, Suzanne. *Hunger Games Trilogy.* Scholastic Press, 2008– . IL YA
Sixteen-year-old Katniss Everdeen accidentally becomes a contender in the annual Hunger Games, a gravely serious competition hosted by the Capitol, in which young boys and girls are pitted against each other in a televised fight to the death.

Ness, Patrick. *Chaos Walking.* Candlewick Press, 2009– . IL YA
Todd, who is one month away from an important birthday, learns the tough lessons of adulthood when he is forced to flee after discovering a secret near the town where he lives.

Westerfeld, Scott. *Uglies Series.* Simon Pulse, c2007– . IL YA
Tally is faced with a difficult choice when her new friend Shay decides to risk life on the outside rather than submit to the forced operation that turns sixteen-year-old girls into gorgeous beauties. She soon realizes that there is a whole new side to the pretty world that she doesn't like.

If You Liked *Little House on the Prairie* by Laura Ingalls Wilder, You May Like . . .

Alcott, Louisa May. *Little Women.* Oxford University Press, 2007. 323p. IL 5–8
The story of the four March sisters—Meg, Jo, Beth, and Amy—and their trials growing into young ladies in a very poor home in nineteenth-century New England.

Aldrich, Bess Streeter. *A Lantern in Her Hand.* Puffin Books, 1997. 251p. IL YA, Lexile: 1020
After marrying Will Deal and moving to Nebraska, Abbie endures the difficulties of frontier life and raises her children to pursue the ambitions that were once her own.

Brink, Carol Ryrie. *Caddie Woodlawn.* Simon & Schuster Books for Young Readers, 1973. 275p. IL 5–8, Lexile: 890
An eleven-year-old tomboy experiences a series of adventures while growing up on the Wisconsin frontier in the mid-nineteenth century.

Cather, Willa. *My Antonia.* Houghton Mifflin, 1995, c1918. 244p. IL AD, Lexile: 1010
A successful lawyer remembers his boyhood in Nebraska and his friendship with an immigrant Bohemian girl.

Conrad, Pam. *Prairie Songs.* HarperTrophy, 1987, c1985. 167p. IL 5–8, Lexile: 780
Louisa's life in a loving pioneer family on the Nebraska prairie is altered by the arrival of a new doctor and his beautiful, tragically frail wife.

Cushman, Karen. *The Ballad of Lucy Whipple.* Clarion Books, c1996. 195p. IL 5–8, Lexile: 1030
In 1849, twelve-year-old California Morning Whipple, who renames herself Lucy, is distraught when her mother moves the family from Massachusetts to a rough California mining town.

Donnelly, Jennifer. *A Northern Light.* Harcourt, c2003. 389p. IL YA, Lexile: 700
In 1906, sixteen-year-old Mattie is determined to attend college and be a writer despite the wishes of her father and boyfriend. When she takes a job at a hotel, the death of a guest renews her determination to live her own life.

Erdrich, Louise. *The Birchbark House.* Hyperion Paperbacks for Children, 2002, c1999. 244p. IL 5–8, Lexile: 970
Omakayas, a seven-year-old Native American girl of the Ojibwa tribe, lives through the joys of summer and the perils of winter on an island in Lake Superior in 1847.

Erdrich, Louise. *The Game of Silence.* HarperCollins, c2005. 256p. IL 5–8, Lexile: 900
Nine-year-old Omakayas and her family, members of the Ojibwa tribe, are forced to leave their island on Lake Superior in 1850 when white settlers move into the territory. She eventually comes to realize that the things most important to her are her home and way of life.

Ferber, Edna. *So Big.* Harper Perennial Modern Classics, 2010, c1924. 252p. IL AD
This story focuses on Selina De Jong, a farmer in High Prairie, and her marriage, widowhood, eventual success as a truck farmer, and son Dirk.

If You Liked *Little House on the Prairie* by Laura Ingalls Wilder, You May Like . . .

Gray, Dianne E. *Holding up the Earth.* Houghton Mifflin, c2000. 210p. IL 5–8, Lexile: 880
Fourteen-year-old Hope visits her new foster mother's Nebraska farm. Through old letters, a diary, and stories, she gets a vivid picture of the past in the voices of four girls her age who lived there in 1869, 1900, 1936, and 1960.

Holm, Jennifer L. *Boston Jane: An Adventure.* Random House, 2010, c2001. 247p. IL 3–6
Schooled in the lessons of etiquette for young ladies of 1854, Miss Jane Peck of Philadelphia finds little use for manners during her long sea voyage to the Pacific Northwest and while living among the American traders and Chinook Indians of Washington Territory.

Hurwitz, Johanna. *The Unsigned Valentine and Other Events in the Life of Emma Meade.* HarperCollins, 2006. 167p. IL 3–6, Lexile: 810
In early twentieth-century Vermont, fifteen-year-old Emma confides in her diary both her hopes of becoming a farmer's wife one day and her frustrations with her parents' belief that she is too young to be courted by the handsome Cole Berry.

Ingold, Jeanette. *The Big Burn.* Harcourt, 2003, c2002. 301p. IL 5–8, Lexile: 860
Three teenagers battle the flames of the Big Burn of 1910, one of the century's biggest wildfires.

Ingold, Jeanette. *Mountain Solo.* Harcourt, 2005, c2003. 309p. IL YA, Lexile: 810
Tess, a violin prodigy who has been playing since age three, throws away all her training and talent to start a new life with her father in Montana, where she realizes having a normal life isn't always so normal.

Jocelyn, Marthe. *Mable Riley: A Reliable Record of Humdrum, Peril, and Romance.* Candlewick Press, 2004. 279p. IL 5–8, Lexile: 890
In 1901, fourteen-year-old Mable Riley dreams of being a writer and having adventures while stuck in Perth County, Ontario, assisting her sister in teaching school, and secretly becoming friends with a neighbor who holds scandalous opinions on women's rights.

Larson, Kirby. *Hattie Big Sky.* Yearling, 2008, 2006. 288p. IL YA, Lexile: 700
After inheriting her uncle's homesteading claim in Montana, sixteen-year-old orphan Hattie Brooks travels from Iowa in 1917 to make a home for herself and encounters some unexpected problems related to the war being fought in Europe.

Laskas, Gretchen Moran. *The Miner's Daughter.* Simon & Schuster Books for Young Readers, c2007. 250p. IL YA, Lexile: 850
Sixteen-year-old Willa, living in a Depression-era West Virginia mining town, works hard to help her family. She experiences love and friendship, and finds an outlet for her writing when her family becomes part of the Arthurdale, West Virginia, community supported by Eleanor Roosevelt.

Lovelace, Maud Hart. *Betsy–Tacy.* HarperTrophy, c2000. 122p. IL 3–6, Lexile: 650
After Tacy Kelly moves into the house across the street from Betsy Ray, the five-year-olds become inseparable friends.

If You Liked *Little House on the Prairie* by Laura Ingalls Wilder, You May Like...

MacLachlan, Patricia. *Sarah, Plain and Tall.* Charlotte Zolotow Book, c1985. 58p. IL 3–6, Lexile: 560
> When their father invites a mail-order bride to come live with them in their prairie home, Caleb and Anna are captivated by their new mother and hope that she will stay.

Montgomery, L. M. *Anne of Green Gables.* Knopf, Distributed by Random House, 1995. 396p. IL 5–8
> Anne, an eleven-year-old orphan, is sent by mistake to live with a lonely middle-aged brother and sister on a Prince Edward Island farm and proceeds to make an indelible impression on everyone around her.

Oswald, Nancy. *Nothing Here But Stones.* H. Holt, 2004. 215p. IL 5–8
> In 1882, ten-year-old Emma and her family, along with other Russian Jewish immigrants, arrive in Cotopaxi, Colorado. The new residents face inhospitable conditions as they attempt to start an agricultural colony, and lonely Emma is comforted by the horse whose life she saved.

Paterson, Katherine. *Jacob Have I Loved.* HarperCollins, c1980. 216p. IL 5–8, Lexile: 880
> After feeling deprived all her life of schooling, friends, mother, and even her name by her twin sister, Louise finally begins to find her identity.

Peck, Richard. *A Year Down Yonder.* Dial Books for Young Readers, c2000. 130p. IL 5–8, Lexile: 610
> During the recession of 1937, fifteen-year-old Mary Alice is sent to live with her feisty, larger-than-life grandmother in rural Illinois and comes to a better understanding of this fearsome woman.

Stratton-Porter, Gene. *A Girl of the Limberlost.* Indiana University Press, 1984. 479p. IL 5–8, Lexile: 850
> Elnora Comstock, an impoverished young girl growing up on the edge of the Limberlost swamp in Indiana, is a lover of nature who has an opportunity to pay for her education by collecting moths.

If You Liked *Lockdown* by Alexander Gordon Smith, You May Like . . .

Bodeen, S. A. *The Compound.* Feiwel and Friends, 2008. 248p IL YA, Lexile: 570

Fifteen-year-old Eli and his family are locked inside a radiation-proof compound built by his father to keep them safe following a nuclear attack. As the family's situation steadily disintegrates over the course of six years, Eli begins to question his future, as well as his father's grip on sanity.

Doctorow, Cory. *Little Brother.* Tor, 2008. 382p. IL YA, Lexile: 900

Interrogated for days by the Department of Homeland Security in the aftermath of a major terrorist attack on San Francisco, California, seventeen-year-old Marcus is released into what is now a police state, and decides to use his expertise in computer hacking to set things right.

Farmer, Nancy. *The House of the Scorpion.* Atheneum Books for Young Readers, c2002. 380p. IL 5–8, Lexile: 660

In a future where humans despise clones, Matt enjoys special status as the young clone of El Patron, the 142-year-old leader of a corrupt drug empire nestled between Mexico and the United States.

Fisher, Catherine. *Incarceron.* Dial Books, 2010, c2007. 442p. IL YA, Lexile: 600

To free herself from an upcoming arranged marriage, Claudia, the daughter of the Warden of Incarceron, a futuristic prison with a mind of its own, decides to help a young prisoner escape.

Grant, Michael. *Gone.* HarperTeen, c2008. 558p. IL YA, Lexile: 620

In a small town on the coast of California, everyone older than the age of fourteen suddenly disappears. The result is a battle between the remaining town residents and the students from a local private school, as well as between those who have "The Power" and are able to perform supernatural feats and those who do not.

Haddix, Margaret Peterson. *Among the Hidden.* Simon & Schuster Books for Young Readers, c1998. 153p. IL 3–6, Lexile: 800

In a future where the Population Police enforce the law limiting a family to only two children, Luke has lived all his twelve years in isolation and fear on his family's farm, until another "third" convinces him that the government is wrong.

Key, Watt. *Alabama Moon.* Farrar Straus Giroux, 2006. 294p. IL 5–8, Lexile: 720

After the death of his father, ten-year-old Moon Blake is removed from the Alabama forest where he was raised and sent to a boys home. There, for the first time, he has contact with the outside world and learns about friendship, love, and humanity.

Kostick, Conor. *Epic.* Viking, 2007, c2004. 364p. IL YA, Lexile: 880

On New Earth, a world based on a video role-playing game, fourteen-year-old Erik persuades his friends to aid him in some unusual gambits to save Erik's father from exile and to safeguard the futures of their families.

Malley, G. R. *The Declaration.* Bloomsbury, 2007. 300p. IL YA, Lexile: 930

In 2140 England, where drugs enable people to live forever and children are illegal, teenaged Anna, an obedient "Surplus" training to become a house servant, has her world view challenged when she meets Peter and discovers that her birth parents are trying to find her.

If You Liked *Lockdown* by Alexander Gordon Smith, You May Like . . .

Myers, Walter Dean. *Lockdown.* Amistad, c2010. 247p. IL YA, Lexile: 730
Teenage Reese, serving time at a juvenile detention facility, gets a lesson in making it through hard times from an unlikely friend with a harrowing past.

Ness, Patrick. *The Knife of Never Letting Go.* Candlewick Press, 2008. 479p. IL YA, Lexile: 860
Todd, who is one month away from an important birthday, learns the tough lessons of adulthood when he is forced to flee after discovering a secret near the town where he lives.

Patneaude, David. *Epitaph Road.* Egmont USA, 2010. 266p. IL YA, Lexile: 720
In 2097, men are a small and controlled minority in a utopian world ruled by women. Fourteen-year-old Kellen must fight to save his father from an outbreak of the virus that killed ninety-seven percent of the male population thirty years earlier.

Sedgwick, Marcus. *Revolver.* Roaring Brook Press, 2010, c2009. 204p. IL YA, Lexile: 890
Fourteen-year-old Sig is stranded at a remote cabin in the Arctic wilderness with his father, who died just hours earlier after falling through the ice, when a terrifying man arrives, claiming Sig's father owes him a share of a horde of stolen gold and that he will kill Sig if he does not get his money.

Shusterman, Neal. *Unwind.* Simon & Schuster Books for Young Readers, c2007. 335p. IL YA, Lexile: 740
Three teens embark upon a cross-country journey to escape from a society that salvages body parts from children ages thirteen to eighteen.

Smelcer, John E. *The Trap.* Holt, 2006. 170p. IL 5–8, Lexile: 1100
In alternating chapters, seventeen-year-old Johnny Least-Weasel, who is better known for brains than brawn, worries about his missing grandfather, and the grandfather, Albert Least-Weasel, struggles to survive, caught in his own steel trap in the Alaskan winter.

Strasser, Todd. *Boot Camp.* Simon Pulse, 2008, c2007. 238p. IL YA, Lexile: 750
After ignoring several warnings to stop dating his teacher, Garrett is sent to Lake Harmony, a boot camp that uses unorthodox and brutal methods to train students to obey their parents.

If You Liked *Matched* by Ally Condie, You May Like ...

Adlington, L. J. *Cherry Heaven.* Greenwillow Books, c2008. 458p. IL YA, Lexile: 830
Kat and Tanka J leave their war-torn city, move with their adoptive parents to the New Frontier, and are soon settled into a home called Cherry Heaven. They become alarmed when Luka, an escaped factory worker, confirms their suspicion that New Frontier is not the utopia it seems to be.

Adlington, L. J. *The Diary of Pelly D.* Greenwillow Books, 2008, c2005. 282p. IL YA, Lexile: 770
Toni V, a construction worker on a futuristic colony, finds the diary of a teenage girl whose life has been turned upside down by holocaust-like events, and he begins to question his own beliefs.

Bacigalupi, Paolo. *Ship Breaker.* Little, Brown, 2010. 326p. IL YA, Lexile: 690
In a futuristic world, teenaged Nailer scavenges copper wiring from grounded oil tankers for a living. When he finds a beached clipper ship with a girl in the wreckage, he has to decide whether he should strip the ship for its wealth or rescue the girl.

Bodeen, S. A. *The Compound.* Feiwel and Friends, 2008. 248p. IL YA, Lexile: 570
Fifteen-year-old Eli and his family have been locked inside a radiation-proof compound built by his father to keep them safe following a nuclear attack. As the family's situation steadily disintegrates over the course of six years, Eli begins to question his future, as well as his father's grip on sanity.

Dashner, James. *The Death Cure.* Delacorte Press, c2011. 384p. IL YA
In a final effort to complete the blueprint for the cure, Thomas must rely on the Gladers, with full memories restored. Thomas does not trust Wicked, however, and he remembers much more than they realize.

Dashner, James. *The Maze Runner.* Delacorte Press, c2009. 375p. IL YA, Lexile: 770
Sixteen-year-old Thomas wakes up with no memory in the middle of a maze and realizes he must work with the community in which he finds himself if he is to escape.

DeStefano, Lauren. *Wither.* Simon & Schuster Books for Young Readers, c2011. 358p. IL YA, Lexile: 800
After modern science turns every human into a genetic time bomb, with men dying at age twenty-five and women dying at age twenty, girls are kidnapped and married off to repopulate the world.

Doctorow, Cory. *Little Brother.* Tor, 2008. 382p. IL YA, Lexile: 900
Interrogated for days by the Department of Homeland Security in the aftermath of a major terrorist attack on San Francisco, California, seventeen-year-old Marcus is released into what is now a police state, and decides to use his expertise in computer hacking to set things right.

Dunn, Mark. *Ella Minnow Pea: A Novel in Letters.* Anchor Books, 2002, c2001. 208p. IL AD
The language-loving inhabitants of a South Carolina island interpret the falling of the letter "Z" from a beloved monument as a divine warning not to use the letter any longer. But catastrophe is imminent when the other letters in the monument—which contains the entire alphabet—begin falling one by one.

If You Liked *Matched* by Ally Condie, You May Like . . .

Fisher, Catherine. *Incarceron.* Dial Books, 2010, c2007. 442p. IL YA, Lexile: 600
To free herself from an upcoming arranged marriage, Claudia, the daughter of the Warden of Incarceron, a futuristic prison with a mind of its own, decides to help a young prisoner escape.

Grant, Michael. *Gone.* HarperTeen, c2008. 558p. IL YA, Lexile: 620
In a small town on the coast of California, everyone older than the age of fourteen suddenly disappears. The result is a battle between the remaining town residents and the students from a local private school, as well as between those who have "The Power" and are able to perform supernatural feats and those who do not.

Haddix, Margaret Peterson. *Among the Hidden.* Simon & Schuster Books for Young Readers, c1998. 153p. IL 3–6, Lexile: 800
In a future where the Population Police enforce the law limiting a family to only two children, Luke has lived all his twelve years in isolation and fear on his family's farm, until another "third" convinces him that the government is wrong.

Hautman, Pete. *Hole in the Sky.* Simon Pulse, 2005, c2001. 215p. IL YA, Lexile: 700
In a future world ravaged by a mutant virus, sixteen-year-old Ceej and three other teenagers seek to save the Grand Canyon from being flooded, while trying to avoid capture by a band of renegade survivors.

Kostick, Conor. *Epic.* Viking, 2007, c2004. 364p. IL YA, Lexile: 880
On New Earth, a world based on a video role-playing game, fourteen-year-old Erik persuades his friends to aid him in some unusual gambits to save Erik's father from exile and to safeguard the futures of their families.

Kostick, Conor. *Edda.* Viking, 2011. 440p. IL YA
In the virtual world of Edda, ruler Scanthax decides he wants to invade another virtual world, embroiling the universes of Edda, Saga, and Epic in war, with only three teenagers to try to restore peace.

Kostick, Conor. *Saga.* Viking, 2008. 367p. IL YA, Lexile: 780
On Saga, a world based on a video role-playing game, fifteen-year-old Ghost lives to break rules. When the Dark Queen who controls Saga plots to enslave its people and those of New Earth, Ghost and her airboarding friends, along with Erik and his friends from Epic, try to stop her.

Lloyd, Saci. *The Carbon Diaries 2015.* Holiday House, 2009, c2008. 330p. IL YA, Lexile: 690
In 2015, England becomes the first nation to introduce carbon dioxide rationing in a drastic bid to combat climate change. Sixteen-year-old Laura documents the first year of rationing as her family spirals out of control.

Lowry, Lois. *The Giver.* Houghton Mifflin, 1993. 180p. IL 5–8, Lexile: 760
Given his lifetime assignment at the Ceremony of Twelve, Jonas becomes the receiver of memories shared by only one other member of his community—and discovers the terrible truth about the society in which he lives.

Readalikes

If You Liked *Matched* by Ally Condie,
You May Like . . .

O'Brien, Caragh M. *Birthmarked.* Roaring Brook Press, 2010. 362p. IL YA, Lexile: 800
Sixteen-year-old Gaia Stone is a midwife who dutifully delivers at least three babies a month and hands them over to the Enclave, a community within walls where the children are adopted and live with conveniences that are not available to the outside world. She begins to question her loyalty to the group after her mother is brutally taken away from her by the people she serves.

O'Brien, Robert C. *Z for Zachariah.* Simon Pulse, 2007, c1974. 249p. IL YA
Seemingly the only person left alive after the holocaust of a war, a young girl is relieved to see a man arrive into her valley—until she realizes that he is a tyrant and she must somehow escape from him.

Pearson, Mary. *The Adoration of Jenna Fox.* Henry Holt, 2008. 266p. IL YA, Lexile: 570
In the not-too-distant future, when biotechnological advances have made synthetic bodies and brains possible but illegal, a seventeen-year-old girl, recovering from a serious accident and suffering from memory lapses, learns a startling secret about her existence.

Pfeffer, Susan Beth. *The Dead and the Gone.* Harcourt, 2008. 321p. IL YA, Lexile: 680
After a meteor hits the moon and sets off a series of horrific climate changes, seventeen-year-old Alex Morales must take care of his sisters alone in the chaos of New York City.

Ryan, Carrie. *The Dark and Hollow Places.* Delacorte Press, c2011. 376p. IL YA
Alone and listening to the moaning of the Dark City dying around her, Annah wants to find her way back home, to her sister and family and their village in the Forest of Hands and Teeth.

Ryan, Carrie. *The Dead-Tossed Waves.* Delacorte Press, c2010. 407p. IL YA, Lexile: 790
Gabry lives a quiet life in a town trapped between a forest and the ocean, hemmed in by the dead who hunger for the living. She becomes alarmed, however, when her mother Mary's secrets, a cult of religious zealots who worship the dead, and a stranger from the forest who seems to know Gabry threaten to destroy her world.

Ryan, Carrie. *The Forest of Hands and Teeth.* Delacorte Press, c2009. 310p. IL YA, Lexile: 900
Through twists and turns of fate, orphaned Mary seeks knowledge of life, love, and especially what lies beyond her walled village and the surrounding forest, where dwell the Unconsecrated, aggressive flesh-eating people who were once dead.

Shusterman, Neal. *Unwind.* Simon & Schuster Books for Young Readers, c2007. 335p. IL YA, Lexile: 740
Three teens embark upon a cross-country journey to escape from a society that salvages body parts from children ages thirteen to eighteen.

Stevermer, Caroline. *River Rats.* Magic Carpet Books, 1996. 305p. IL 5–8, Lexile: 690
Nearly twenty years after the holocaust called the Flash has destroyed modern civilization, Tomcat and a group of other orphans face danger as they steer an old steamboat over the toxic waters of the Mississippi River.

If You Liked *Matched* by Ally Condie, You May Like...

Weaver, Will. *Memory Boy: A Novel.* HarperTrophy, 2003, c2001. 230p. IL YA, Lexile: 570
Sixteen-year-old Miles and his family must flee their Minneapolis home and begin a new life in the wilderness after a chain of cataclysmic volcanic explosions creates dangerous conditions in their city.

Series

Collins, Suzanne. *The Hunger Games Trilogy.* Scholastic Press, 2008–2010. IL YA
Contains *The Hunger Games*, in which sixteen-year-old Katniss Everdeen becomes a contender in a gravely serious competition hosted by the Capitol, in which young boys and girls are pitted against each other in a televised fight to the death; *Catching Fire*, in which Katniss and Peeta win the competition and become the faces of an impending rebellion; and *Mockingjay*, in which Katniss and her family and friends are in danger because the Capitol holds her responsible for the unrest.

Westerfeld, Scott. *Uglies Series.* Simon Pulse, 2005– . IL YA
Tally is faced with a difficult choice when her new friend Shay decides to risk life on the outside rather than submit to the forced operation that turns sixteen-year-old girls into gorgeous beauties. She soon realizes that there is a whole new side to the pretty world that she doesn't like.

If You Liked *Nick and Norah's Infinite Playlist* by Rachel Cohn, You May Like . . .

Brooks, Kevin. *Candy.* The Chicken House/Scholastic, 2005. 364p. IL YA, Lexile: 640
Joe, an English boy from the right side of the tracks, is poised to get everything he has ever wanted, but he risks it all when he falls for Candy and is drawn into her seedy, dangerous world.

Castellucci, Cecil. *Beige.* Candlewick Press, 2007. 307p. IL YA, Lexile: 540
Katy, a quiet French Canadian teenager, reluctantly leaves Montreal to spend time with her estranged father, an aging Los Angeles punk rock legend.

Chbosky, Stephen. *The Perks of Being a Wallflower.* MTV Books/Pocket Books, c1999. 213p. IL YA, Lexile: 720
Charlie, a freshman in high school, explores the dilemmas of growing up through a collection of letters he sends to an unknown receiver.

Cohn, Rachel. *Naomi and Ely's No Kiss List: A Novel.* Knopf, c2007. 230p. IL YA, Lexile: 850
Although they have been friends and neighbors all their lives, straight Naomi and gay Ely find that their relationship becomes severely strained during their freshman year at New York University.

Dessen, Sarah. *This Lullaby: A Novel.* Viking, 2002. 345p. IL YA, Lexile: 820
Remy, a master at getting rid of boyfriends before any emotional attachments form, finds herself strangely unwilling to free herself from Dexter, a messy, disorganized, impulsive musician whom she suspects she has come to love.

Going, Kelly. *Fat Kid Rules the World.* G. P. Putnam's Sons, c2003. 187p. IL YA, Lexile: 700
Seventeen-year-old Troy—depressed, suicidal, and weighing nearly three hundred pounds—gets a new perspective on life when Curt, a semi-homeless teen who is a genius on guitar, asks Troy to be the drummer in a rock band.

Jones, Patrick. *Nailed.* Walker, 2006. 216p. IL YA, Lexile: 920
An outcast in a school full of jocks, sixteen-year-old Bret struggles to keep his individuality through his interest in drama and music, while trying to reconnect with his father.

Korman, Gordon. *Born to Rock.* Hyperion Paperbacks, 2008, c2006. 261p. IL YA, Lexile: 780
High school senior Leo Caraway, a conservative Republican, learns that his biological father is a punk rock legend.

Krovatin, Christopher. *Heavy Metal and You.* PUSH Books, c2005. 186p. IL YA, Lexile: 730
High schooler Sam begins losing himself when he falls for a preppy girl who wants him to give up getting wasted with his best friends, and even his passion for heavy metal music, to become a better person.

Lane, Dakota. *The Orpheus Obsession.* Katherine Tegen Books, c2005. 273p. IL YA, Lexile: 840
Sixteen-year-old Anooshka Stargirl, whose home life is less than rosy, meets a rock singer named Orpheus and finds her obsession with him drawing her into his world.

From *101 Great, Ready-to-Use Book Lists for Teens* by Nancy J. Keane. Santa Barbara, CA: Libraries Unlimited. Copyright © 2012.

If You Liked *Nick and Norah's Infinite Playlist* by Rachel Cohn, You May Like . . .

Lyga, Barry. *The Astonishing Adventures of Fanboy & Goth Girl.* Houghton Mifflin, 2006. 311p. IL YA, Lexile: 710

A fifteen-year-old "geek" who keeps a list of the high school jocks and others who torment him, and pours his energy into creating a great graphic novel, encounters Kyra, Goth Girl, who helps change his outlook on almost everything, including himself.

Manning, Sarra. *Guitar Girl.* Speak, 2005, c2003. 217p. IL YA

As her band, The Hormones, becomes an international sensation, seventeen-year-old Molly begins to question the high cost of fame.

Meno, Joe. *Hairstyles of the Damned.* Punk Planet Books, c2004. 270p. IL AD

Brian Oswald and his best friend, Gretchen, become involved in the punk rock scene in Chicago and begin hanging with various outcast groups to fit in.

Nelson, Blake. *Rock Star, Superstar.* Speak, 2005, c2004. 229p. IL YA, Lexile: 530

When Pete, a talented bass player, moves from playing in the high school jazz band to playing in a popular rock group, he finds the experience exhilarating, even as his new fame jeopardizes his relationship with his girlfriend Margaret.

O'Malley, Bryan Lee. *Scott Pilgrim. 1, Scott Pilgrim's Precious Little Life.* Oni Press, 2004. IL YA

Twenty-three-year-old Scott Pilgrim has the perfect life playing guitar in a rock band and dating a cute high school girl until he meets Ramona Flowers, an unforgettable rollerblading delivery girl whose seven evil ex-boyfriends Scott must defeat if he wants to win her love.

Portman, Frank. *King Dork.* Delacorte Press, 2008, c2006. 344p. IL YA, Lexile: 1060

High school loser Tom Henderson discovers that *The Catcher in the Rye* may hold the clues to the many mysteries in his life.

Watts, Leander. *Beautiful City of the Dead: A Novel.* Graphia, c2006. 254p. IL YA

After joining a heavy metal band, high school student Zee learns that she is a god of water and is called upon to fight sinister forces that want her powers for their own.

Westerfeld, Scott. *The Last Days: A Novel.* Razorbill, c2006. 286p. IL YA, Lexile: 820

Five New York teenagers try to concentrate on their new band while the city suffers from a mysterious epidemic that is turning people into cannibals.

If You Liked *The Perks of Being a Wallflower* by Stephen Chbosky, You May Like . . .

Alexie, Sherman. *The Absolutely True Diary of a Part-time Indian.* Little, Brown, 2009, c2007. 230p. IL YA, Lexile: 600
> Budding cartoonist Junior leaves his troubled school on the Spokane Indian Reservation to attend an all-white farm town school, where the only other Native American is the school mascot.

Barnes, John. *Tales of the Madman Underground.* Speak, 2011, c2009. 532p. IL YA, Lexile: 1040
> Karl Shoemaker, starting his senior year in Lightsburg, Ohio, in 1973, vows to break out of the therapy group he has been forced to attend during school hours and become "normal."

Brothers, Meagan. *Debbie Harry Sings in French.* Henry Holt, 2008. 234p. IL YA, Lexile: 560
> When Johnny completes an alcohol rehabilitation program and his mother sends him to live with his uncle in North Carolina, he meets Maria, who seems to understand his fascination with the new wave band Blondie. He also learns about his deceased father's youthful forays into "glam rock," which gives him perspective on himself, his past, and his current life.

Burgess, Melvin. *Smack.* Square Fish, 2010, c1996. 327p. IL AD, Lexile: 750
> After running away from their troubled homes, two English teenagers move in with a group of squatters in the port city of Bristol and try to find ways to support their growing addiction to heroin.

Cohn, Rachel. *Nick & Norah's Infinite Playlist.* Knopf, c2006. 183p. IL YA, Lexile: 1020
> High school student Nick O'Leary, a member of a rock band, meets college-bound Norah Silverberg and asks her to be his girlfriend for five minutes to help him avoid his ex-sweetheart.

Foer, Jonathan Safran. *Everything Is Illuminated.* Houghton Mifflin Harcourt, 2010. 647p. IL AD
> A young Jewish man named Jonathan Safran Foer goes in search of the woman who saved his grandfather from the Nazis and is aided by information provided to him by Alex Perchov, a native Ukrainian translator.

Frank, Hillary. *Better Than Running at Night.* Houghton Mifflin, c2002. 263p. IL YA, Lexile: 580
> Ellie, having endured a lonely high school existence, tries to make a place for herself as a freshman art student at the New England College of Art and Design.

Go Ask Alice. Simon & Schuster Books for Young Readers, c1971. 159p. IL YA
> This anonymous work is based on the diary of a fifteen-year-old drug user, which chronicles her struggle to escape the pull of the drug world.

Going, Kelly. *Fat Kid Rules the World.* G. P. Putnam's Sons, c2003. 187p. IL YA, Lexile: 700
> Seventeen-year-old Troy—depressed, suicidal, and weighing nearly three hundred pounds—gets a new perspective on life when Curt, a semi-homeless teen who is a genius on guitar, asks Troy to be the drummer in a rock band.

Green, John. *Looking for Alaska: A Novel.* Dutton, c2005. 221p. IL YA, Lexile: 930
> For sixteen-year-old Miles, his first year at Culver Creek Preparatory School in Alabama includes good friends and great pranks, but is defined by his search for answers about life and death after a fatal car crash.

If You Liked *The Perks of Being a Wallflower* by Stephen Chbosky, You May Like . . .

Green, John. *Paper Towns*. Dutton Books, c2008. 305p. ILYA, Lexile: 850
One month before graduating from his Central Florida high school, Quentin "Q" Jacobsen basks in the predictable boredom of his life—until the beautiful and exciting Margo Roth Spiegelman, Q's neighbor and classmate, takes him on a midnight adventure and then mysteriously disappears.

Hopkins, Ellen. *Crank*. Margaret K. McElderry Books, 2004. 537p. IL YA, Lexile: NP
Kristina Georgia Snow's life is turned upside down when she visits her absentee father, gets turned on to the drug "crank," becomes addicted, and is led down a desperate path that threatens her mind, soul, and her life.

Jenkins, A. M. *Repossessed*. HarperTeen, c2007. 218p. IL YA, Lexile: 700
A fallen angel, tired of being unappreciated while doing his pointless, demeaning job, leaves Hell, enters the body of a seventeen-year-old boy, and tries to experience the full range of human feelings before being caught and punished. Meanwhile, the boy's family and friends puzzle over his changed behavior.

Jones, Patrick. *Nailed*. Walker, 2006. 216p. IL YA, Lexile: 920
An outcast in a school full of jocks, sixteen-year-old Bret struggles to keep his individuality through his interest in drama and music, while trying to reconnect with his father.

Klass, David. *You Don't Know Me: A Novel*. Farrar, Straus and Giroux, 2001. 262p. IL YA, Lexile: 970
Fourteen-year-old John creates alternative realities in his mind as he tries to deal with his mother's abusive boyfriend, his crush on a beautiful, but shallow classmate, and other problems at school.

Korman, Gordon. *Born to Rock*. Hyperion Paperbacks, 2008, c2006. 261p. IL YA, Lexile: 780
High school senior Leo Caraway, a conservative Republican, learns that his biological father is a punk rock legend.

Kuehnert, Stephanie. *Ballads of Suburbia*. Pocket Books/MTV Books, 2009. 344p. IL YA
An aspiring film writer tells about her troubled teen years in the Chicago suburbs when she and her friends tried to escape the pain of their lives through rock music and drugs.

Kwasney, Michelle D. *Blue Plate Special*. Chronicle Books, c2009. 366p. IL YA
Madeline, Desiree, and Ariel—three young women who live in different decades—struggle with similar issues related to family, men, self-respect, empathy, and forgiveness.

Leitch, Will. *Catch: A Novel*. Razorbill, c2005. 286p. IL YA, Lexile: 720
Teenager Tim Temples must decide whether he wants to leave his comfortable life in a small town and go to college.

Levithan, David. *Boy Meets Boy*. Knopf, 2005, c2003. 185p. IL YA, Lexile: 730
Paul's simple high school life is confused by his desire for another boy who seems unattainable, until Paul's friends help him find the courage to pursue the object of his affections.

If You Liked *The Perks of Being a Wallflower* by Stephen Chbosky, You May Like...

Portman, Frank. *King Dork.* Delacorte Press, 2008, c2006. 344p. IL YA, Lexile: 1060
High school loser Tom Henderson discovers that *The Catcher in the Rye* may hold the clues to the many mysteries in his life.

Rich, Jamie S. *Cut My Hair.* Oni Press, 2002, c2000. 236p. IL YA
Nineteen-year-old Mason, a comic book store employee and avid punk fan, thinks his life is improving when he meets and falls in love with Jeane, until events surrounding the music scene with which he is fascinated threaten his happiness.

Runyon, Brent. *The Burn Journals.* Vintage Books, 2005, c2004. 327p. IL AD, Lexile: 690 (Non-fiction)
At age fourteen, Brent Runyon set himself on fire and sustained burns over eighty percent of his body. This account describes the months of physical and mental rehabilitation that followed as he attempted to pull his life together.

Standiford, Natalie. *How to Say Goodbye in Robot.* Scholastic Press, 2009. 276p. IL YA, Lexile: 560
After moving to Baltimore and enrolling in a private school, high school senior Beatrice befriends a quiet loner with a troubled family history.

Tharp, Tim. *The Spectacular Now.* Knopf, c2008. 294p. IL YA, Lexile: 790
In the last months of high school, charismatic eighteen-year-old Sutter Keely lives in the present, staying drunk or high most of the time. That situation could change when he starts working to boost the self-confidence of a classmate, Aimee.

Thomas, Rob. *Rats Saw God.* Simon Pulse, 1996. 202p. IL YA, Lexile: 970
In hopes of graduating, Steve York agrees to complete a hundred-page writing assignment that helps him sort out his relationship with his famous astronaut father and the events that changed him from promising student to troubled teen.

Vizzini, Ned. *It's Kind of a Funny Story.* Miramax Books/Hyperion Paperbacks, 2006. 444p. IL YA, Lexile: 700
New York City teenager Craig Gilner succumbs to academic and social pressures at an elite high school and enters a psychiatric hospital after attempting suicide.

Wiess, Laura. *Such a Pretty Girl.* Pocket Books/MTV Books, 2007. 212p. IL AD, Lexile: 780
Haunted by flashbacks, fifteen-year-old Meredith learns that three years in prison has not changed the abusive father who molested her.

Wittlinger, Ellen. *Hard Love.* Aladdin Paperbacks, 2001, c1999. 224p. IL YA, Lexile: 680
After starting to publish a magazine in which he writes his secret feelings about his lonely life and his parents' divorce, sixteen-year-old John meets an unusual girl and begins to develop a healthier personality.

If You Liked *The Perks of Being a Wallflower* by Stephen Chbosky, You May Like . . .

Zarr, Sara. *Story of a Girl: A Novel.* Little, Brown, 2007. 192p. IL YA, Lexile: 760
During the summer after her sophomore year, Deanna Lambert tries to come to terms with the reputation with which she was slapped in the eighth grade when she was caught by her father in the backseat of a car with a high school senior. Along the way, she struggles with her still-strained relationship with her father and her changing feelings for her best friend, Jason.

Zusak, Markus. *Getting the Girl.* Push, 2004, c2001. 250p. IL YA, Lexile: 620
Tired of being the underdog, Cameron Wolfe hungers to become something worthwhile. He finally finds a girl with whom he can share his words and feelings—his popular brother Rube's ex-girlfriend.

Zusak, Markus. *I Am the Messenger.* Knopf, 2006. 357p. IL YA, Lexile: 640
After capturing a bank robber, nineteen-year-old cab driver Ed Kennedy begins receiving mysterious messages that direct him to addresses where people need help, which helps him start to get over his lifelong feeling of worthlessness.

If You Liked *Push* by Sapphire, You May Like...

Hopkins, Ellen. *Crank.* Margaret K. McElderry Books, 2010, c2004. 537p. IL YA, Lexile: NP
Kristina Georgia Snow's life is turned upside down when she visits her absentee father, gets turned on to the drug "crank," becomes addicted, and is led down a desperate path that threatens her mind, soul, and her life.

Hopkins, Ellen. *Glass.* M. K. McElderry Books, c2007. 681p. IL YA, Lexile: 600
Kristina is determined to break her addiction to drugs so that she can keep her newborn child. When the pull of drugs becomes too strong and her resolve fails, her greatest fears are quickly realized.

Johnson, Angela. *The First Part Last.* Simon & Schuster Books for Young Readers, c2003. 131p. IL YA, Lexile: 790
Bobby's carefree teenage life changes forever when he becomes a father and must care for his adored baby daughter.

Johnson, Angela. *Heaven.* Simon & Schuster Books for Young Readers, c1998. 138p. IL YA, Lexile: 790
Fourteen-year-old Marley's seemingly perfect life in the small town of Heaven is disrupted when she discovers that her father and mother are not her real parents.

Johnson, Angela. *Sweet, Hereafter.* Simon & Schuster Books for Young Readers, c2010. 118p. IL YA, Lexile: 750
Sweet leaves her family and goes to live in a cabin in the woods with the quiet but understanding Curtis, to whom she feels intensely connected, just as he is called back to serve again in Iraq.

Lamb, Wally. *She's Come Undone.* Pocket Books, 1998, c1992. 465p. IL YA, Lexile: 760
A series of tragedies, including the death of her baby brother, her parent's divorce, her mother's nervous breakdown, and her own rape at the age of thirteen, leave Dolores Price wounded both mentally and physically, but she miraculously finds the strength to give herself one more chance at life and love.

Scott, Elizabeth. *Living Dead Girl.* Simon Pulse, 2008. 170p. IL YA, Lexile: 870
Alice, a fifteen-year-old girl who was abducted by Ray when she was ten, lives in fear of what he is going to do to her and hopes death will save her from her real-life nightmare.

From *101 Great, Ready-to-Use Book Lists for Teens* by Nancy J. Keane. Santa Barbara, CA: Libraries Unlimited. Copyright © 2012.

Readalikes

If You Liked *Ranger's Apprentice* by John Flanagan, You May Like . . .

Barry, Dave. *Peter and the Starcatchers*. Disney Editions/Hyperion Books for Children, c2004. 451p. IL 5–8, Lexile: 770
> Peter, an orphan boy, and his friend Molly fight off thieves and pirates to keep a secret safe away from the diabolical Black Stache and his evil associate Mister Grin.

Collins, Suzanne. *Gregor the Overlander*. Scholastic, c2003. 312p. IL 3–6
> Eleven-year-old Gregor and his two-year-old sister are pulled into a strange underground world populated by humans, giant spiders, bats, cockroaches, and rats. Gregor's anxiety about finding his way home is quelled, however, when he finds a prophecy that foretells of his role in the Underland's future.

Curley, Marianne. *The Named*. Bloomsbury, 2002. 332p. IL YA, Lexile: 850
> The first in a fantasy trilogy, this story focuses on Ethan, a boy for whom the lines separating his lives as a regular student struggling with homework, and a Guardian of Time charged with fighting the forces of evil, begin to blur after his classmate Isabel is assigned as his apprentice.

Farmer, Nancy. *The Sea of Trolls*. Atheneum Books for Young Readers, c2004. 459p. IL 5–8, Lexile: 670
> After Jack becomes apprenticed to a Druid bard, he and his little sister Lucy are captured by Viking Berserkers and taken to the home of King Ivar the Boneless and his half-troll queen, leading Jack to undertake a vital quest to Jotunheim, home of the trolls.

L'Homme, Erik. *Quadehar the Sorcerer*. Scholastic, 2006, c2003. 275p. IL 3–6, Lexile: 780
> Robin Penmarch lives a regular life in the Lost Isle, where he and his friends are protected from an ever-present danger by magic and knights in armor—until one day Robin's rare, magical potential is accidentally revealed in the presence of Quadehar the Sorcerer.

Paver, Michelle. *Wolf Brother*. HarperCollins, c2004. 295p. IL 5–8, Lexile: 660
> Twelve-year-old Tarak and his guide, a wolf cub, set out on a dangerous journey to fulfill an oath the boy made to his dying father—to travel to the Mountain of the World Spirit seeking a way to destroy a demon-possessed bear that threatens all of the clans.

Turner, Megan Whalen. *The King of Attolia*. Greenwillow Books, c2006. 387p. IL 5–8, Lexile: 840
> Eugenides, still known as the Thief of Eddis, faces palace intrigue and assassins as he strives to prove himself both to the people of Attolia and to his new bride, their queen.

Series

MacHale, D. J. *Pendragon*. Aladdin Paperbacks, 2002–2004. IL 5–8
> Fourteen-year-old Bobby Pendragon, who is apprenticed to his Uncle Press, a Traveler responsible for solving interdimensional conflict, must travel from one territory to another to stop an evil enemy named Saint Dane.

If You Liked *Ranger's Apprentice* by John Flanagan, You May Like...

Reeve, Philip. *Mortal Engines Quartet.* Scholastic Press, c2004– . IL YA

Tom is a third-class apprentice in a distant future in which technology has been lost and tiered cities move about the Earth on caterpillar tracks, often absorbing smaller locales. He has many dangerous adventures after being pushed off London by Thaddeus Valentine, a historian who is trying to resurrect an ancient atomic weapon.

Sage, Angie. *Septimus Heap.* Katherine Tegen Books, c2005– . IL 3–6

Jenna learns that she is a princess found as a baby. Now she and Septimus, who was taken at birth by the midwife, are being threatened by the evil wizard, DomDaniel, who intends to finish off the entire royal line.

Stewart, Paul. *Edge Chronicles.* David Fickling Books, 1998– . IL 5–8

Young Twig lives in the Deepwoods among the Woodtrolls, but he isn't one of them. In a brave attempt to find out where he truly belongs, Twig wanders into the mysterious, dangerous world beyond the Deepwoods.

Stroud, Jonathan. *The Bartimaeus Trilogy.* Disney/Hyperion Books, 2004–2007. IL 5–8

This trio of books follows the adventures of Nathaniel, a young magician, as he makes a rapid rise through the government of an alternative Britain. He is aided by the witty and wise-cracking Bartimaeus, a djinni Nathaniel first summons to assist him in a plan of revenge, and who later plays an important role in saving London and the entire country.

If You Liked *Twilight* by Stephenie Meyer, You May Like . . .

Klause, Annette Curtis. *The Silver Kiss.* Bantam Doubleday Dell Books for Young Readers, 1992, c1990. 198p. IL YA, Lexile: 690

Zoe, a teenage girl dealing with her mother's impending death, receives an unexpected visit from a beautiful young man named Simon. She eventually learns that he is a three-hundred-year-old vampire seeking to avenge his mother's death.

Pauley, Kimberly. *Sucks to Be Me: The All-True Confessions of Mina Hamilton, Teen Vampire (Maybe).* Mirrorstone, c2009. 297p. IL YA, Lexile: 740

Sixteen-year-old Mina is forced to take a class to help her decide whether to become a vampire like her parents—which also means that she faces a choice between her best friend and her current crush and the potential new friends and possible boyfriends in her vampire class.

Schreiber, Ellen. *Vampire Kisses.* HarperCollins, c2003. 197p. IL YA, Lexile: 700

Sixteen-year-old Raven, an outcast who always wears black and hopes to become a vampire some day, falls in love with the mysterious new boy in town and is eager to find out if he can make her dreams come true.

Smith, L. J. *Night World.* Simon Pulse, 2008. IL YA

In this book series, *Secret Vampire* tells the tale of Poppy, who asks her secret lover James to make her immortal after she is diagnosed with terminal cancer; *Daughters of Darkness* describes the lives of three vampire sisters; and *Spellbinder* tells of two witch cousins who fight over their high school crush.

Vande Velde, Vivian. *Companions of the Night.* Magic Carpet Books/Harcourt, 1995. 212p. IL YA, Lexile: 870

When sixteen-year-old Kerry Nowicki helps a young man escape from a group of men who claim he is a vampire, she finds herself faced with some bizarre and dangerous choices.

Westerfeld, Scott. *The Last Days: A Novel.* Razorbill, c2006. 286p. IL YA, Lexile: 820

Five New York teenagers try to concentrate on their new band while the city suffers from a mysterious epidemic that is turning people into cannibals.

Westerfeld, Scott. *Peeps: A Novel.* Razorbill, c2005. 312p. IL YA, Lexile: 840

Cal Thompson, who is a carrier of a parasite that causes vampirism, must hunt down all of the girlfriends he has unknowingly infected.

Series

Shan, Darren. *Cirque du Freak Collection.* Little, Brown, 2002–2003. IL 5–8

Darren Shan's life is forever changed after he meets Mr. Crepsley at a freak show and becomes a vampire.

If You Liked *Warriors* by Erin Hunter, You May Like . . .

Adams, Richard. *Watership Down.* Scribner, 1996, c1972. 429p. IL YA, Lexile: 880
This classic novel chronicles the adventures of a group of rabbits searching for a safe place to establish a new warren where they can live in peace.

Avi. *Poppy.* HarperTrophy, 2001, c1995. 159p. IL 3–6, Lexile: 670
Poppy, a deer mouse, urges her family to move next to a field of corn big enough to feed them all forever, but Mr. Ocax, a terrifying owl, has other ideas.

Bell, Clare. *Ratha's Creature: The First Book of the Named.* Firebird, 1983. 259p. IL YA
Twenty-five million years in the past, a society of intelligent cats pushed close to extinction meets an enemy band of raiding predatory cats in a decisive battle that will determine the future for both groups.

Clement-Davies, David. *Fire Bringer.* Firebird, 1999. 498p. IL 5–8, Lexile: 840
Rannoch, who was born with a fawn mark the shape of an oak leaf on his forehead, is destined to lead the deer out of the Lord of the Herd's tyranny, but first he must complete a journey through the Great Land.

DiCamillo, Kate. *The Tale of Despereaux: Being the Story of a Mouse, a Princess, Some Soup, and a Spool of Thread.* Candlewick Press, 2003. 267p. IL 3–6, Lexile: 670
The adventures of Despereaux Tilling, a small mouse of unusual talents; the princess whom he loves; the servant girl who longs to be a princess; and a devious rat determined to bring them all to ruin.

Jacques, Brian. *Redwall.* Philomel Books, 2007, c1986. 351p. IL 5–8, Lexile: 800
A collection of three adventure fantasy stories in the Redwall series, including "The Wall," "The Quest," and "The Warrior."

O'Brien, Robert C. *Mrs. Frisby and the Rats of NIMH.* Atheneum, 1971. 233p. IL 3–6, Lexile: 790
With nowhere else to turn, a field mouse asks the clever escaped lab rats living under the rosebush to help save her son, who lies in the path of the farmer's tractor, too ill to be moved.

Oppel, Kenneth. *Silverwing.* Aladdin Paperbacks, 2007, c1997. 216p. IL 5–8, Lexile: 660
When a newborn bat named Shade (but sometimes called "Runt") becomes separated from his colony during migration, he grows in ways that prepare him for even greater journeys.

Said, S. F. *Varjak Paw.* Yearling, c2003. 254p. IL 3–6, Lexile: 500
Guided by the spirit of his legendary Mesopotamian ancestor, Jalal, a pure-bred cat named Varjak Paw leaves his home and pampered existence and sets out to save his family from the evil Gentleman who took their owner, the Contessa, away.

Wallace, Bill. *The Legend of Thunderfoot.* Simon & Schuster Books for Young Readers, c2006. 150p. IL 3–6, Lexile: 610
Humiliated by the name given to him after a rattlesnake bite left him with gigantic, swollen feet, Thunderfoot, a roadrunner, takes the advice of Berland, a wise gopher tortoise, and sets out to prove a name doesn't mean everything.

If You Liked *Warriors* by Erin Hunter, You May Like . . .

White, E. B. *Stuart Little.* HarperTrophy, c1973. 131p. IL 3–6, Lexile: 920
The adventures of the debonair mouse Stuart Little, who sets out in the world to seek out his dearest friend, a little bird who stayed a few days in his family's garden.

Williams, Tad. *Tailchaser's Song.* DAW Books, 2000, c1985. 375p. IL YA, Lexile: 860
Fritti Tailchaser, a ginger tomcat of courage and curiosity, becomes alarmed as cats begin vanishing mysteriously. When his catfriend, Hushpad, disappears, he sets out on a magical quest to rescue her.

Series

Collins, Suzanne. *Underland Chronicles.* Scholastic Press, 2004– . IL 3–6
When eleven-year-old Gregor is pulled into a strange underground world, he triggers an epic battle involving humans, bats, rats, cockroaches, and spiders while on a quest foretold by ancient prophecy.

Lasky, Kathryn. *Guardians of Ga'Hoole.* Scholastic, c2004– . IL 3–6
A band of owls go on a quest for the mythic Great Ga'Hoole Tree in an attempt to acquire the powers that will enable them to defeat the evil that threatens their kingdom.

If You Liked *Wintergirls* by Laurie Halse Anderson, You May Like...

Bauer, Joan. *Squashed.* Speak, 2005. 194p. IL YA, Lexile: 930
As sixteen-year-old Ellie pursues her two goals—growing the biggest pumpkin in Iowa and losing twenty pounds from her own body weight—she strengthens her relationship with her father and meets a young man with interests similar to her own.

Bell, Julia. *Massive.* Simon Pulse, 2006. 261p. IL YA
Carmen has been shaped by her mother to believe that true beauty and success mean being thin, so she begins to take charge of the only thing she can control—what she eats.

Bennett, Cherie. *Life in the Fat Lane.* Ember, 2011, c1998. 265p. IL YA, Lexile: 640
Sixteen-year-old Lara, winner of beauty pageants and Homecoming Queen, is distressed and bewildered when she starts gaining weight and becomes overweight.

Carlson, Melody. *Faded Denim: Color Me Trapped.* THINK Books, c2006. 215p. IL YA
Seventeen-year-old Emily, who originally intended to lose only a few pounds, develops an eating disorder that plagues her until she decides that trusting in God and her friends can help her regain her health.

Does This Book Make Me Look Fat? Clarion Books, 2008. 215p. IL YA
A collection of short stories, poems, and essays about body image, self-esteem, diets, eating disorders, relationships, fashion magazines, and more, with book, movie, and music recommendations.

Eliot, Eve. *Insatiable: The Compelling Story of Four Teens, Food and Its Power.* Health Communications, c2001. 284p. IL 5–8 (Non-fiction)
Recounts the experiences of four high school girls whose feelings of shame, fear, and confusion compelled them to use or refuse food in misguided attempts to feel safe and in control of their lives.

Fairfield, Lesley. *Tyranny.* Tundra Books, c2009. 114p. IL 5–8
Anna records her struggles with anorexia—which she personifies as Tyranny, her tormentor—in her journal, and describes her efforts to overcome her deadly enemy through strength of character.

Friedman, Robin. *Nothing.* Flux, c2008. 232p. IL YA, Lexile: 670
Despite his outward image of a popular, attractive high-achiever bound for the Ivy League college of his father's dreams, high school senior Parker sees himself as a fat, unattractive failure and finds relief from his overwhelming anxiety in ever-increasing bouts of binging and purging.

Friend, Natasha. *Perfect.* Milkweed Editions, 2004. 172p. IL 5–8, Lexile: 590
Following the death of her father, a thirteen-year-old uses bulimia as a way to avoid her mother's and ten-year-old sister's grief, as well as her own.

George, Madeleine. *Looks.* Viking, 2008. 240p. IL YA, Lexile: 1060
Two high school girls—one an anorexic poet and the other an obese loner—form an unlikely friendship.

If You Liked *Wintergirls* by Laurie Halse Anderson, You May Like . . .

Gottlieb, Lori. *Stick Figure: A Diary of My Former Self.* Simon & Schuster Paperbacks, 2009, c2000. 222p. IL AD, Lexile: 1100 (Non-fiction)
    The author shares her childhood diaries, chronicling her experiences as an eleven-year-old anorexic.

Kaslik, Ibi. *Skinny.* Walker, 2004. 244p. IL YA
    After the death of their father, two sisters struggle with a variety of problematic issues, including their family history, personal relationships, and an extreme eating disorder.

Levenkron, Steven. *The Best Little Girl in the World.* Warner, 1997, c1978. 253p. IL YA
    After being a model daughter all her life, fifteen-year-old Francesca suddenly begins to starve herself and is diagnosed as suffering from the psychological disorder known as anorexia nervosa.

Littman, Sarah. *Purge.* Scholastic Press, 2009. 234p. IL YA, Lexile: 950
    When her parents check sixteen-year-old Janie into the Golden Slopes treatment facility to help her recover from her bulimia, she discovers that she must talk about things she has admitted to no one—not even herself.

Lytton, Deborah A. *Jane in Bloom.* Dutton Children's Books, c2009. 182p. IL YA, Lexile: 540
    Devastated when her beautiful, older sister dies from anorexia, twelve-year-old Jane recovers slowly from the tragedy, with help from unexpected sources.

Pettit, Christie. *Empty: A Story of Anorexia.* Revell, c2006. 203p. IL AD (Non-fiction)
    Author Christie Pettit chronicles her fight with anorexia nervosa and describes how counseling and her faith in God helped her overcome the eating disorder.

Sarkar, Dona. *Shrink to Fit.* Kimani TRU, c2008. 251p. IL YA
    Basketball star Leah Mandeville thought losing weight would solve all of her problems on the court and in the game of love. Even though she is getting thinner, however, her troubles seem to be getting bigger.

Shaw, Liane. *Thinandbeautiful.com.* Second Story Press, c2009. 263p. IL YA, Lexile: 790
    Seventeen-year-old Maddie's weight loss begins to spiral out of control after she discovers an on-line community filled with girls like herself, who offer one another support and weight-loss tips that mask their obsession with being thin. When Maddie's parents send her to an eating disorders treatment facility, Maddie refuses to admit she needs help, until a tragedy opens her eyes to her dangerous habits.

Shivack, Nadia. *Inside Out: Portrait of an Eating Disorder.* Atheneum Books for Young Readers, c2007. 64p. IL YA (Non-fiction)
    In this memoir, presented in graphic novel form, the author illustrates her ongoing struggle with an eating disorder she has named Ed.

If You Liked *Wintergirls* by Laurie Halse Anderson, You May Like . . .

Vaught, Susan. *Big Fat Manifesto.* Bloomsbury, 2008. 308p. IL YA, Lexile: 800

High school senior Jamie Carcaterra tries to win a scholarship by sharing her experiences as a fat girl in today's appearance-obsessed high school culture. As she opens her life up to the criticism of her classmates and the media, she begins to wonder if she is being truly honest with herself.

Vrettos, Adrienne Maria. *Skin.* M. K. McElderry, c2006. 227p. IL YA, Lexile: 810

When his parents decide to separate, eighth-grader Donnie watches with horror as the physical condition of his sixteen-year old sister, Karen, deteriorates due to an eating disorder.

Wild, Margaret. *Jinx.* Simon Pulse, 2004, c2002. 215p. IL YA, Lexile: 790

With the help of her understanding mother and a close friend, Jen eventually outgrows her nickname, Jinx, and deals with the deaths of two boys with whom she had been involved.

Wilson, Jacqueline. *Girls under Pressure.* Dell Laurel-Leaf, 2003, c1998. 214p. IL 5–8, Lexile: 740

Ellie learns to deal with her self-image as she battles anorexia.

Zarr, Sara. *Sweethearts: A Novel.* Little, Brown, 2008. 217p. IL YA, Lexile: 720

Jennifer Harris, years after being the tormented outsider on the playground, has reinvented herself as Jenna Vaughn, a popular girl with what seems to be the perfect life. When a childhood friend reenters her life, she is forced to confront the most traumatic event of her past and question who she really is.

Professional Resources

Reading Lists

Barr, Catherine. *Best Books for Children: Preschool through Grade 6.* Libraries Unlimited, c2010. 1901p.

> Collects information on nearly 25,000 fiction and non-fiction titles—covering topics such as biographies, history, science, and recreation—for children from prekindergarten through the sixth grade, with brief annotations, bibliographic data, grade-level appropriateness, and review citations.

Barr, Catherine. *Best Books for Children: Supplement to the Eighth Edition: Preschool through Grade 6.* Libraries Unlimited, 2007. 445p.

> Presents details on more than 4,200 books for children from prekindergarten through sixth grade, providing bibliographic information, brief summaries, and review citations, and includes author/illustrator, title, and subject/grade level indexes.

Barr, Catherine. *Best Books for High School Readers: Grades 9–12.* Libraries Unlimited, 2009. 1075p.

> Contains annotated listings of approximately 15,000 recommended books for high school readers culled from fiction and non-fiction titles published through 2008. Each entry includes the ISBN, length and price, grade level, review citations, audio availability, and more.

Barr, Catherine. *Best Books for Middle School and Junior High Readers: Grades 6–9.* Libraries Unlimited, 2009. 1242p.

> Contains annotated listings of approximately 15,000 recommended books for middle school and junior high readers, including fiction, plays, literary history and criticism, biographies, philosophy and religion, guidance and personal development, and other genres. Each listing includes the ISBN, length and price, grade level, and review citations.

Bartel, Julie. *Annotated Book Lists tor Every Teen Reader: The Best from the Experts at YALSA.* Neal-Schuman Publishers, c2011. 270p.

> Presents annotated lists of books for young adults, with lists separated by genre, reading level, theme, and format.

Best Books for Young Adults. American Library Association, 2007. 346p.

> Presents twenty-seven themed, annotated lists of fiction and non-fiction books for young adults and an annotated list of the Best Books for Young Adults Committee selections spanning 1966–2007, and discusses contemporary trends in teen literature.

Bodart, Joni Richards. *Radical Reads 2: Working with the Newest Edgy Titles for Teens.* Scarecrow Press, 2010. 479p.

> Provides information on approximately one hundred controversial books for teen readers, with each listing being accompanied by publication data, character descriptions, a booktalk, lists of subject areas and major themes, ideas for book reports and booktalks, risks, strengths, and awards, and excerpts from reviews.

Professional Resources

Drew, Bernard A. *100 Most Popular Nonfiction Authors: Biographical Sketches And Bibliographies.* Libraries Unlimited, 2008. 438p.

> Profiles one hundred of today's most popular non-fiction writers, with an overview of each author's personal and professional lives, literary accomplishments, genre, and awards, with reading lists and contact information for each entry.

Fry, Edward Bernard. *The Reading Teacher's Book of Lists.* Jossey-Bass, c2006. 524p.

> Presents more than two hundred lists for elementary and secondary reading teachers, providing exercises, vocabulary, and other teaching tools in eighteen topic areas, including phonics, word play, study skills, and assessment.

The Librarian's Book of Lists. American Library Association, 2010. 118p.

> A collection of library-related lists, including "10 Commandments for Borrowers of Books," "15 Favorite Library Postcards," "Stephen Leary's Top 10 Ways to Exit a Library," and "10 Intriguing Paper Defects," among others.

McElmeel, Sharron L. *The Best Teen Reads 2010.* Hi Willow Research & Publishing, 2010. 153p.

> An annotated listing for teens drawn from the pool of books that have been tapped as award winning or received star reviews from professional reviewing sources or endorsements from professional teenagers, featuring overviews of several genres, each with notes on representative books. The book includes lists of recommended audio materials, award winners, theme books, and book packages.

Nieuwenhuizen, Agnes. *Right Book, Right Time: 500 Great Books for Teenagers.* Allen & Unwin, 2007. 355p.

> Contains reviews and recommendations of five hundred books for teenagers, including Australian and international titles; listings are grouped by genre.

Pearl, Nancy. *Book Crush: For Kids and Teens: Recommended Reading for Every Mood, Moment, and Interest.* Sasquatch Books, c2007. 288p.

> Presents lists of recommended book titles in 118 categories, including dogs, girl power, family, boys, dolls, friends, dancing, love, and many others.

Quick and Popular Reads for Teens. American Library Association, 2009. 228p.

> Contains annotated lists of recommended young adult books for reluctant readers and provides advice on library programming, displays, and readers' advisories.

Reisner, Rosalind. *Read on—Life Stories: Reading Lists for Every Taste.* Libraries Unlimited, c2009. 175p.

> Contains brief summaries of nearly 450 published memoirs from throughout history, grouped based on the categories of story, character, setting, language, and mood.

Schwedt, Rachel E. *Core Collection for Children and Young Adults.* Scarecrow Press, 2008. 207p.

> Presents a book list containing selected children's and young adult literature, and provides annotations while also listing awards, subjects, and character themes. The lists cover the classics, fantasy, historical, non-fiction, picture books, poetry, and more.

Professional Resources

Strouf, Judie L. H. *The Literature Teacher's Book of Lists.* Jossey-Bass, c2005. 553p.
 Contains 254 lists that may be used by literature teachers to develop instructional materials and plan lessons for middle school, secondary, and college students, providing information on a variety of topics under the headings of literature, books, genres, poetry, drama, themes, literary periods, potpourri, and student activities and teacher tips.

Thomas, Rebecca L. *Popular Series Fiction for Middle School and Teen Readers: A Reading and Selection Guide.* Libraries Unlimited, 2009. 710p.
 Presents a comprehensive fiction resource guide for middle and high school readers covering more than eight hundred series, along with annotations, character lists, grade levels, genre, and more.

Trupe, Alice. *Thematic Guide to Young Adult Literature.* Greenwood Press, 2006. 259p.
 Identifies thirty-two themes in young adult literature and features critical discussions of three or more representative novels in each category. The book also includes lists of other recommended titles.

Zbaracki, Matthew D. *Best Books for Boys: A Resource for Educators.* Libraries Unlimited, 2008. 189p.
 Profiles five hundred fiction and nonfiction books that will be interesting and motivating for boys, with entries organized by genre. Each listing includes information on the book's plot, reading level, and author.

Index

About the Author

NANCY J. KEANE is a school librarian whose goal is to get students reading. In addition to her work in the school, Nancy has hosted a children's literature television show that featured children from the area talking about their favorite books. The show also showcased local authors and storytellers. Nancy has authored several books on creating and using booktalks.

Nancy is the author of an award-winning website *Booktalks: Quick and Simple* (http://www.nancykeane.com/booktalks). This site has proved to be indispensable to librarians and teachers. The database includes more than 5,000 ready-to-use booktalks, and additional contributions from educators are welcomed. Additionally, Nancy's wiki, *ATN Reading Lists,* consists of nearly 2,000 thematic lists culled from suggestions from several professional e-mail discussion lists. The wiki is an open collaborative through which educators from around the world can share their lists.

Nancy received a BA from the University of Massachusetts, Amherst; an MLS from the University of Rhode Island; and an MA in educational technology from George Washington University. She is currently an EdD candidate at Rivier College. She is an adjunct faculty member at New Hampshire Technical Institute, Plymouth State University, and University of Rhode Island and teaches workshops around the country.

10/14 ① 4/14
10/15 ① 4/14
8/16
9/18 ② 12/17